DISCIPLINES OF EDUCATION

Disciplines of Education

IVOR MORRISH

B.D., B.A., Dip.Ed.(Lond.), B.A.(Brist.)
Senior Lecturer and Librarian
Bognor Regis College of Education

London
GEORGE ALLEN & UNWIN LTD
RUSKIN HOUSE MUSEUM STREET

PRINTED IN GREAT BRITAIN
in 11 on 12 point Baskerville type
BY WESTERN PRINTING SERVICES LTD
BRISTOL

To Thelma

AUTHOR'S PREFACE

This book was originally planned to meet some of the needs of students who are faced with the new, imaginative and exciting syllabus, devised by the Institute of Education of London University, for a paper in the General Theory of Education in the Academic Diploma examination. The paper is based on works by Plato, Rousseau, Dewey, Freud, Piaget, Skinner, Durkheim, G. H. Mead and Mannheim, which are of special relevance to education. Because the syllabus has been designed in this broad yet specific way the student is forced to read both widely and in depth, and no single textbook could possibly hope to cover the ground—certainly not one of this length—even if such a thing were desirable.

But students, particularly the ever-increasing number of external ones, require some sort of guide to the books that ought to be read or surveyed, and to books that will assist them to interpret writers in disciplines in which they, as students, may have had little or no training. In order, however, to understand those works of the above-named writers which are "relevant to education", one must also have some idea of the general approach of the thinker to his own discipline, whether it be philosophy, psychology or sociology. Some attempt has been made to provide this in the following pages.

The author feels, however, that this book may have a more general relevance to teachers in training at the present time. The Colleges of Education are busy revising their syllabuses in order not merely to meet the more rigorous demands of the B.Ed., but also in order to give closer definition to what has too often been, in the words of Professor R. S. Peters, "the undifferentiated mush of educational theory". It is hoped, therefore, that this work may at least provide for all students concerned with education some guiding lines on how the "mush" may be differentiated.

Bognor Regis   IVOR MORRISH
Sussex

ACKNOWLEDGEMENT

My debt to other authors, and their publishers, is obvious on almost every page of this book. I would like, therefore, to express my grateful thanks to them all for permission to quote from their works. I have tried to acknowledge all my sources in the notes, but if anyone has been in advertently omitted I hope that they will forgive me.

I.M.

CONTENTS

12   CONTENTS

PART THREE: SOCIOLOGICAL

CHAPTER 1

INTRODUCTION

In its discussion of the aims of Higher Education, the Robbins Report, published in October 1963, submits that there are four main objectives:

(a) The instruction of skills suitable to play a part in the general division of labour.
(b) The promotion of the general powers of the mind.
(c) The advancement of learning.
(d) The transmission of a common culture and common standards of citizenship[1].

Colleges and institutions which have existed for the training of teachers have always recognized, of course, that they were attempting to pass on skills suitable to play a part in the profession of teaching. Indeed, this has undoubtedly been the main emphasis, and some have even been persuaded that this was the only aim of any great importance. Certainly many students have said, and repeated almost *ad nauseam*, when anything else has been presented to them beyond what they regard as *their* subject: "What is the use of all this? We shan't be teaching this anyway. I shan't have time to analyse a child to find out why he behaves in a particular way. Why don't they tell us how to control a class? Why don't they give us the stuff to teach, and give it in a form that we can teach? Why don't they give us more practice in teaching?" In fact, students in training, and many of them after they have become teachers, have felt and believed that "the instruction of skills suitable to play a part" in the classroom was not merely the chief aim, but the sole aim of a college for training teachers.

In the past, the almost indecent haste with which a teacher was "trained" certainly lent some validity to this view. In fact, the emergency scheme for training teachers in thirteen months, after the Second World War, produced for the teaching profession a body of men and women no less adapted in the *skills* of teaching than those who previously had taken a two-year course. It is true, however, that it was a more highly concentrated and stream-lined course, and it involved in the main older and generally more experienced students. But the fact remains that the latest "skills" in teaching were mediated no less to these 36,000 "dilu-tees", as they were at first stigmatized by some sections of the pro-fession, than to other students who took two years. In its final report on the scheme[2], the Ministry underlined the keenness, singleness of purpose, and capacity for sustained effort of the emergency-trained students, their greater maturity, their wide range of talents and accomplishments, their vitality and genuine interest in their fellows, their conviction regarding the importance of schools, and their powers of initiative and organization. All this, and the steadying effect in most cases of domestic respon-sibilities, had helped to get the skills across in a minimum of time.

No one would deny the importance of the "skills" of any pro-fession, and perhaps because of their somewhat lower level in the academic sphere the training colleges have naturally empha-sized this important side of their work. But one of the miscon-ceptions in the past concerning the training of teachers, expressed not least by the teachers themselves, has been that their training should be an almost exclusively "practical" one. The idea that a student who will eventually teach infants, or even juniors, should treat a subject in a very superficial way, and study nothing in depth, has often resulted in uneducated as well as unskilled teachers.

The second point made by the Robbins Report in connexion with all forms of Higher Education was that

"we must postulate that what is taught should be taught in such a way as to promote the general powers of the mind"[3].

It goes on to say that the aim should be not mere specialists, but rather cultivated men and women. The renaming of training colleges as "colleges of education" has underlined to some extent this particular point. It is a regrettable fact that in the past many trained teachers have been uneducated; it would be an even more regrettable possibility that students emerging from the renamed colleges of the future might be equally uneducated and mentally undisciplined, unless greater emphasis were placed upon the "promotion of the general powers of the mind".

The very busyness of our institutions, and the economic pressures which still demand a maximum output of teachers in a minimum of time, all militate against a gradual, healthy and even leisurely development of our students' mental capacities. And it often happens that students in training are left with time to do almost everything except just read and think. Three years, broken into by periods of teaching practice, are all too short a time for the promotion of the general powers of the mind. Moreover, if our future teachers are to be of the quality and standard which one of the most important professions in the country should demand, then a fourth year for the purposes of graduating as Bachelors of Education should not be a remote possibility for the very few, but an almost accepted procedure for the majority. One can agree with the statement made by the Robbins Report that

"although we cannot go as far as those who advocate an all-graduate profession, it would not be acceptable simply to allow the present situation to continue"[4].

But it would be equally true to say that the more graduates the profession possesses, the more likely it is to be a profession held in some regard, as well as a profession with a maximum of individuals who have been intellectually stretched and disciplined. The disciplines of education require specialists to promote them, just as much as the disciplines of philosophy, psychology and sociology or history require specialists to promote them. Yet "education" has remained, for many years, a somewhat amorphous collocation of disparate material in which a bit of philosophy or philosophizing, a smattering of psychology, and an unduly self-conscious acceptance of the need for some social orientation, have been entertained *en passant* as it were.

At a time when thought was held in the grip of witchcraft, superstition, magic and a constricting theology, Francis Bacon wrote his *Advancement of Learning* (1605)[5], in which he emphasized the need for a scientific approach to learning in order to discover new truths. Nearly 360 years later the Robbins Report considers that one of the aims of Higher Education is the "advancement of learning", and that "the search for truth is an essential function of institutions of higher education and the process of education is itself most vital when it partakes of the nature of discovery"[6].

The discovery of truth, both for the individual in his personal development, as well as for the improvement of society, is one of the important objectives of teacher-training, or rather of the education of teachers. And although we obviously no longer remain at the Baconian level in our search and process of discovery, it would be tragic indeed if it were ever thought that the "advancement of learning" was the sole prerogative of research institutions or of university students pursuing post-graduate studies. If our reconstituted Colleges of Education are producing the majority of the teachers for our society, then they, as much as any other institutions of Higher Learning, should be concerned in the search for truth, and in research into the various methods, skills and disciplines employed in educational theory and practice; and they should, in consequence, be afforded both time and facilities for this important purpose. If such research is to be done in anything but the most light-hearted and superficial manner, there will be a need for an ever-increasing emphasis upon the disciplines involved in serious educational study—the disciplines of philosophy, psychology, sociology, history and comparative analysis.

The final objective of Higher Education as envisaged by the Robbins Report is the transmission of a common culture and common standards of citizenship. It goes on to say that

"we believe that it is a proper function of higher education, as of education in schools, to provide in partnership with the family that background of culture and social habit upon which a healthy society depends"[7].

If our society is not to be a split society with discrete elements, possessing their own cultures and sub-cultures, then there must be some means of transmitting a common culture with agreed and acceptable standards. This does not mean a static society, nor does it mean that all sub-cultures must be rejected; what it does mean is the necessity for the inculcation of a sense of fluidity, as well as of judgement, in the minds of those who are educating. Only in this way can they learn to seize upon what is lasting, or even of utilitarian value, in the sub-cultures of their society, and to integrate it into the main culture which is being transmitted. This does presuppose an understanding at some level of the society in which the educator lives, as well as some appreciation of the nature and background of his pupils, and of any possible aims or ideals in his society. In his *Inaugural Address at St Andrew's University*, which he gave in 1867, John Stuart Mill said that

"Not only does education include whatever we do for ourselves and whatever is done for us by others for the express purpose of bringing us nearer to the perfection of our nature; it does more: in its largest acceptation it comprehends even the indirect effects produced on character, and on the human faculties, by things of which the direct purposes are quite different; by laws, life, nay, even by physical facts not dependent on human will; by climate, soil, and local position".

And in his summing-up he suggested that the core of education was

"the culture which each generation purposely gives to those who are to be its successors, in order to qualify them for at least keeping up, and if possible for raising, the level of improvement which has been attained"[8].

If our teachers are to keep up with the highest level of culture of their time, they will need to have a wide knowledge; if they are to assist in the raising of the level of improvement which has been attained, they must have more than knowledge, they must have skill, understanding, discernment and sound judgement. The General Theory of Education is naturally concerned with all these things, but it can achieve its purpose best by breaking down the field of inquiry into a number of areas in which specific disciplines are involved.

Professor D. J. O'Connor, in *An Introduction to the Philosophy of Education*[9], holds that "education" refers to a set of techniques for the purpose of imparting skills, knowledge and attitudes, and to a set of theories which claim to justify or explain the use of these techniques—these functions relate chiefly to psychology. It also refers, he says, to a set of ideals and values expressed in the purposes for which these skills, knowledge and attitudes are imparted—this is most relevant to philosophy. And he goes on to add that in some sense the "aim of education must be the same in all societies"[10]; it is concerned with the continuity and growth of each society. Yet, education is also very much a relative term. It will have different meanings for different eras, different countries, different societies and different groups. That is why, in any discussion of the aims of education today, we cannot afford to talk for any length of time *in vacuo*: education is concerned with a particular people, at a particular time and in a particular society. The rapidly developing discipline of comparative education clearly demonstrates this fact. We are, therefore, faced with concrete needs and situations in a society which is rapidly expanding and losing its old parochialism and insularity. Change, rapid change, is being brought about by scientific investigation and imagination, by invention and experiment, and even simply by novel and daring thinking; change is being effected by an entirely new concept of the nature of man, and of his physical, mental and spiritual functions; and change is also being anticipated by the thorough examination, analysis and evaluation of social structures, groups and institutions.

Because of this rapid change, when we come to a consideration of education, its theory and its aims, we must inevitably envisage not merely the age and state of society in which we are now living, but also the era and type of society into which we are now evolving. We are, as educators, very much concerned with the foreseeable future[11]. This view of education does impose upon the individual educator an integrated and orientated concept of life and its problems. It is not academic perversity or vested interests which insist that the future educator should have something more than just a nodding acquaintance with the disciplines of philosophy, psychology and sociology. If we are to educate for our society we must know and understand that society: we must, in fact, be educated ourselves. The study of individual philosophers (such as Plato, Rousseau and Dewey), of individual psychologists (such as Freud, Piaget and Skinner), and of individual sociologists (such as Durkheim, G. H. Mead and Mannheim), will do much both to "educate the educator" and to give that "total" view of our society and its problems which we as educators need. This is not a mere dilettante study—the aim, at least, is not to "do a bit" of philosophy, psychology and sociology: it is to enter fully into these disciplines and their methodology, always with an eye, of course, upon their more specific link with educational theory and practice.

Because education has become such a vast subject, with ramifications as broad as life and society, it has become necessary to break it down and study it from particular points of view. It would be fatal, however, if educators were to regard themselves simply as philosophers, or psychologists, or sociologists in the classroom. It is the function, therefore, of a course in the General Theory of Education to present these various approaches synoptically, and to try and integrate them. The integration, it is true, cannot be effected in a short conclusion at the end of the course; it is something which should be achieved in the mind of the student as he looks at education from these various points of view.

In his *Some Tasks for Education*, Sir Richard Livingstone said that "modernity is a question, not of date, but of outlook"[12]. Now it would be true to say that some of the finest and most constructive thinking about education has been done by educators steeped in both philosophy and classics. Many of the issues which Socrates and Plato raised are still in principle the same as those which exercise our minds today; and a closer look at Plato may, indeed, help to clarify the problems themselves even though no particular solution may be found already "built-in" for modern times. Of Rousseau, Lytton Strachey has said that

"He believed that it was necessary to start altogether afresh. And what makes him so singularly interesting a figure is that, in more than one sense, he was right. It *was* necessary to start afresh; and the new world which was to spring from the old was to embody, in a multitude of ways, the visions of Rousseau"[13].

It is, perhaps, true to say that almost every serious educational thinker since the time of Rousseau owes something to his general influence and revolutionary approach. Dewey was pre-eminently an academic philosopher, however we may think of him in active and "pragmatic" terms. In his *Education in a Divided World*, Professor J. B. Conant remarks that Dewey was largely responsible for building a bridge between the discipline of philosophy and the schools of education, which seemed "the most likely way to improve the training of teachers"[14]. There is a sense in which the philosophy of education propounded by Dewey can never date. He regarded education as growth, and the sole purpose of growth through education was (he thought) to encourage further mental, moral and physical development. Whether this in itself can provide an adequate criterion for further educational theory and practice, or whether an additional criterion is necessary to establish the nature and direction of growth, we must leave until we come to a more detailed consideration of Dewey. What *is* more important to note here is that the principles enunciated by Dewey are still vital for any serious consideration of the general theory of education.

If you accept the Rousseauian creed that children should be educated according to their nature, you must clearly begin to make some scientific study of the nature of childhood and child development. In 1893 James Sully founded the British Association for Child Study, which was one of the first attempts to harness psychology to education. According to A. D. C. Peterson[15] the first real attempt in this country to put the new psychological theories "in a form that would be useful to the practical teacher" was made by Sir John Adams in his *Herbartian Psychology Applied to Education*[16]. The psychological principles of Herbart had, in fact, quite a considerable effect upon the techniques of teaching and education; but more important still, perhaps, they gave popularity to the *idea* of psychology and to its embryonic jargon. The psychological theories and psycho-analytic methods of Freud firmly underlined the importance of understanding fully the human mind in all its various aspects and phases of development, whether conscious or unconscious, if the child were to be helped through its obsessions, phobias, complexes and neuroses, as well as its many educational problems. J. S. Ross has made this judgement of the use to which Freud's theories have been put:

"The teaching of Freud was a godsend to the postwar apostles of naturalism, both in the educational sphere and outside of it; it was believed to have proved the soundness of their case for untrammelled self-expression and for entire freedom from restraint. Books on psycho-analysis applied to education flooded the market and found many eager readers. Educational systems informed by psycho-analysis aim at free, natural development through the prevention of repression, and its resulting state of unconscious conflict and neurosis"[17].

Our study of Freud will reveal that whilst the general popularization of his teaching led to a great deal of half-baked ideas concerning "free discipline", the real and lasting benefit of his work is found in a deeper understanding of the causes of delinquency in childhood and adolescence, and of some of the ways in which such causes might be avoided, as well as the manner in which problem children generally might be handled.

Many advances have been made in the realms of psychology since Freud began his researches. One of the great, outstanding pioneers in this country was Susan Isaacs who devoted her life to the study of children, the problems of their intellectual growth, and emotional and social development. Other psychologists, such as Burt, Spearman, Thomson, P. E. Vernon and many others, have been concerned in experimental work and in establishing valid and standardized tests for anthropometric research.

Piaget has been concerned, by methods of research, observation, and thousands of organized experiments, with the mental processes and concepts of children from their earliest days. Much of Piaget's "developmental psychology" has still to be adequately described, analysed and assessed, but he seeks to investigate the growth of logical thinking in the child, the development of his moral judgement, and the evolution of his conceptions of number, space, geometry, physical causality and of the world. Piaget's work has had far-reaching effects both in a deeper understanding of the child mind, and in a reconsideration of curricula and teaching methods in such divergent realms as mathematics and religious education.

We live in a world of machines, of automation and of programming. Many people view these things with either distaste or fear, or perhaps both. When, however, these media are applied to the mental processes of instruction and learning, there are those who see the adumbration not merely of a new era but also of a soulless society. Professor Skinner of Harvard University is one of the most brilliant researchers in behaviouristic and experimental psychology today, and his work has led to much of the modern development in the field of teaching machines and programmed instruction. As E. B. Fry has pointed out in his standard work on the theme:

"Teaching machines and programmed instruction methods are not monsters designed to enslave thought and turn teachers and students into robots. In fact, many educators see these methods as liberating devices that allow for many more individual differences than the lock-step instruction now found in large classes, required text-books, motion pictures, and television. With these methods teachers can be freed from many clerical tasks of paper correction and the repetition of mountains of curriculum details that must be covered"[18].

Education can no more be divorced from society and social change than it can be cut off from novelty in philosophical ideas or psychological experiment. This was recognized by the French sociologist, Durkheim, as long ago as 1913 when he became the first Professor in the Science of Education and Sociology at the Sorbonne, Paris. Even as early as 1902 Durkheim had drawn attention to the ever-changing nature of society and of social ideals, and to the impact of such developments upon society, but his work as an educational thinker has been neglected until recently.

The American thinker, George H. Mead, was particularly concerned with the "self", which he regarded as a social rather than as a purely psychological phenomenon. He maintained that our very sense of difference from other people, whom we internalize in a web of relations, was a social product. Mead was also concerned with the problem of communication; to him language was a principle of social organization making the distinctively human society possible. It has been said of Mead that, perhaps more than any other, he has helped to define the opportunities of social psychology and he has proposed the dimensions that help constitute the facts of someone's action when he is in the presence of others. Since for him the essence of *all* human experience is social, his theories must have importance in a consideration of the aims of education.

Mannheim was bred on concepts of organization, ideologies, systems and paradigmata. He came to England as a refugee from Nazi totalitarianism; but he was thoroughly imbued with the idea that if one wanted a "free", democratic society one had to plan and organize for it. Just as we had planned for war so we must plan for peace. His *Diagnosis of Our Time* is a classic in social examination in order to demonstrate how post-war society could be planned, ruled by an *élite*, and yet preserve the essential freedoms of the individual. Mannheim saw that ultimately a planned society would depend upon a transformation of man; and education was, he felt, the chief means of bringing this about.

It should be clear from the foregoing not only that education has many divisions and sub-divisions, but also that, in order to make any assessment of its aims and objectives we must know a great deal about the growth and development of the child and of society, and much about their multifarious and interrelated problems. In all disciplines our aims are best achieved by the precept "divide and conquer". And so in education we have found it most effective to study our problems via philosophy, psychology and sociology. The differentiation of method and discipline is inevitable if the child, in the long run, is to get the education which is, at once, the best for each separate individual and for society as a whole. This is an age of analysis and differentiation: the difficulty is that we get so involved at times with the problems of our particular piece of analysis that we may fail to see it within the total perspective. The "General Theory of Education" is concerned to reintegrate the main findings of the various disciplines involved in the process, and to try and make some estimate of their total effect upon the theory and practice of education within the schools of our society.

REFERENCES

1. Robbins Report: *Higher Education*. H.M.S.O., October 1963, pp. 6–7.
2. Min. of Ed. Pamphlet No. 17: *Challenge and Response*. H.M.S.O., 1950.
3. *Op. cit.*, p. 6, para. 26.
4. *Ibid.* p. 112, para. 327.
5. Bacon, F.: *The Advancement of Learning*. J. M. Dent, Everyman Lib.
6. *Op. cit.*, p. 7, para. 27.
7. *Ibid.* p. 7, para. 28.
8. *Vide* Cavenagh, F. A.: *James and John Stuart Mill on Education*. History of Education Series, C.U.P., 1931.
9. *Vide* O'Connor, D. J.: *An Introduction to the Philosophy of Education*. Routledge, 1957, pp. 5–6.
10. *Ibid.* p. 6.

11. *Vide* Ottaway, A. K. C.: *Education and Society.* Routledge, 1960 (4th Impression), Chapter V, "The Educational Needs of Our Future Society".
12. Livingstone, R.: *Some Tasks for Education.* O.U.P., 1946, p. 5.
13. Strachey, Lytton: *Landmarks in French Literature.* H.U.L., 1939, pp. 185–6.
14. Conant, J. B.: *Education in a Divided World.* O.U.P., 1948, pp. 147–8.
15. Peterson, A. D. C.: *A Hundred Years of Education.* Duckworth, 1952, p. 71.
16. *Vide* Adams, J.: *Herbartian Psychology Applied to Education.* Heath, 1897.
17. Ross, J. S.: *Modern Trends in Education.* Melrose, 1950, p. 32.
18. Fry, E. B.: *Teaching Machines and Programmed Instruction.* McGraw-Hill, 1963, p. viii.

BIBLIOGRAPHY

Although this book is not directly concerned with the disciplines of the History of Education and Comparative Education, the following lists of books are appended as a general guide to these particular fields.

A. BOOKS ON THE HISTORY OF EDUCATION

Adamson, J. W.: *A Short History of Education.* C.U.P., 1919.
— : *English Education 1789–1902.* C.U.P., 1930.
Archer, R. L.: *Secondary Education in the Nineteenth Century.* C.U.P., 1921.
Barnard, H. C.: *A History of English Education from 1760.* U.L.P., 1961 (2nd Edition; 2nd Impression, 1963).
Birchenough, C.: *History of Elementary Education in England and Wales from 1800.* U.T.P., 1938 (2nd Edition).
Boyd, W.: *The History of Western Education.* A. & C. Black, 1964 (7th Edition).
Curtis, S. J.: *History of Education in Great Britain.* U.T.P., 1963 (5th Edition).
— :*Education in Britain, 1900–1950.* Andrew Dakers, 1952.
Curtis, S. J. & Boultwood, M. E. A.: *An Introductory History of English Education since 1800.* U.T.P., 1964 (3rd Edition).
— : *A Short History of Educational Ideas.* U.T.P., 1965 (4th Edition).

Dent, H. C.: *Growth in English Education 1946–52*. Routledge, 1954.

Hans, N.: *New Trends in Education in the Eighteenth Century*. Routledge, 1951.

Jarman, T. L.: *Landmarks in the History of Education*. Cresset Press, 1951.

Kerr, J.: *Scottish Education, School and University*. C.U.P., 1910.

Lester Smith, W. O.: *Education in Great Britain*. O.U.P., H.U.L., 1958 (3rd Edition).

Meyer, A. E.: *An Educational History of the Western World*. McGraw-Hill, 1965.

Morgan, A.: *Rise and Progress of Scottish Education*. Oliver & Boyd, 1927.

Peterson, A. D. C.: *A Hundred Years of Education*. Duckworth, 1952.

Raymont, T.: *A History of the Education of Young Children*. Longmans, 1957.

Rusk, R. R.: *A History of Infant Education*. U.L.P., 1933.

B. BOOKS ON COMPARATIVE EDUCATION

Baron, G.: *Society, Schools and Progress in England*. Pergamon Press, 1966.

Bentwich, J.: *Education in Israel*. Routledge, 1965.

Bereday, G. Z. F. *et al.*: *The World Year Book of Education: The Education Explosion*. Evans, 1965.

Bereday, G. Z. F.: *The Changing Soviet School*. Constable, 1960.

—: *The Politics of Soviet Education*. Stevens, 1960.

Counts, G. A.: *The Challenge of Soviet Education*. McGraw-Hill, 1957.

Dixon, C. W.: *Society, Schools and Progress in Scandinavia*. Pergamon Press, 1966.

Dore, R. P.: *Education in Tokugawa Japan*. Routledge, 1965.

Dropkin, S. et al.: *Contemporary American Education*. Collier-Macmillan, 1965.

Foster, P. J.: *Education and Social Change in Ghana*. Routledge, 1965.

Fraser, W. R.: *Education and Society in Modern France*. Routledge, 1963.

Grant, N.: *Soviet Education*. Penguin Books (Pelican), 1964.

Halls, W. D.: *Society, Schools and Progress in France*. Pergamon Press, 1966.

Hans, N.: *Comparative Education*. Routledge, 1958 (3rd Edition; 3rd Impression, 1964).

—: *The Russian Tradition in Education*. Routledge, 1963.

Hartford, E. F.: *Education in these United States.* Collier-Macmillan, 1964.

Holmes, B.: *Problems in Education: A Comparative Approach.* Routledge, 1965.

Kandel, I. L.: *The New Era in Education: A Comparative Study.* Harrap, 1955.

King, E. J.: *Other Schools and Ours.* Holt, Rinehart, 1963.
—: *World Perspectives in Education.* Methuen, 1963.
—: *Communist Education.* Methuen, 1963.
—: *Society, Schools and Progress in U.S.A.* Pergamon Press, 1966.

Kitchen, H. (ed.): *The Educated African.* Heinemann, 1965.

Kline, G. L.: *Soviet Education.* Routledge, 1957.

Lewis, L. J.: *Society, Schools and Progress in Nigeria.* Pergamon Press, 1966.

Mallinson, V.: *An Introduction to the Study of Comparative Education.* Heinemann, 1965 (2nd Edition).
—: *Power and Politics in Belgian Education.* Heinemann, 1965.

Moehlman, A. H.: *Comparative Educational Systems,* Prentice-Hall, 1964.

N.A.S. (ed.): *Education in Europe.* N.A.S., 1963.

Redl, H. B. (ed.): *Soviet Educators on Soviet Education.* Collier-Macmillan, 1964.

Samuel, R. H. *et al.*: *Education and Society in Modern Germany.* Routledge, 1949 (2nd Impression, 1962).

Unesco (ed.): *World Survey of Education.* Evans Bros., 1966 (Reprint).

PART ONE

Philosophical

CHAPTER 2

PHILOSOPHY AND EDUCATION

A. THE NATURE OF PHILOSOPHY

In his *Introduction to the Philosophy of Education* Professor D. J. O'Connor puts forward the view that philosophy is "not a body of knowledge of a positive kind", such as law, biology, history or geography, but rather "an activity of criticism or clarification"[1]. H. L. Elvin, in *Education and Contemporary Society*, argues that

"Philosophy is a technique for thinking, and is especially concerned with examining our assumptions and defining our concepts. Social philosophy and the philosophy of education are concerned with the assumptions we make and the concepts we use in thinking about society and education"[2].

Both these statements appear to reject the traditional view of metaphysics, namely, that philosophical investigation could give a knowledge and understanding of such ultimate and transcendent "realities" as the existence of God, or some ultimate Ground of the Universe, the freedom of the human will, or the relation that exists between the mind and the body. Philosophy, according to the views expressed by Elvin and O'Connor, is an activity and a technique which may be applied, in fact, to any subject matter at all. Thus we have, for example, the philosophy of history, the philosophy of science, the philosophy of religion, and the philosophy of education; sometimes we hear of meta-history, and many years ago Ernst Mach used the term "meta-geometry" for this philosophical sort of analysis of some geometrical problems.

Although, however, since the 1920's the classical metaphysical approach has received some severe blows from the Wittgenstein

School, from the logical atomists and Bertrand Russell, and from the so-called logical positivists and Professor A. J. Ayer, there are still those who believe that philosophy has a function other than sheer analysis. Labels of any kind are dangerous and open to misinterpretation, and our study in the disciplines and general theory of education, if it does nothing else, should at least make us wary of categorizing anybody or any particular line of thought. We shall, no doubt, use labels, but we shall also be aware that different philosophers, psychologists, sociologists and educationists frequently use the same terms with differing connotations. Different writers also classify the various "types" of philosophy, or "schools" of philosophy in a variety of ways. Neither life nor thought is ultimately reducible to precise classification and definition. To give but two examples, Plato has been termed both an "idealist" and a "realist", whilst Rousseau has been classified as a "naturalist", an "idealist", or some synthetic composition of both. In the long run, educational philosophy, insofar as it follows the classical metaphysical pattern, tends to be eclectic; that is it tends to select and utilize elements in all philosophies and to apply them in a variety of ways both inside and outside the classroom. Or, again, it may seek to synthesize and organize into some new system the best that it finds in all philosophies.

In the past, philosophy has concerned itself with three main lines of inquiry, and these lines are still very clearly defined in many University syllabi for the honours school in philosophy. They are referred to as ontology, epistemology and teleology:

(a) *Ontology* is the philosophical inquiry into the ultimate nature of Being itself, its origin and its essence. This is the whole question of Reality—What *is* Reality? What is the *Ground* of all existence? What is it "to be"? What is it that exists, and in what does its existence consist? These questions must inevitably lead on to an examination of the nature of man and life, the nature of man's essence and being, and the different kinds of life (e.g. mental, physical, spiritual, etc.).

(b) *Epistemology* is the philosophical inquiry into the problem of knowing and of knowledge, and an examination of the essence, origin and limitations of knowledge. What *is* knowledge? Are there different kinds of knowledge (conceptual, perceptual, intuitional, etc.)? And what is the relation between knowledge and being? Different schools of epistemology have arisen, such as rationalism, empiricism, transcendentalism and so on.

(c) *Teleology* is subsidiary to, and derived from, ontology and epistemology. It is the philosophical inquiry into the problem of purpose, and therefore value. What is the purpose of life, its aim? Is there some end towards which Creation painfully but inexorably moves? What are the values involved in both being and knowing?

Logic has usually been regarded as the tool, or part of the methodology for reaching conclusions in philosophical inquiry.

Those philosophers who are generally referred to as "logical positivists" (though many of them repudiate the label), or who at least belong to the analytical school, regard much of the foregoing type of inquiry as a waste of time. To them it is axiomatic, by the verification principle, that if a statement has "meaning" it can be verified in experience. The "Reality", the thing-in-itself, the Being of Being, the Platonic "Forms" of Truth, Beauty and Goodness—all these are meaningless, and all discussion concerning them is simply beating the air. They are not, and cannot by their very nature be, a part of sense experience, and so are unverifiable. Such things are in fact "nonsense", in the strictly technical sense of the word; i.e. they are not amenable to verification through sense-experience, and therefore have no objective meaning for us. In his *Critique of Logical Positivism*, Professor C. E. M. Joad appears at times to ignore Professor Ayer's technical use of the word "nonsense" in relation to the emotive theory of values. Joad equates "nonsense" in Ayer's usage with "nonsensical" in more popular usage, that is, "a meaningless set of noises which cannot, one would suppose, give us any information about anything" [3]. But if I say that I can see beautiful and radiant angels riding upon healthy, pink elephants, when no one else can see them, I am certainly giving expression to a judgement (both of fact and of value) which I cannot verify, and which is, therefore, technically "nonsense". It may yet be far from "nonsensical" or "a meaningless set of noises which cannot ... give us any information about anything", since my statement may reveal a great deal about myself and about the things I "really do see", but which just aren't there. And there seems to be no reason why the same sort of argument should not be used about what appear to be more sober value-judgements, such as, "This picture is beautiful". If I say that a picture is beautiful and others consider that it is ugly, or moderate, or indifferent, we seem to be in the realm of the unverifiable. It is, therefore, "nonsense"; it is neither true nor false; it is the expression of an emotion. But it is certainly not "nonsensical". If everybody were to say that "this picture is beautiful", then (I suppose) Ayer would say that this was a statement of value which was "significant"; and that

"in so far as statements of value are significant, they are ordinary 'scientific' statements; and that in so far as they are not scientific, they are not in the literal sense significant, but are simply expression of emotion which can be neither true nor false"[4].

There is something almost as indeterminate and uncertain about our value-judgements as there is about the path or position of an electron—which is about as close as we have got to the thing-in-itself. When, however, our value-judgements become "significant" they may, says Ayer, be equated with "scientific" statements.

In a lecture which he gave before the International Congress of Philosophy at Bologna on April 6, 1911, Emile Durkheim spoke on the subject of "Value Judgements and Judgements of Reality"[5]. Towards the end of his lecture, in which he has attempted to show how factual-judgements and value-judgements are related, he says:

"Thus the faculty of judgement functions differently according to the circumstances, but these differences do not impair the essential unity of the function"[6].

In his analysis of this lecture, in the Introduction to *Sociology and Philosophy*, Professor J. G. Peristiany, sums up Durkheim's view in the following words:

"A *judgement of reality* is a judgement of existence, as when I state that a certain object has weight. It also expresses the partiality of a person to an object, as when I express a preference for wine. A *judgement of value* expresses a relation between a

ducation"[9]. It is perhaps best to say, with H. L. Elvin,
that our approach to thinking about philosophical problems and
social questions should be "philosophical problems and
analysing the terms we use (such as "to the extent of
"truth", etc.), and of asking ourselves why", "patriotism",
"desirable" and others as "undesirable" consider some aims
we may agree with Professor L. A. Reid f "wrong"[10];
that "teachers ought (at times) to think as we must accept
they can" about their assumptions, and exami losophically as
detail[11]; and we can certainly accept what them in some
O'Connor has said, whether we accept his general position or
not, that

"Most of the catchwords and slogans of the educational reformer
are fossilized value judgements: 'education according to nature',
'education for democracy', 'equality of opportunity', 'education
for citizenship', and the rest. It is of the greatest importance that
directives of this sort should not remain mere slogans. They should
be explicitly formulated, related to practice *and recognized for
what they are*. An undiagnosed value judgement is a source of
intellectual muddle"[12].

If, after all this, the reader does not know what philosophy is,
it may well be because philosophers are not agreed as to the nature
of their subject. But at least the "philosophical approach"
should be plain—it involves a rigorous, analytical examination of
all our assumptions, without prejudice and with as little emotion
as possible, and then, as practising teachers at any level, the
attempt at some verification by the empirical application of any
conclusions we may have reached.

B. CLASSICAL SCHOOLS OF PHILOSOPHY

It is important for any student of educational theory at least to
know what the great schools of philosophy of the past have been
trying to say, and also how these philosophical standpoints,
through their adoption by educationists and reformers, have affected educational practice. In his *Introduction to the Philosophy
of Education*, S. J. Curtis has outlined the ways in which different
writers on the subject have classified the various schools of philo-

socially *held* ideal, nor a subjective apprec iation
ing the *na* ture of . 'This is an heroic action'
an *objective* eva ome sacred and judgements
of value. Objec ocial ideal"[7].
when they *reflec*

Peristiany a dds real" there is no difference of n
is, *in its own* wa e and judgements of reality.
judgements o of value" are "sociological" th
such "*judgem* suggesting that Durkheim wa s a
fic"; *and with* time, he does seem to have a
tivist" *before his* question of "statements of value" t
approach to the
fessor Ayer.

The analytical school, at any rate, claims that ph
philosophy is con cerned solely with the analysis of c
ing; its proposition ns are not factual, but linguistic i
It is not concern ed with the "description of the b
physical or ment al objects", but with the expression
tions. In fact, phil osophy is a "department of logic",fo

"we shall see that the characteristic mark of a purely
quiry is that it is c oncerned with the formal consequer
definitions and not with questions of empirical fact"[8]

There is no doubt that philosophy has always been ha
great deal by unve rifiable and speculative thinking; it
produced tightly-k nit, hermetically-sealed, almost un
"positions" and sy tems, in which discussion was baull
the start because of diametrically opposed premisses; ar
resulted in argumen ts which often became duologue rati
dialogue, and some imes quite impassioned defence of fa
dogma, rather than in a logical and calculated examina
evidence.

Despite the great service which such an analytic appro
provided, there are s till problems of being, knowing, purpo
value in which most people have some interest, and some pe
such as educationists have a great deal. Whether we cal
"philosophy", or " metaphysics", or even meta-educati
largely an academic question for the pundits. Ayer has re
philosophy to logic, Dewey defined it as "the general theo

B

sophical thought[13]. In the main, four types stand out for consideration—idealism, realism, naturalism and pragmatism. J. S. Brubacher refers to idealism and realism as forms of essentialism, whilst naturalism and pragmatism are forms of progressivism [14]. There are objections to every form of classification, and thinkers obviously overlap the various divisions, but as a cut-and-dried categorization Brubacher's seems to account for the facts as well as most, if not historically, then functionally. The essentialist function is to inquire after the nature of Reality itself, the essence of Being; the function of the progressivist philosophy is concerned much more with the development or evolution of what is *given*, rather than with questions of its ultimate origin and nature. There are obviously assumptions on both sides, but in broad terms essentialism is interested in ontology, whilst progressivism, though at times thoroughly utilitarian, is more immediately concerned with questions of teleology. The teleology of essentialism is largely derivative. Thus, for example, if after having searched for the ultimate essence I find some concept of God, I may then conceive it as the purpose of life to glorify him and serve him for ever; if, however, I accept that such a search is fruitless anyway, I may assume that man's nature is basically good and that life's purpose is progressively to elicit and develop that nature to the full.

I. Idealism

There are many misconceptions about the philosophy of idealism, most of which derive from the name itself, which really ought to be "Idea-ism". Any concern which this philosophy may have with ideals *qua* ideals is secondary and derivative. According to idealism the ultimate reality of the Universe is both intelligible and expressible in terms only of ideas rather than in terms of spatial matter. We cannot know our environment directly, only indirectly, and the physical world depends for its very existence, or at least for its organizational form, upon mind or spirit. Thus, idealism concludes that the Universe is entirely an embodiment and expression of Mind. Bishop Berkeley (1685–1783), for example, began with the fact that the qualities of objects, e.g. their colour, size, shape, weight, etc., change with the conditions of our perception; and hence, he suggested, they are in reality ideas in our mind, or, when we are absent, in the Mind of God. In opposition to realism and materialism, idealism insists that the basic and essential "thing-in-itself" is the very stuff of the Universe, is mental and not material, is Mind not Matter.

Idealism accepts values as having reality; such values are axiomatic or given; they are intrinsic and not extrinsic or instrumental. There are absolute values of Truth, Beauty and Goodness which are discoverable, and in the works of Plato we shall see this developed into the Doctrine of Forms or Ideas, which were to him the eternal principle of things. Everything else represented simply the decaying flux of material representations, the particular objects perceived by the senses. It is worth while noting here that some thinkers have referred to Plato's doctrine as "realism" because he considered that his Forms were real existents, i.e. that they had separate existence and essential reality. This, however, is an unsatisfactory use of the term and leads simply to confusion.

One of the great exponents of idealism, Immanuel Kant (1724–1804), distinguished two worlds: there was the world of morals, the noumenal world, in which the freedom of the will reigned supreme; and there was the world of concepts and their relations, the phenomenal world, in which the law of casuality was the controlling factor. It is sometimes argued that Kant left a dualism in which noumena and phenomena were unreconciled, and that in his system there was no satisfactory justification for the assumption of a reality outside of experience. But, in fact, Kant argued that the two apparently opposing factors of freedom and causality were reconciled in a suprasensible world, in the Absolute or World-Soul, which is revealed in a unifying, eternal and spiritual force. Kant is just another example of the difficulty of rigidly classifying philosophers; insofar as he asserted that some element other than ourselves is implied in our experience of the external world, he is a realist, and opposed to the subjective idealism of Bishop Berkeley; insofar as he affirms that this "other" is never experienced as it is independently of us, but is moulded by the principles of understanding and intuition, he is an idealist. This external "other" is conditioned by our thought, and if we were to disappear it would be a different "other"—even if it didn't disappear altogether. Kant is, in consequence, sometimes referred to as an objective idealist, and sometimes as a critical realist.

II. Realism

The very existence of idealism as a philosophy implies its opposite —realism. Idealism had a long run of popularity among philosophers, but during the nineteenth century it came under constant fire from both the traditional, or essentialist side, and from the progressive side, and realist philosophy began to reassert itself. Realism maintains that the objects of sense-perception, or of knowledge, exist independently of the perceiver or knower. Knowledge is merely the process of discovery of the objective world. Realism received a great boost from the development of the natural sciences and the virtually infinite multiplication and examination of factual data: in this way the objectivity of the external world was increasingly emphasized. There were "things" to be discovered, to be analysed, to be correlated, to be forced into some pattern of cosmic coherence; and with the vast development of technology and the improved techniques of instrumentation it became increasingly possible to examine the "real" world, from galaxies in infinite space to pions and muons in the atomic structure. Many of these elements may be elusive, but they are no longer felt to be undiscoverable or simply "mental". Thus idealism asserts that only "ideas" have ultimate reality: realism, *per contra*, asserts that only "things" have real existence.

III. Naturalism

Naturalism is opposed to idealism in that it believes that we are restricted to the phenomenal world of scientific investigation. Its general outlook is an evolutionary and progressive one, both in relation to life at large and to man in particular. Man is the product of organic evolution, and throughout Nature may be discerned a physical and mental continuity. This continuity is governed by the operation of natural forces and natural laws. During the nineteenth century, naturalism grew largely in opposition to the very pessimistic view, supported by the Church doctrine of Original Sin, that human nature was essentially evil and depraved. In the ethical field, naturalism took the view that goodness, or rightness, consists in some natural quality, such as the production of general happiness.

The catch-phrase of the moment was, "Back to Nature"—back to the essential and inherent qualities within us, back to the natural as opposed to the artificial, back to the dynamic, progressive forces of Nature. It is at this point that we should remember D. J. O'Connor's warning note about "fossilized value judgements"[15]. The word "nature" was used by Rousseau in about five different ways, and this fact underlines the importance of the analytical approach to philosophical questions. There is implicit in this philosophical doctrine a biological determinism, which, in turn, must inevitably affect the trend of educational thought based upon it. One can, presumably, unfold only what is already enfolded, and this seems to have been the view of Rousseau (as we shall see later) that, since the child is "by nature" good, if we allow him to unfold in a natural way, he will develop into a "good" man and a "good" citizen. But since the philosophy of naturalism is based upon biological determinism, it would seem rather pointless, if not "nonsense", to speak of values within its context. Life is what it is by its very nature, and it is impossible to elicit any criterion of value from this, or somewhat dreamily or in utopian manner to speak of how life ought to be.

IV. Pragmatism

Pragmatism[16] insists upon the validity of empirical methods, and upon the necessity of changing hypotheses in the light of new discovery. It believes that the ultimate test of what is right or true must be sought in the practical consequences (hence "pragmatic" and "pragmatism"), and that the whole meaning of any conception is also expressed in its practical consequences. Like naturalism, it is opposed to idealist philosophy and is also influenced largely by evolutionary principles. Pragmatism regards everything as dynamic and changing, and so, apart from this assumption and the criterion of what is "right" or "true", it can possess no predetermined body of doctrines. Its "truths" must be established pragmatically and experientially; and the "good life" is not one one laid up in heaven and based upon a collection of "absolutes", "ideas" or "forms", but is quite simply "the life that is good to live". The only test that can be applied is the quite practical one—"Does it *work*?" If it works, it is good.

We are not here going to enter into a long critique of pragmatism, but it should be at once clear that the criterion, "does it work?", is no less "nonsense" than to ask "ought I to do this?" or "does this correspond with the ideal?" To ask whether something *works*, in this way, implies something more than just "has it happened?" It does, in fact, imply a value-judgement regarding the effect of certain activity in relation to the doer and the contextual situation in which the act is done. If the criterion means simply, "does it work for me?", then it is no more than a doctrine of selfish and egocentric behaviour. If it means, "does it work for others as well as myself?", it implies a knowledge of what is "good" for others as well as for oneself; and this, in turn, implies not only a great deal of knowledge of other people, what they like, want, and need, but it also passes beyond its own limits to some further standard of judgement—unless we are really to accept that the behaviour of a successful criminal is acceptable in this philosophy because it meets the requirements of the pragmatic test, to the extent that it works for the criminal. In fact, few pragmatists would accept that criminal behaviour is "right" or "good", however successful, and they must, therefore, have assumptions other than purely pragmatic ones. Another criticism, of course, is that we very often do not know the effect of our actions, whether immediate or remote, and we may have to wait an infinitely long time before we know whether or not they have "worked". In fact, whilst this may well be the criterion for many of our actions, it is clearly not so for many others.

Under a philosophy of pragmatism, however, the aim of life is to create a fairer, better, and more equitable environment for all mankind, by general experimentation and by the successful solution of problems. Such a philosophy fits in well with the ideas of behaviourism generally and with "trouble-shooting", whether in the industrial field or in the realms of technology. Certainly man possesses the power to adapt his environment to his own needs: but he must know what his essential needs are, he must be fully aware of those things that pertain to his peace of mind, and to a life of happiness lived in harmony with, and in the social context of, similar beings with similar needs, hopes and ambitions. Much of man's failure pragmatically may possibly be attributed to his own lack of awareness of the object of his pragmatism; just as many idealists may be so involved in utopian ideals about the "kingdom of heaven" that the only thing they succeed in raising is hell on earth.

Perhaps there is something of "truth" in all these philosophies, just as there may be "truth" in all religions. One may contemplate the "ideal" without necessarily be day-dreaming, although the novice should beware; a perpetual state of contemplation of the ideal could make one unfit for daily life. Professor M. V. C. Jeffreys quotes the story of St Theresa of Avila who, when addresing a novitiate, said, "My daughter, we do not want ecstasies here; we want someone who can wash up"[17]. And even Plato's philosopher-kings, after a long period of the contemplation of the Vision of the Good, returned to the intellectual and spiritual troglodytes in order to share with them their greater vision. On the other hand, a life of dishwashing pragmatism could be very frustrating, busy and purposeless—however much we might convince ourselves that it was "working". Somewhere a balance must be sought between the contemplative and the active, between the ideal and the real, between value and fact. One is reminded of the Zen monk who was enjoying his contemplation, and yet was dissatisfied with his progress. Anxious for further instruction he approached the Master and requested, "Would you kindly give me some instruction?" To which the Master answered. "Have you eaten your breakfast yet?" "I have", returned the monk. "All right, then go and clean your bowl." A judicious interpenetration of reflection and activity is one of the essentials of education.

C. EXISTENTIALISM AND PERSONALISM

To lump together such names as those of Kierkegaard, Heidegger, Sartre, Camus, Jaspers, Berdyaev, Marcel, Mounier, Buber, Maritain, Tillich and John Macmurray, and to call them all existentialists, or personalists, may be useful in general terms, but an examination of the men themselves quite apart from their writings reveals the fact that we have here people of a great divergence of religious belief and commitment—from atheists and agnostics to Quaker, Catholic, Orthodox and Lutheran persuasion[18]. The ramifications of the philosophy of the "existential" would (following Professor E. A. Tiryakian and Paul Tillich) take us back to the nihilism and naturalism of Nietzsche [19], but we must be content with a very brief reference to its origins in its attempt to overcome the depressing depersonalization of modern society. S. J. Curtis has summarized this tendency in his remarks concerning Kierkegaard (1813–55):

"Even a century ago, Kierkegaard, though the Denmark of his day had scarcely been affected by the industrial revolution, raised his voice against the growing tendency to lose sight of the individual in the masses. He was not thinking of the tyranny of the dictator but he was alarmed at forces in the democratic state which in the process of moulding public opinion were crushing the individual, the newspaper, and the ballot box. Since his time we should have to add the cinema, the radio and television, and organized propaganda of different kinds"[20].

Karl Jaspers is particularly concerned with this social situation, since, for him, "man only exists in and through society"[21], and his deep sense of history will not allow him to isolate the individual from the social (and historical) family of which he is a member. Moreover, the self is revealed only in existential communication with others; but unfortunately the mass society in which man finds himself stifles belief and communication; technology has uprooted man and left him

"devoid of specific character and cultural heritage, without foundations and empty"[22].

It is because of this fundamental need for rebirth of vital communication, and social communion and community[23], that the philosophies of the "existential" and of personalism have found root and have developed.

Paul Tillich defines the existential attitude as

"one of involvement in contrast to a merely theoretical or detached attitude. 'Existential' in this sense can be defined as participating in a situation, especially a cognitive situation, with the whole of one's existence. This includes temporal, spatial, historical, psychological, sociological, biological conditions. And it includes the finite freedom which reacts to these conditions and changes them"[24].

Thus we see in the great variety of existential and personalist philosophers, from the time of Kierkegaard on, that there are two main themes of agreement. Against the great superstructures of systematized philosophy they revolt, not in the analytical and coldly logical terms of the logical positivists, but in terms of the individual or *person*. Against the ever-increasing mass movements

in man's society, and in the context of its increasingly complex
nature, these philosophers point once more to the person. The
idealists have their "ideas", the realists have their "things", and
the logical positivists their "words", "definitions" and "meanings"; but the existentialists and personalists have shifted the
centre of interest to people. It is fascinating to note that in the
atmosphere of "existential thinking", atheists, agnostics, humanists, Jews and Christians of all sects find themselves using the
same sort of terminology to express their concern, not for doctrines or dogmas, but for the human situation, for people in their
Angst or despair; an atmosphere in which love, sympathy, mutual
respect, communion, dialogue and empathy are seen not as ideas,
ideals or values but as the very nature of the total situation. Tillich
has expressed the fundamental meaning of the "existential"; he
has also stated precisely how he views idealism and naturalism:

"Idealism and naturalism are alike in their attitude to the existing
person; both of them eliminate his infinite significance and make
him a space through which something else passes"[25].

The first great emphasis, then, in these philosophies is the person. The second is the person in relation. We have already
mentioned Jaspers' concern for social awareness as well as the
importance of the individual in the mass. Here there is a great
emphasis upon *involvement*; we must participate in a situation
with the whole of our being; we must exert our will in choice,
"for man finds himself in the act of choosing". There is emphasis also here on being and becoming, not in "essentialist" terms,
but in "existentialist" ones; we don't argue about life and its
meaning, we just live it to the full, we maximize our participation
in it and in our communication or dialogue with others. "Existence precedes essence" is frequently quoted as a catch-phrase of
the existentialists, and it is just as capable of becoming "fossilized" as any other catch-phrase; but its meaning is clear. Philosophers have considered the ontological question from before the
time of Socrates; but they have projected the mystery of being
into the Blue Inane; the mystery of being is in everyday life[26],
it is the mystery of becoming. "Man is the crystallized potenti-
ality of existence"[27], his destiny lies in becoming a person.

In this involvement in situations, in life and in people, there is
an *I-Thou* relation, of man to nature, of man to man, and of

man to God. Our relation to things, to objects, may be expressed as an *I-It* relation; but when we are involved with people, our relationship should not be as one with things, for every human being is another person and should be treated as such; which means that our great problem, in the words of Wilhelm Dilthey, is "a rediscovery of the *I* in the *Thou*"[28]. As we live in other people, and live again their experiences, so we establish this *I-Thou* relationship; a relationship termed by Buber "dialogical" or "dialogue". It is in dialogue that we really have this communion with others, or establish community. It is a truism that people can be as much alone in a crowd as they can be locked in their own rooms, and Buber has warned us that

"The life of dialogue is not one in which you have much to do with men, but one in which you really have to do with those with whom you have to do. . . . He who can be unreserved with each passer-by has no substance to lose; but he who cannot stand in a direct relation to each one who meets him has a fulness which is futile"[29].

D. PHILOSOPHY AND EDUCATION

Thought inevitably goes into life and action; our sense of purpose, or lack of it, will guide our actions; our concept of values and our view or vision of the totality of existence will make us the sort of person we are, and will affect our "dialogical" relationship with other people. If you believe that there are spiritual values, that there is an after-life, and that this present life is in some sense a preparation for it, your aims and practice in education are likely to be modified by it, even though you never take a class in Religious Education. If you believe that this life is all that there is, then the maximization of economic, social and technological functions *may* seem to you to be the sole aim of the educative process; or, as a humanist, you may feel that there are certain virtues and values worth mediating to others. It is not unlikely that, if there is any sort of real relationship between educator and educand, the "philosophy of life" (whether in technical or common-sense terms) of teachers will be reflected in their pupils. We will briefly look at each of the main philosophies in turn, and see how they might affect, or have affected, educational thought and method.

Idealism really begins with Socrates and Plato, who not only were educationists of their own time, but also have affected education in various ways ever since. Idealism stresses man's dignity, and regards the development of the individual personality and the fullest self-realization of each child as some of education's chief aims. The educator's problem is to discover what *is* the highest level of development in each case, and to try and find some means of enabling the pupil to reach it.

One of the finest expressions of idealism as an educational philosophy is to be found in the work of Friedrich Froebel (1782–1852), particularly in his *Education of Man*, in which he maintains that there is a unity transcending the opposition between work and play, for both are means to the individual's self-realization.

"Man works only that his spiritual divine essence may assume outward form, and that thus he may be enabled to recognize his own spiritual, divine nature and the innermost being of God"[30].

Froebel was influenced by the Hegelian dialectic of thesis, antithesis, and synthesis, and he saw in education a means of synthesizing human personality and universal values. In Froebel's fundamental concept of the *Kindergarten* there is an analogy of the school and the garden; the teacher is the careful gardener who tends his pupils as if they were plants. The "garden" is an environment or situation in which the whole school provides a means by which the pupil may fulfil his own being, may "grow" and develop according to the laws of his own nature. Both the external means—the environment—and the internal significance of work, play and activity are media for evolving the inner, spiritual life of the child. Here the task of education is seen as the development of the child's innate capacities, and of his ability to appreciate the absolute values of Beauty, Truth and Goodness.

Whilst the conception of *Naturalism*, as seen in J.-J. Rousseau's *Emile*, was never fully put into practice in any school—even if it could—it is true to say that many of the ideas propounded by Rousseau, as we shall see in Chapter 4, have moulded the educational philosophy of many reformers in the nineteenth and twentieth centuries. Rousseau emphasized the need to study the child so that his education could be adapted to his characteristic needs. The child is the datum of the educational process. In general, Naturalism emphasizes the importance of growth, freedom, interest and activity in education, and it underlines the individual's autonomous development. It is obvious that the naturalist philosophy has made a great deal of use of the prominence given in recent years to the doctrine of the heredity of intelligence. Nature has already decided what we are going to be like: nurture has very little hand in it; this again has developed a determinist attitude in education itself, and it has taken the form of sorting out, through Intelligence Tests etc., what nature has already established. The tripartite system of secondary education has represented largely an unwarrantable naturalistic conclusion. Naturalism has also exercised a considerable influence upon the development of teaching methods; paedocentricism, or child-centred education, is naturalistic and many modern methods have some relationship to it, from the Play Way to A. S. Neill's methods at Summerhill.

One of the first and greatest exponents of *Pragmatism* was John Dewey (1859–1952), who is discussed more fully in Chapter 5. Pragmatism, in general, taught that there are two sides of education, the psychological and the social, neither of which should be subordinated or neglected. The psychological nature of the individual child is the starting point, and the teacher should then study the social situation in order that the child's activities may be properly interpreted and may be directed into social channels. The data of education for the pragmatist are, therefore, the organism and the environment; and the interaction between the individual pupil and his environment is *experience*. Pragmatism is, therefore, concerned with practical experience and empirical data, and it is through continuous interaction with his environment that the individual learns, by degrees, to control it and modify it.

Thus, to the pragmatist, education is an active process of experiencing; but it is an active experiencing, since experience itself may be reformed towards a more significant social meaning. Education becomes, in this theory, an end in itself and must not be controlled by any aims external to the learner; it is development from within. Again, pragmatism is opposed to formal indoctrination and the sort of education which tries to train individuals for specific types of adult life and occupation. The educative process must centre upon the child's own needs, purposes and interests; they cannot be assigned by a teacher. There must be a spontaneity and wholeheartedness about the child's purposes, and they must derive from his own felt needs as stimulated by problematic situations. Even so devoted a follower of the pragmatic line, however, as W. H. Kilpatrick (b. 1871), of Teachers' College, Columbia University, believed that coercion had to be used on occasion:

"Do we therefore conclude that coercion is never to be used? The answer is no. In certain situations and with certain background matters it seems wise to use compulsion, as for example, with compulsory attendance at school. But even here, if we rely solely on compulsion to make children come to school, we shall not succeed; what goes on in school must commend itself to the learners or legal compulsions will not continue to work. Or again, where certain behaviour is necessary because of its effects on the child or on others, it is true that at times, at school or at home, positive coercion may be necessary for the sake of the wider values involved"[31].

Perhaps the greatest and most characteristic contribution of pragmatism to the practice of education is to be found in the Project Method, which is the full expression of this theory.

Truth, then, according to pragmatism, is reached through experience, and learning comes very close to verification, to "truth-finding"; and so the child must experiment and experience if he is to find the truth for himself. The educational aim is within itself, it is the *creation* of new values rather than the attainment of old ones; and the educator's main task is to assist the pupils in every way possible to develop values for themselves, and this he can do by providing the "right environment" and the "right type" of experience.

Pragmatist philosophy in educational practice has always come in for severe criticism. It is argued that the pragmatist's rejection of spiritual values and assumptions, of any predetermined or external standards, of any external authority, inevitably leads to the adoption of lowered standards of achievement and of character formation. It is suggested that progress is a question of values and criteria, and that the pragmatist has no such general criteria for total progress, since he has no final values. It is sometimes said that "pragmatism is a method and not a philosophy, and that a true philosophy of education must have goals more definite than that provided by 'growth'". This is perhaps altogether fair, and W. H. Kilpatrick has provided a defen some extent, in two chapters of his *Philosophy of Education*, one on the "Philosophy of Educational Method", and the other entitled, "Correlatives: Philosophy of Life; the Educative Process" [32]. It is not possible here to summarize those chapters in full, but Kilpatrick is well aware of the criticisms made of pragmatism and of its criterion, and he here appears to go outside the pragmatic field to provide what he terms "Basic Value-Assumptions" and "Strategic Guiding Principles"[33]. He suggests that

"acceptance of moral obligation becomes essential to satisfactory social living. Only on such a basis can we have a decent civilization"[34].

And of the "Philosophy of Educational Method" he says:

"Gaining knowledge and skills are important, even necessary, but building inclusive character of the kind to live democratically is the crux of it all; this 'living and learning method', properly used, does so build character; and it does this far and away better than can any amount of mere knowledge as such"[35].

Realism in education was largely a reaction against studies that had become chiefly theoretical and which depended mainly on book-learning. It was a movement against mere verbalism, and its war-cries were "things before words", and "action not abstraction". This was a swinging of the pendulum against "chalk and talk". But, as with most educational philosophies, it represented an exaggeration. In fact, most children love "words", and regard them as things to be manipulated and controlled; they are as essential to a child's mental development as things themselves, and what is required is a proper balance between the two. As R. S. Peters has remarked:

"Any method which can create interest in what is worth while should not be debarred—even talk and chalk, if employed by a man who is good at it"[36].

The aim should be to work at "things" and "words" together, and to recognize that verbal studies and so-called "real" studies are no more opposed than a text-book on chemistry and the chemicals in the laboratory—provided they are used together.

The realist approach to education usually emphasizes the value of vocational education and guidance as being related to the "real" world outside the school, and maintains that there should be close co-operation between the school and the community outside.

The philosophies of *Personalism*, with the exception of those of Gabriel Marcel and Martin Buber, have been almost silent on the problems of education as such, although they clearly have implications for education. Buber's comments on education are to be found in two chapters in *Between Man and Man*[37]. Buber had already discussed in chapter one what he meant by dialogue, its implications, and its limitations—which are the limits of the individual's awareness. Buber places considerable emphasis on this question of awareness:

"Each of us is encased in an armour which we soon, out of familiarity, no longer notice. There are only moments which penetrate it and stir the soul to sensibility. And when such a moment has imposed itself on us and we then take notice and ask ourselves, 'Has anything particular taken place? Was it not of the kind I meet every day?' then we may reply to ourselves, 'Nothing particular, indeed, it is this every day, only we are not there every day'"[38].

One is reminded a little of the Zen student who, after seven years of arduous training, was asked, "And to what does your Zen training lead?" He replied, "Nothing miraculous, so far as I know; but I wake up in the morning and the world seems so beautiful that I can hardly stand it". This awareness of Nature, of the Other, is vital to true dialogue, true understanding and true being.

"Only he who himself turns to the other human being and opens himself to him receives the world in him. Only the being whose otherness, accepted by my being, lives and faces me in the whole compression of existence, brings the radiance of eternity to me. Only when two say to one another with all that they are, 'It is *Thou*', is the indwelling of the Present Being between them"[39].

This *I-Thou* relationship, this interprenetration of personalities, is beautifully expressed by Dante when he addresses Foulquet of Marseilles, in Book III of *The Divine Comedy*:

Why grants it not the longing prayer in me?
I would not wait for thee to make demand,
Could I in-thee me as thou in-meëst thee[40].

This is dialogue; it is a relation between persons which is characterized, in more or less degree, by the element of inclusion; and,
to Buber, the relation in education is "one of pure dialogue"
[41].

Education is also "essentially education of the character"[42].
The genuine educator is concerned with the whole person, both
as he now is and also what he may become. But if he is to affect
the whole being of his pupil he must do it in the whole of his own
being; this requires, not a moral genius, but a man wholly alive,
"able to communicate himself directly to his fellow men"[43].
Firstly, the confidence of the pupil must be won, and then he
will give up his resistance to being educated, and he then "accepts
the educator as a person"[44]. It is not the educational intention
of the teacher that is educationally fruitful, but this meeting of
person with person. Nor is it of any use, in seeking to educate
character, to point to eternal values.

"Men who have so lost themselves to the collective Moloch cannot be rescued from it by any reference, however eloquent, to the
absolute whose kingdom the Moloch has usurped"[45].

Buber emphasizes the importance of awakening in young people
the courage to be, the courage to shoulder life again, and to accept
full responsibility for everything they meet. Finally, through
genuine education of character there comes a genuine education
for community.

It is not the writer's purpose to enter into a discussion as to
what the aims of education really are, or whether, as R. S. Peters
has argued, education can have no ends beyond itself[46]; it is
left to the reader to follow up the various arguments and sources
which have been quoted. Perhaps it should be emphasized again
that the approach in the realm of the philosophy of education is
at present less at the metaphysical level and more at the analytical.
Philosophy, as was said at the beginning of this chapter, is
viewed more as a technique of criticism, thinking and clarification. Not everyone is prepared to reduce it to a department of
logic, but few are anxious, on the other hand, to erect a synthetic,

or synoptic, overall system of life's purpose, and then apply it to education. Philosophy is used in a somewhat empirical and practical way for discussing and probing current educational problems. Thus, for example, Professor G. H. Bantock has said that one of the most pressing problems of the moment in education, and in the whole of our social life, is the search for

"an 'authority' that will give strength and meaning to man's free development of himself that will allow man to come to his true 'self' . . . which, in the last resort, is what education implies"[47].

This, then, is a subject for analysis at the philosophical level, beginning with a discussion on what "authority" means, and why "authority" is necessary anyway if a person really wants to be "free"; which leads to a consideration of what we really mean by "freedom" in a modern society; and if man has a "true 'self'" as distinct from the "himself" for which *he* is seeking free development, what is the nature of these various "selves", which are connected in some way, but which are apparently different? Words and phrases like "equality", "equality of opportunity", "parity of esteem", "total education", "integration", and "discipline", and problems such as moral and religious education, liberal, technical and vocational education, the curriculum, and so on, are all the subject matter of a philosophy of education. And if some of these terms have become "fossilized", then at least our future educators should be made aware of the extent of the fossilization. It may well turn out to be that the claim that we have an educational system in which all children have "equality of opportunity" may simply mean that all children are granted equal opportunity to display their unequal capacity. Such hollow-sounding expressions should not be mouthed as if they were the very cornerstone of the whole of our educational system.

    This, in turn, raises the very important question of *élites*, and whether some are not inevitably, by heredity and social environment, "more equal than others". And, finally, in our anxiety to make sure that our pupils are getting somewhere (e.g. "getting on", "improving", "likely to make the grade", "has acquired ten O Levels", "should go far"), have we failed to ask what may conceivably be the more important question, "*Who* is going where?"? Perhaps, as Professor Peters has hinted,

"To be educated is not to have arrived at a destination; it is to travel with a different view"[48].

REFERENCES

1. O'Connor, D. J.: *An Introduction to the Philosophy of Education.* Routledge, 1957, p. 4.
2. Elvin, H. L.: *Education and Contemporary Society.* C. A. Watts & Co., 1965, p. 65.
3. Joad, C. E. M.: *A Critique of Logical Positivism.* Victor Gollancz, 1950, p. 117.
4. Ayer, A. J.: *Language, Truth and Logic.* Victor Gollancz, 1954, 2nd Edition, p. 103.
5. *Vide* Durkheim, E.: *Sociology and Philosophy.* Cohen & West, 1965 (Revised Edition), pp. 80–97.
6. *Ibid.* p. 96.
7. *Ibid.* p. xxv. and note 1. My italics.
8. Ayer, A. J.: *Op. cit.*, p. 57.
9. Dewey, J.: *Democracy and Education.* Macmillan, 1923, p. 383.
10. *Vide* Elvin, H. L.: *Op. cit.*, pp. 83–7; and Chapter IV *passim.*
11. *Vide* Reid, L. A.: *Philosophy and Education.* Heinemann, 1962, p. 41. (Particularly Chapter III, "Values in Life and Education"; and Chapter IV, "The Justification of Judgements of Value".)
12. O'Connor, D. J.: *Op. cit.*, p. 107.
13. Curtis, S. J.: *An Introduction to the Philosophy of Education.* U.T.P., 1958 (Reprinted 1963). *Vide* Chapter III, pp. 55–89.
14. Brubacher, J. S.: *Modern Philosophies of Education.* McGraw-Hill, 1939.
15. *Vide* O'Connor, D. J.: *Op. cit.*, p. 107.
16. *Vide* Chapter 5 on "John Dewey" for greater detail.
17. Jeffreys, M. V. C.: *Glaucon.* Pitman, 1950, p. 96n.
18. For a useful brief account of "Personalist Philosophy" *vide* Curtis, S. J.: *Op cit.*, pp. 81–9; *vide* also Curtis, S. J. & Boultwood, M. E. A.: *A Short History of Educational Ideas.* U.T.P., 1965 (4th Edition), pp. 604–20, and Reid, L. A.: *Op. cit.*, pp. 65–7.
19. *Vide* Tiryakian, E. A.: *Sociologism and Existentialism.* Prentice-Hall, 1962, pp. 89–103; and Tillich, P.: *The Courage to Be.* Collins, Fontana Lib., 1962 (2nd Imp. 1964) *passim.*

20. Curtis, S. J.: *An Introduction to the Philosophy of Education*, p. 84.
21. Jaspers, K.: *Man in the Modern Age*. Routledge, 1951, p. 149.
22. —: *The Origin and Goal of History*. Routledge, 1953, p. 128.
23. *Vide* Buber, M.: *Between Man and Man*. Collins, Fontana Lib. 1961, *passim*.
24. Tillich, P.: *Op. cit.*, p. 124.
25. *Ibid.* p. 136.
26. *Vide* Buber, M.: *Op. cit.*, p. 11.
27. *Ibid.* p. 102.
28. Hodges, H. A.: *Wilhelm Dilthey*—An Introduction. Routledge, 1944, p. 114.
29. Buber, M.: *Op. cit.*, pp. 38–9.
30. Froebel, F.: *The Education of Man*. Appleton & Co., 1909, p. 32.
31. Kilpatrick, W. H.: *Philosophy of Education*. Macmillan, 1951 (Reprinted 1963), pp. 269–70.
32. *Ibid.* Chapter XXI, pp. 283–98, and Chapter XXIX, pp. 420–32.
33. *Ibid.* pp. 420–4.
34. *Ibid.* p. 421.
35. *Ibid.* p. 298.
36. Peters, R. S.: *Education as Initiation* (Studies in Education). Univ. of Lond. Inst. of Ed., published by Evans Bros., 1964, pp. 45–6.
37. Buber, M.: *Op. Cit.*, Chapter III "Education" and Chapter IV "The Education of Character", pp. 109–47.
38. *Ibid.* p. 28.
39. *Ibid.* pp. 49–50.
40. Dante: *The Divine Comedy: Book III—Paradise*. Penguin Books (Pelican), 1962. Translated by Sayers, D. L. and Reynolds, B., Canto XI, ll. 79–81, p. 127.
41. Buber, M.: *Op cit.*, p. 125.
42. *Ibid.* p. 132.
43. *Ibid.* p. 134.
44. *Ibid.* p. 135.
45. *Ibid.* p. 139.
46. Peters, R. S.: *Op. cit.*, p. 47.
47. Bantock, G. H.: *Freedom and Authority in Education*. Faber, 1952, p. 183. Of course, this is not intended to be a criticism of Professor Bantock who clearly knows what he means by these terms.
48. Peters, R. S.: *Op. cit.*, p. 47.

BIBLIOGRAPHY

A. GENERAL BOOKS ON THE PHILOSOPHY OF EDUCATION

Brameld, T.: *Patterns of Educational Philosophy*. World Book Co., 1950.
—: *Philosophies of Education in Cultural Perspective*. Holt, 1955.
Brubacher, J. S.: *Modern Philosophies of Education*. McGraw-Hill, 1939.
Burns, H. & Brauner, C.: *Philosophy of Education*. Ronald Press, N.Y., 1962.
Butler, J. D.: *Four Philosophies and Their Practice in Education and Religion*. Harper, 1951.
Curtis, S. J.: *An Introduction to the Philosophy of Education*. U.T.P., 1958 (Reprinted 1963).
Horne, H. H.: *The Philosophy of Education*. Macmillan, 1927.
Kilpatrick, W. H.: *Philosophy of Education*. Macmillan, 1951 (Reprinted 1963).
Lenz, J.: *Philosophy of Education*. Harper, 1947.
Neff, F. C.: *Philosophy of Education*. Prentice-Hall, 1965.
O'Connor, D. J. *An Introduction to the Philosophy of Education*. Routledge, 1957.
Phenix, P. H.: *Philosophy of Education*. Holt, 1958.
Reid, L. A.: *Philosophy and Education*. Heinemann, 1962.
Rusk, R. R.: *The Philosophical Bases of Education*. U.L.P., 1928, 2nd Edition, 1956.
Weber, C. O.: *Basic Philosophies of Education*. Holt, 1960.

B. OTHER BOOKS OF REFERENCE

Ayer, A. J.: *Language, Truth and Logic*. V. Gollancz, 1954, 2nd Edition (10th Imp.).
Bantock, G. H.: *Education and Values*. Faber, 1965.
—: *Freedom and Authority in Education*. Faber, 1952.
Barnes, W. H. F.: *The Philosophical Predicament*. A. & C. Black, 1950.
Brameld, T.: *Towards a Reconstructed Philosophy of Education*. Holt, 1955.
Buber, M.: *Between Man and Man*. Collins, Fontana Lib., 1961.
Childs, J. L.: *American Pragmatism and Education*. Holt, 1956.
Dewey, J.: *Experience and Education*. Macmillan, 1938.

Dobinson, C. H. (ed.): *Education in a Changing World*. O.U.P., 1951.

Elvin, H. L.: *Education and Contemporary Society*. C. A. Watts, 1965.

Hardie, C. D.: *Truth and Fallacy in Educational Theory*. C.U.P., 1942.

Hollins, T. H. B. (ed.): *Aims in Education*. Manchester Univ. Press, 1964.

Horne, H. H.: *The Democratic Philosophy of Education*. Macmillan, 1932.

Jacks, M. L.: *Total Education*. Kegan Paul, 1946.

Jeffreys, M. V. C.: *Glaucon, An Enquiry into the Aims of Education*. Pitman, 1950.

Joad, C. E. M.: *A Critique of Logical Positivism*. Gollancz, 1950.

Judges, A. V. (ed.): *Education and the Philosophic Mind*. Harrap, 1957.

Kneller, G. F.: *Existentialism and Education*. Phil. Lib. Inc. N.Y., 1958.

Macmurray, J.: *The Self as Agent*. Faber, 1957.

—: *Persons in Relation*. Faber, 1957.

Mounier, E.: *Personalism*. Routledge, 1952.

Niblett, W. R. (ed.): *Moral Education in a Changing Society*. Faber, 1963.

—: *Education, Bias and Indoctrination*. Univ. of Leeds, 1954.

—: *Education and the Modern Mind*. Faber, 1954.

Nunn, T. P.: *Education: Its Data and First Principles*. Arnold, 1945.

Peters, R. S.: *Authority, Responsibility and Education*. Allen & Unwin, 1959; 2nd Edition 1963.

—: *Education as Initiation*. Univ. Lond. Inst. of Ed., published by Evans Bros., 1964.

Reid, L. A.: *Creative Morality*. Allen & Unwin, 1937.

—: *Ways of Knowledge and Experience*. Allen & Unwin, 1961.

Ross, J. S.: *Groundwork of Educational Theory*. Harrap, 1952.

Rusk, R. R.: *Doctrines of the Great Educators*. Macmillan, 1954, 2nd Edition.

Thomson, G. H.: *A Modern Philosophy of Education*. Allen & Unwin, 1929.

Urban, W. M.: *Beyond Realism and Idealism*. Allen & Unwin, 1949.

Whitehead, A. N.: *The Aims of Education*. Benn, 1962.

—: *Adventures of Ideas*. Macmillan, 1933.

CHAPTER 3
PLATO (427–347 B.C.)

A. PLATO'S LIFE AND TIMES

Plato was a member of an old and distinguished family which had a large number of political connexions in Athens. In particular, through his stepfather, he had a link with Pericles, who died during the year before Plato was born, i.e. 428 B.C. Pericles gave his name to the great age of Athenian history, and much of the Athenian "democracy" was obviously indebted to him. Little is known of Plato's early life, and we can only assume that he received the normal education of a Greek youth; that of learning to read and write, and pursuing a study of the poets[1]. Plato grew up in Athens during the time of the Peloponnesian War, which lasted from 431 to 403 B.C.; a war between Athenian democracy and the "arrested oligarchic tribalism of Sparta"[2], which resulted in defeat and humiliation for Athens, and in the breakdown of the confederation which Pericles had done so much to strengthen.

The downfall of Athens was followed by the Spartan oligarchic revolution. A commission of Thirty was appointed ostensibly in order to frame a new Constitution, but in the event they sought to retain power in their own hands and to use it for the final destruction of their enemies. There followed a reign of terror and tyranny for eight months, until the Thirty were eventually expelled and killed, and the democratic constitution was once more restored. Despite its general moderation and its discrimination, it was this democracy that put Socrates to death in the year 399 B.C. on charges of impiety and a deliberate policy of attempting to subvert and corrupt the young. This event had a deep and lasting effect upon Plato who had expected to go into politics; but he became disgusted with it all and drew back, as he says, from the wickedness of the times.

Socrates and his Influence (469–399 B.C.): It is probable that
Plato was quite young when he met Socrates whom he represents
in his Socratic Dialogues as a friend of the family. Yet, in spite of
his considerable influence, Socrates has left us nothing in writing.
One is reminded somewhat of a modern parallel in the great
George Herbert Mead who, when he died at the age of sixty-
eight in 1931, had not published a single book and comparatively
few articles. It was Mead's avid and admiring students who
managed, between them, to record his lectures almost *verbatim*.
The method of Socrates, the Socratic dialectic, was an attempt at
showing how contradictory and confused many of the contemporary and conventional notions of morality, politics and religion
were. The "irony" of Socrates, expressed both in *The Republic*
and elsewhere, has been accepted by different critics as an expression of humility or as one of a consciousness of his own superiority; at any rate, Socrates claimed that his greater wisdom existed in the fact that he was aware of his own ignorance, whereas
his listeners were unaware of theirs. And the simple cure for
ignorance was knowledge: if only we *knew* what was right the
problems that faced both society and the individual would be
solved. It was, indeed, the duty of all men to seek and find true
knowledge, both in order to be themselves and to help society.
But in order to do this they must first of all know themselves, for
true knowledge was itself true goodness[3].

The Socratic method of cross-examination, which Plato reproduces in the Dialogues, with its intense, and not infrequently
irritating, penetration of verbal connotation and definition, was
regarded as highly unorthodox, and inevitably led in many minds
to scepticism and agnosticism. To many Athenians, particularly
those who saw safety in authoritarianism and dogma, all this
"modern nonsense" was highly dangerous[4]. If their society
were to remain stable and intact, a greater respect for its conventions and institutions was essential. But one thing is perfectly
clear, namely that, although Socrates sought to provoke and agi-
tate the minds of his young and intelligent hearers, he was not himself a complete sceptic about moral principles. K. R. Popper[5]
has described Socrates as the champion of the "Open Society", of
democracy; he was a man who emphasized the equalitarian
theory of human reason as a universal medium for the communication of all ideas and principles; a philosopher who, in a time of

utter sophistry and intellectual dishonesty, laid great stress on self-searching and self-criticism; a supporter of a strictly egalitarian theory of justice; a moralist who proposed that it is better to be the victim of injustice than to inflict injustice upon others; an individualist who propounded a creed of individualism and preached a belief in the human individual as an end in himself.

Socrates strongly opposed the contemporary Sophists on moral questions and their casuistry, and he endeavoured to demonstrate that back of every particular action one must presuppose some general ideas or principles which are universal or eternal, for all people and for all time. Such cardinal virtues as temperance, courage, wisdom and justice are not the pawns of individual interpretation: they are the basic and essential ideas which are the very foundation for particular forms of society and social activity, for which any individual may find the *imprimatur* in his own experience when soundly analysed. If "Virtue is Knowledge", as Socrates believed, then virtue is also teachable and ought to be taught.

Plato and his Academy: Plato's own disillusionment at the political scene led him to the conclusion that all existing States were badly governed, and that it would require really drastic treatment to reform them. The only hope of finding justice for either the individual or society at large lay in true philosophy, and

"Until philosophers are kings, or the kings and princes of this world have the spirit and power of philosophy, and political greatness and wisdom meet in one, and those commoner natures who pursue either to the exclusion of the other are compelled to stand aside, cities will never have rest from their evils—no, nor the human race, as I believe—and then only will this our State have a possibility of life and behold the light of day"[6].

Plato travelled to Cyrene, Egypt, and Phoenicia and served in the Athenian army. He wrote his first Dialogues, including his defence of Socrates and the *Gorgias*, in which he provided an analysis of the respective merits of philosophy and politics, and finally rejected the latter. In 388–387 B.C. he visited Southern Italy and there became acquainted with the Pythagorean philosophers, who influenced him in the Orphic-Pythagorean belief in an After-Life and in their emphasis upon mathematics as a philosophic discipline. In Sicily he obtained a first-hand acquaintance with the "Tyranny" of Dionysius I of Syracuse.

In 386 B.C. Plato founded the Academy where he taught until his death in 347 B.C. The object of this "University" was to train a new type of politician who might become the sort of philosopher-ruler outlined in *The Republic*. A few years before, in 390 B.C., Isocrates (436–388 B.C.) had established another School in his own house near the Lyceum. There he taught rhetoric and, in general, prepared his pupils for the political life. Plato, on the other hand, sought to continue the work of Socrates and taught philosophy.

The Sophists[7] were travelling lecturers and teachers who sought to cover the whole field of knowledge; but

"since success in life is what most men want, and since the ability to persuade your neighbour is always an important element in success, and was particularly important in the Greek democracies, they all taught rhetoric, the art of self-expression and persuasion"[8].

Many of them were particularly interested in political theory and ethics, and in arguing casuistical situations; and whilst Thrasymachus, who is portrayed in Book I of *The Republic*, may not be a typical Sophist he certainly represents one type of Sophist who liked to expatiate at length in a somewhat authoritarian manner, who would certainly not be self-depreciatory in the Socratic "ironical" manner, and who was not very anxious to engage in the more rigorous analysis of Socratic dialectic. Many of the Sophists were superficial in their treatment of their subjects, and somewhat sciolistic, but by no means all of them could be accused of this lack of depth. There was, however, a premium upon rhetoric as opposed to sound discussion, and ability in declaiming was regarded almost as a sign of culture and "higher education".

In 367 B.C., on the death of Dionysius I, Plato was invited to go to Syracuse in order to train Dionysius II who was then twenty-eight, as a philosopher-statesman. Plato decided to go, but his visit was unsuccessful, and a year later he returned, somewhat disillusioned, to Athens. Almost twenty years later, at the time of his death, he was still seeking the perfect philosopher-king of his dreams in the various courts of his society and in his Academy.

B. PLATO'S PHILOSOPHY OF IDEALISM

The aim of Plato's Academy was, as we have said, to train philosopher-statesmen, and *The Republic* was a statement of that aim, and so dealt at some length with the means to be employed; that is, it dealt with education. Since the ills and the disruptions of society would not be eliminated until philosophers ruled, the education of such philosophers became the most important of political activities. If only they could be properly trained, and given power, the details of administration could then be left in their capable hands.

Moreover, because the Ideal State is to be governed by philosophers, philosophy itself plays a large part in *The Republic*. The most important feature in that philosophy is the belief in Two Worlds; there is the everyday, physical world in which we live; this is the world of phenomena, of change and appearance; and there is the world of eternals, of absolutes, "ideas" or Forms. It is important that the philosopher should have a true sense of values: these values are absolute, and their ultimate source and standard is Absolute Goodness, or the Form of the Good. The vision of the Form of the Good is what some have termed "the Vision of God", but that is not to say that the Form of the Good and God are necessarily the same. The experience of the Form of the Good is, however, mystical—even religious; it is a state of knowledge and yet it is incapable of being communicated in ordinary language.

The Form of the Good is supreme and is the fount and source of the very existence of all other Forms, and of their value. Plato cannot describe the Form of the Good directly, but in Book VI he does it indirectly by means of a simile or analogy in which the Good is compared to the Sun. In the Visible World of changing phenomena, the Sun is the Source of Light and Growth, and it gives visibility to the objects of sense, and the power of seeing to the faculty of sight, namely, the eye. In the Intelligible World of Forms, the Good is the Source of Truth and Reality, and it gives intelligibility to the objects of thought, and the power of knowing to the faculty of knowledge, namely, the mind.

Also in Book VI Plato provides the analogy of the Divided Line and expands the Sun simile a little further. The Physical World is a world of Opinion, in which both Illusion and Belief play a part. The realm of Illusion is one of images and shadows;

but higher up the scale is the realm of Belief, which is concerned with the sense-objects, or physical things, responsible for the shadows of the world of Illusion. The Intelligible World is the realm of Knowledge, which at the lower levels uses the objects of the physical world as illustrations, and so develops mathematical reasoning. But the highest realm of knowledge is to be found in the "dialectic", the pure thought and intelligence which goes entirely beyond the world of physical things to the rarefied realm of Forms and "ideas".

The Simile of the Cave, in Book VII, provides a more picturesque and vivid elucidation of the Platonic metaphysic. Imagine human beings dwelling in an underground cave which is open towards the light. They have been there from childhood with their necks and legs chained, and they are able to look only into the cave. At a distance there is a fire, and between the fire and the denizens of the cave there is a raised bank and a low wall is built along the way, just like a screen over which players might show their puppets. Behind the wall there are moving figures, who hold various objects, images of men and animals, ikons of stone and wood; some of the passers-by are talking and some are silent. We see only the shadows, the phantasmagoria of fading visions. The sounds we hear are vague, confused and fleeting. If we were to be dragged up the steep ascent into the Light, into the presence of the Sun, we would be "blinded with excess of light". It is given only to the few to make the ascent of the mind from Illusion to Pure Thought, and then only slowly and by stages. And when the philosopher, who achieves this and has the experience of the Supreme Vision, has stayed awhile, he is required to return to the cave and to save his fellows. In this return his very unwillingness is his chief qualification.

In Plato's philosophy, then, true knowledge is of the eternal, the unchanging. There is no denial of the physical phenomena of sense-experience; it is merely that these have no reality or existence of their own; they derive their reality from the Forms of which they are but copies or, rather, from the essence of which in some mystical way they are a part. Plato's Doctrine of Forms or Ideas has traditionally been termed "Idealism", because it is concerned with "ideas", and those ideas are seen in an "ideal" or universal application. Others have preferred to call his philosophy "realism" because his ideas are "real", that is, they have an absolute existence outside the mind of man. But if the term "realism" is here used it must not be identified with the "realism" of common sense[9]. Others have suggested that his philosophy should really be termed "Idea-ism". The term which appears to be least objectionable, however, is that adopted by K. R. Popper:

"I use the name *methodological essentialism* to characterize the view, held by Plato and many of his followers, that it is the task of pure knowledge or 'science' to discover and to describe the true nature of things, i.e. their hidden reality or essence"[10].

Popper distinguishes this form of methodology from *methodological nominalism*, whose function it is to describe how a thing behaves in a variety of circumstances; and, in particular, whether there are any regularities in its behaviour.

The fact is, of course, that there are both realistic and idealistic aspects in the philosophy of Plato and in that of Aristotle, but "in their fundamentals they transcend both"[11]. And short of creating an entirely new "grammar" of metaphysics, with a precise classification of each philosopher agreed upon by all, it would be best to leave Plato in the "idealist" school provided that there is a complete understanding of what "idealist" connotes in this context.

C. PLATO ON MORALITY

Plato's *Republic* has been called a work on politics, a treatise on educational philosophy, a Utopia, a sociological diagnosis, and a large number of other things. It is also a study in ethics or morality. The main question that leads to the final construction of *The Republic* is a moral one; "What is the meaning of Justice?" This ethical inquiry is concerned with both the individual and the society; with the moral behaviour of the individual in society and with the manner in which society as a whole behaves in a "moral" way in regard to individuals. "What is right?" "What is the right thing to do in this situation?" "Why should I obey the dictates of the Law?" "Why should I be good?" These are some of the questions that *The Republic* looks at, and which it answers step by step, and in sometimes objectionable ways, throughout its construction of the ideal society. Glaucon, for example, proffers an answer in the form of the "Social Contract" theory, arguing that we are good or moral because it pays us to be, or because, through *force majeure*, we have to be. If we were given the opportunity would we not all act differently? Adeimantus supports Glaucon in his arguments and suggests that we obey the dictates of our society for purely mercenary reasons. It is left to the great Socrates to demonstrate that there is something intrinsic about morality; it is preferable *per se* to immorality. In moral behaviour we are not concerned with motives of self-interest. "Virtue is Knowledge"; morality is a question of knowing what is right: because if we really *knew* we would do it.

In *The Republic* Plato looks for justice, or morality, in the harmonious functioning of the various departments of society. Society is the individual "writ large", and justice is to be found in the face-to-face relationships between every member of that society. Similarly, the happiness of the individual, his full development and well-being, are to be secured by the harmony within himself, and by doing what is right and avoiding what is wrong. The reward of virtue is the individual and social fulfilment that it brings. Individual fulfilment means that each part of the human being is harmoniously operating with every other part. Plato does not seek to make any exhaustive analysis of the mind; and what he had to say about its function would undoubtedly be regarded by psychologists today as unscientific. His view of human nature is tripartite: the intellectual, spirited and appetitive elements; but his usage is largely metaphorical and utilitarian.

Thus Plato answers the main question, "What is Justice?", by saying that in the individual it consists in keeping a proper balance between the intellectual, the spirited and the appetitive elements; between mind, will and emotion. Each will then be performing its own function or doing its job. "So perhaps justice is, in a certain sense, just this minding of one's own business"[12]. True morality, says Plato, really consists in giving full satisfaction to those impulses within us, but not at the expense of one another: none must be allowed to dominate; but they must each find their due place in the human constellation of impulses in order to produce "the good life". Similarly, when each class and element in society is fulfilling its proper function, social justice has been achieved.

There has, for hundreds of years, been a sort of "archaic tradition" about Plato. New interpretations have from time to time appeared, including quite novel and unconventional ones such as

E. J. Urwick's *The Message of Plato*[13], but only very rarely
have they been strongly opposed to his general teaching, or ad-
versely critical of his moral position. It is almost refreshing, therefore to read K. R. Popper's very different approach[14]. Popper
regards Plato's account as a collectivist, tribal, and utilitarian
theory of morality.

"Plato recognizes only one ultimate standard, the interest of the
state. Everything that furthers it is good and virtuous and just;
everything that threatens it is bad and wicked and unjust. Actions
that serve it are moral; actions that endanger it, immoral. In
other words, Plato's moral code is strictly utilitarian; it is a code
of collectivist or political utilitarianism. *The criterion of morality
is the interest of the state.* Morality is nothing but political
hygiene"[15].

So Thrasymachus was right after all, and justice is nothing else
than the interest of the stronger: might is right! It is not surprising that classicists rallied to the defence of Plato. But there are
certainly some passages in *The Republic* which strongly support
Popper's view, that Plato's picture is one of a closed totalitarian
society, in which certain devices of propaganda, certain myths concerning man's birth and place in society, and a certain casuistical
opportunism towards "truth" are the rule. It has been argued in
our time, and not always by totalitarian societies, that it may be
"right" at times to give the public misinformation, or information which is less than the whole truth, for the security of the State,
or for the further entrenchment of the government. Popper believes that Plato was sincere in his totalitarianism[16], but that it
was a totalitarianism in which the State had its own concepts of
truth and morality. It is a little difficult to rebut this when *The
Republic* blandly states:

"Then if any one at all is to have the privilege of lying, the rulers
of the State should be the persons; and they, in their dealings
either with enemies or with their own citizens, may be allowed to
lie for the public good. But nobody else should meddle with anything of the kind"[17].

Pro bono publico—what crimes are committed in thy name!
    From the foregoing it would almost seem as if only those who
best know the truth are really fit to lie. One can perhaps argue

that the best secret service agents, and those most fitted to deceive and prevaricate, or engage in counter-espionage, are those who know the most, who are in possession of the total picture. But this hardly fits in with Plato's philosopher-kings who have seen the Sun itself, have had a Vision of the Form of the Beautiful and the Good, and have now returned to mediate their vision to those less fortunate. In a sense, however, all that they say will be less than the truth of the Vision that they have received, but Plato's "privilege of lying" suggests a deliberate perversion of the truth that they know. And Popper, in turn, suggests that this is for propaganda purposes, for the controlling of the masses.

D. PLATO ON SOCIETY AND POLITICS

1. *The Social Strata:* In his discussion of "Totalitarian Justice" Popper considers the principal elements in Plato's political programme[18], and the first one that he enumerates is the strict division of the classes; that is,

"the ruling class consisting of herdsmen and watchdogs must be strictly separated from the human cattle"[19].

There were, in reality, in Plato's ideal Republic only two classes— the Rulers and the Rest. There was a sort of "efficiency bar" among the ruling classes, who were divided into the Guardians and the Auxiliaries. The function of the Guardians was to rule, to make decisions and to determine policy; the function of the Auxiliaries was at all times to help the Guardians, to execute their commands, and to serve as a sort of military police. Guardians and Auxiliaries pursued the same sort of life, and had to undergo the same rigorous training and education. And just as promotion was possible from Auxiliary to Guardian, so it was equally possible for an unworthy Guardian to be demoted to an Auxiliary. Plato wanted the rule of "the best", and this, he believed, could only be achieved by careful selection and breeding. He was quite aware that mistakes would arise, and he made provision for them—there was this possibility of inter-traffic between Guardians and Auxiliaries. But he sought primarily a ruling group who would be an *élite*, an aristocracy of intellect and talent.

The Rest, the second-class citizens, comprised everyone other than the *élite* already mentioned. They were all those engaged in farming, manufacturing, trading—all the economic activities of the Republic—everyone, rich and poor alike. It was their function to be governed and to provide for the sum-total needs of the community in the economic and material realm. The prime virtue of the Rest was obedience to the dictates of the Guardians and the control of the Auxiliaries, who in their turn would ensure that the Rest were "happy" within their society, for

"our aim in founding the State was not the disproportionate happiness of any one class, but the greatest happiness of the whole"[20].

They would also ensure that the work of the Rest did not degenerate through either excessive wealth or excessive poverty[21]. It is frequently argued by critics of *The Republic* that the position of the Rest was little better than that of slaves, who were a common feature of the Athenian society. But when we speak of "slaves", particularly in relation to Plato's *Republic*, we do well to pause and look at, not the acknowledged slaves in our present world society, but the virtual slaves in our contemporary economic and industrial system. As R. C. Lodge has commented:

"And when we consider the modern harshness and ultra-ruthlessness, it looks as though the advantage, morally speaking, is with the comparatively easy conditions depicted by Plato . . . the charge that Plato's civilization is utterly different from ours because its labour is slave-labour, while our labour is something else, is a charge which must be dropped because it is not in accord with the facts of present-day life"[22].

2. *The Family and Ownership of Property:* We have already noted that the differences of wealth among the Rest were to be brought to an absolute minimum. Wealth, according to Plato, had a corrupting influence—those who had too little spent their lives in desperate unhappiness trying to get enough; those who had too much became indolent and dissolute. As far as the Guardians were concerned Plato would introduce an ascetic principle: both private property and the family were to be abolished. A man who is to govern others, and control the destinies of his society, must be free from disaffecting private interests and claims. No man who is concerned with the acquisition of wealth, or who is emotionally disturbed by the disquieting, and often

c

disrupting, affairs of the family could be trusted to place himself wholeheartedly at the disposal of the State and its service. As long as one has property there is a tendency to live in, and for, that property; to become involved in its varying vicissitudes, and to be taken up with personal worries and considerations. The Guardians must have none of these: they must live only for the State.

The abolition of the family derived also from the principle maintained by Plato that the sexes were equal. In their reproductive functions men and women were obviously different, but apart from this "accident" of nature they should be permitted to follow the same lines of social development. They should have the same sort of education, similar careers, and equal opportunities. Instead of family units for the Guardians Plato envisaged State Nurseries; even sexual intercourse itself should be strictly regulated, and there should be a certain number of regular "marriage festivals" each year, when suitable partners would be mated in order to produce the best types of Guardian. This upper-class stud-farm for humans had all the qualities of a loveless, dutiful, State-conscious, self-sacrificing Experimental Unit about it. What they did, they did—just as they lied—for the public good.

It is, of course, true that many of the differences between men and women, other than the purely biological ones, may be socially conditioned. Yet, when all allowances have been made, the sexes are in very essence different; and to seek to force them into precisely the same mould as men, to give them precisely the same jobs to do, even to give them exactly the same sort of education may, as H. D. P. Lee has pointed out, result simply in the production of a class of "inferior men"[23].

3. *The Guardians or Philosopher-Rulers:* The whole system of education as outlined in *The Republic* is geared to the production of the Guardian, the best type of ruler that society can evolve. After the long course of training as outlined by Plato there is left a group, a small number, an *élite*, who have satisfactorily passed all their examinations and tests. They have attained to wisdom through their learning and knowledge; but they are not only informed and wise, they are also good, for "Virtue is Knowledge".

These Philosopher-Rulers are clearly the cream of their society, the intellectual *élite*. But strangely enough, having been trained for the job of ruling, they do not wish to rule. Some sixty years or more before Plato was born, the Chinese philosopher Confucius was giving utterance to something very similar. Talking of the virtue *Te*, or moral power, he said that the greatest power by which men ruled was the power of moral example; everything, therefore, depended upon the men at the top. They must be completely without personal ambition, for, indeed, "only those are worthy to govern who would rather be excused". Plato's Philosopher-Rulers would rather be excused: they have had a supreme vision of the Form of the Good in the Kingdom of Ideas, and such a vision of the Beautiful-Good can but leave a man enraptured and unwilling to return to the images and shadows of the realm of physical things. He would rather contract out and live the remainder of his days in pleasant and peaceful contemplation.

But they have been trained for a function, and that function is, through their superior wisdom, knowledge and understanding, to serve their society through government. Their reluctance does them credit—there is here no "vaulting ambition which o'erleaps itself"; no quest for power that corrupts. These men are worthy rulers because they have first established order and harmony within themselves, and therefore they are able to disseminate it throughout the society over which they rule.

Plato wanted an aristocracy of talent. Two books in recent years have indicated certain movements in our own society in the same direction. James Burnham's *The Managerial Revolution* describes the control, and the need for control, of society by special ability; Michael Young's *The Rise of the Meritocracy* adumbrates, however satirically, a society in which intellectual "merit" rules supreme[24]. Somewhat cynically, one feels, K. R. Popper concludes his chapter on the Philosopher-King with the words:

"I think we must face the fact that behind the sovereignty of the philosopher king stands the quest for power. The beautiful portrait of the sovereign is a self-portrait. . . . We may even begin to feel a little sorry for Plato, who had to be satisfied with establishing the first professorship, instead of the first kingship, of philosophy"[25].

E. PLATO ON EDUCATION

I. The Aims of Education

Rousseau said that *The Republic* was the finest treatise on education ever written. To Plato education was a social process, and as such it sought to adjust the individual to his society. But it was also the path to the vision of Absolute Truth, or the Form of the Good and the Beautiful. That "beatific" vision was a personal experience, a vision of the individual soul; and, therefore, education was also an individual process. Education was concerned with righteousness, with truth in the soul, with the Beautiful-and-the-Good; it was concerned with justice both individual and social but it was not concerned with the social success which very much formed the aims of the Sophists.

Plato believed very strongly in the principle of Recollection or Reminiscence. The Vision of Truth and Goodness were, in fact, already within us; it was largely a question of the teacher helping to turn the eye of his students inward towards the light. No wonder Rousseau, with his "inner light", thought that this was the finest treatise on education ever written! In his most unusual and very unorthodox treatment, *The Message of Plato*, E. J. Urwick tries to relate Plato's teaching with Indian philosophy and practice, and regards Plato as an exponent of the Gnana Yoga or Wisdom Path. He says:

"He is not concerned with any of those 'excellences of mind' which may be produced by training and discipline: his only aim is to open the eye of the soul, to bring into activity the hidden power of spiritual vision which lies dormant in everyone of us . . ."[26].

The true art of the teacher lies, says Plato, in setting the right objects before the pupil so that his vision may be cleared, the "doors of perception" may be opened, and the mud and the mire of worldly preoccupations may be uncovered. And so he is led to that Vision of Goodness which is already intrinsically within him; he recalls to remembrance the former life or experience which he had.

The art of making the soul beautiful, says Plato, is to set it in the context of beautiful things; and so music and art find a pride of place in the educational process. And this process goes on through life, so long as man is capable of responding to any stimulus in his environment, so long as he remains an active participator in his experience and able to learn from it and to make personal adjustments in his development. As one stage ends, so another begins. At the age of thirty-five the official training of the future Guardian is said to be over; but even after the Guardian has contributed fifteen years of his energetic life to government, he must (at the age of fifty) return to the study of philosophy and contemplate the Realm of Eternity. Plato speaks of the illumination of the soul, the slow turning of the self to the pure light of the Sun, and the acquisition of wisdom. This is a mystical, almost poetical, realm and it is not surprising that Urwick found parallels with Yoga thought. It all recalls that intuitive poem by Dylan Thomas:

> Light breaks on secret lots,
> On tips of thought where thoughts smell in the rain;
> When logics die,
> The secret of the soil grows through the eye,
> And blood jumps in the sun;
> Above the waste allotments the dawn halts[27].

But before this illuminating experience is elicited the individual must undergo a great deal of arduous effort and strict discipline.

For Plato Knowledge and Truth are cosmic, and the unity of the world and of the Universe is an ultimate postulate of his thought. To *know* something is to see it clearly as a part of the divine or universal scheme of things; it is purposeful, and to discover its purpose is to participate in its ultimate Form, which is also the chief aim of education. Every scheme, every idea, every purpose that we fully know becomes a part of our experience; and gradually the integrated scheme of the Universe unfolds before our eyes in the fulness of our human experience. This is the sum-total of the curriculum and the subject-matter of education. But to *know* is to *do*. To know the ultimate Form of the Good is to know what to do and why we should do it. Virtue is knowledge, and knowledge issues in action.

II. *The Training of Auxiliaries and Guardians*

1. *The Stages of Education in* The Laws: In *The Laws*[28] Plato works out a scheme of Nursery education (3–6 years), Primary

education (6–10 years), and Secondary education (10–16 years). It should be noted that some critics do not accept the Platonic authorship of *The Laws*, whilst those who do regard it as one of his latest works. In this scheme Plato leaves a gap between the ages of sixteen and twenty-five, at which age young men are permitted to marry and to serve as associates to the inspectors of the country in their peregrinations. Education in *The Laws* appears to be for all the populace and not merely the future rulers.

Education begins at birth, children being carried in arms by nurses until they are three years old, when they may begin to walk. *Nursery* education now begins. As the child grows so it will jump and shout, and these activities should be trained gradually, by the use of rhythm, tune and a sense of time, into singing and dancing. Children now begin to develop games together in a natural, unorganized way, and from time to time nurses should take them to the village temples. At the age of six boys and girls must be separated. *Primary* education now commences, and studies are begun in more earnest, taking the form chiefly of physical drill. Both girls and boys are taught archery, the use of the sling and riding; games are used as a means to an end—for the purpose of creating better soldiers and citizens for the State.

Secondary education begins at the age of ten when a tutor is appointed to escort the child to school, to watch over him, and if necessary to punish him, for he is that

"most unmanageable of all animals, who, just before he possesses (what other animals do not possess) a spring of thought, still turbid and unsettled, is full of wiles, full of sharpness, and very full of impertinence"[29].

The child must now learn to read and write, to study literature, to acquire some skill with the lyre, work out calculations, including the elements of both arithmetic and geometry, and the rudiments of astronomy. At the age of thirteen the pupil will begin the study of instrumental music. "True astronomy" must be developed to the point where "the student begins to see the 'being and the operation of God'"[30]. This is the element of moral and religious teaching. Generally speaking, in *The Laws* there is a strong advocacy of compulsory education in organized schools for both boys and girls; and it is interesting to note that Plato was here concerned with three age levels in this organized education—nursery, primary and secondary.

2. *The Stages of Education in* The Republic: In *The Republic* there are two stages[31]. The *First Stage* of education is the stage through which alone the great majority of the Auxiliaries ever pass. It is that stage when youth is trained in order to develop character through the emotions, and in order to produce the "spirit" or ethos best suited to the needs of the community, and to the function of the Auxiliary himself within the community. It is primarily a social training and its aim is the preparation of a class of citizens who will adequately and correctly discharge their function as a sort of military police within the State.

The *Second Stage* is that to which only those of maturer years, who have proved themselves worthy of membership of the Guardian class, can attain. During this stage the social element of education loses a great deal of its prominence, and there is a concentration upon the development of wisdom and understanding through the inflexible pursuance of science and philosophy. It is a period during which men who are destined to be statesmen are produced: men who would rather spend their days in the contemplation of Ultimate Reality.

3. *The Place of Gymnastic* (γυμναστική) *and Music* (μουσική) *in Education*: Plato advocates the studies of Gymnastic and Music for the first stage of education. Gymnastic includes a great deal of what today we might call Health Education; that is, it involves medicine and diet as well as the exercise of the body. Music includes a study of literature as well as music proper; in fact, Plato's use of the term "Music" seems to include also a study of the plastic arts. Music is a way of training both mind and character through the media of sound, movement, speech and form.

Plato regards both Music and Gymnastic as working together in their effect upon the individual. In reality

"he who mingles music with gymnastic in the fairest proportions, and best attempers them to the soul, may be rightly called the true musician and harmonist in a far higher sense than the tuner of strings"[32].

Both serve the purpose of training the mind and the character, since they both have a moral as well as a physical and mental effect. Gymnastic is a training of the body for the sake of the mind; it is calculated to elicit qualities of courage and endurance, and is therefore concerned not merely with individual development but also with social training.

Music acts directly upon the mind or soul. Its intention is to provide harmony to the various elements of the human soul and further to elicit the innate power of reasoning. Whilst Music cannot of itself give a man scientific knowledge, it can give "right opinion". The rhythm and diction of poetry, the harmonious strains and mystical melodies of musical instruments, the shapes and colours produced in the development of the arts, plastic and creative—all these appeal to the human soul. But they also have a *moral* quality and dimension which will enter the innermost recesses of the soul, mediating to it a sense of beauty, or imparting to it a sense of deformity, according to their nature.

Because of this moral element in the arts and its inevitable effect upon the individual development, Plato would introduce both reform and censorship in music, in literature and in art. The misrepresentations of the nature of the gods to be found in the poets must be corrected and where necessary expurgated. Thus Plato is concerned in his system of education with questions of religion as well as literary form. The soul is affected by everything with which it comes into contact: the State must, therefore, provide the right sort of environment in which the soul may develop in a healthy, harmonious, good and beautiful way. And Plato concludes that a good, sound education in gymnastic and music carries with it everything else; it is a "law in the heart" requiring no further compulsion (cf. Jeremiah) whether by words, external legislation, or law enforcement in order to ensure its fulfilment in the greater society. Plato believed that if the education were of the right sort, then laws, legislation and litigation would wither away.

"We would not have our guardians grow up amid images of moral deformity, as in some noxious pasture, and there browse and feed upon many a baneful herb and flower day by day, little by little until they silently gather a festering mass of corruption in their own soul. Let our artists rather be those who are gifted to discern the true nature of the beautiful and graceful; then will our youth dwell in a land of health, amid fair sights and sounds, and receive the good in everything; and beauty, the effluence of fair works, shall flow into the eye and ear, like a health-giving breeze from a purer region, and insensibly draw the soul from earliest years into likeness and sympathy with the beauty of reason"[33].

4. *The Higher Studies of the Guardian or Philosopher-Ruler: Dialectic*: The education of the maturer years of the initiate to Guardianship develops from an education through art to an education through mathematics, science, and metaphysics. Already, during the earlier stages of education, youths were trained in the elements of science. Arithmetic, geometry and general science should be presented to the child mind as a sort of amusement, and not by the use of compulsion. This is the way by which to discover the natural bent of the child, and also to find out those who are fit to be selected for more rigorous studies.

At the age of twenty the youth is ready for the life-long education which will elevate him, through a succession of stages, to the contemplation of the Pure Idea. The *Quadrivium* (arithmetic, geometry, astronomy and music) and Dialectic are the subjects of higher study outlined in *The Republic*. Mathematics is the natural link with Plato's "universals" or "Forms", since the things with which it deals are neither the Forms themselves nor yet any sensible particulars; they are intermediate features between the two realms. The units employed by arithmetic are abstractions of the mind; and, according to Plato, the real value of plane and solid geometry depends upon whether it tends, to any extent, "to make more easy the vision of the good"[34]. Astronomy and the harmonies have an equal part to play in this search for the Vision of the Good.

All these studies should occupy a period of ten years, from the ages of twenty to thirty years. Some who followed the earlier stage of education will not be permitted to enter the later stages, which are reserved for those who showed most promise in the earlier stage. Between the ages of thirty and thirty-five Dialectic will be studied; this is the means whereby the realm of pure Forms and the Idea of the Good is at last attained. Dialectic, or Philosophy, is the study of the first principles of Being, and of the Idea of the

Good, which is the cause of Being, and is also the object of knowledge. This represents those branches of Metaphysics usually referred to as Ontology and Epistemology. The teleological element is provided by the fact that the sole *purpose* of human existence or being is to achieve a vision of, and an identity with or participation in, the Form of the Good.

The future Guardians will be proved and tried in their study of Philosophy, and those who lack the true philosophical nature will be relegated to the class of Auxiliaries; those who are successful will become the Philosopher-Rulers and perfect Guardians of the State.

Between the ages of thirty-five and fifty these Guardians must give themselves to the full service of the State. They will command in battle, they will hold important and responsible offices, and throughout they will gain wisdom and a wide experience of life. Right throughout their service they will be tested and tried until, at the age of fifty, those who emerge with distinction may be permitted to reach the goal:

"the time has now arrived at which they must raise the eye of the soul to the universal light which lightens all things, and behold the absolute good; for that is the pattern according to which they are to order the State and the lives of individuals, and the remainder of their own lives also; making philosophy their chief pursuit, but, when their turn comes, toiling also at politics and ruling for the public good, not as though they were performing some heroic action, but simply as a matter of duty"[35].

In this life of perfect activity they must work for their fellow men, and in the light of the perfect knowledge that they have achieved, as a matter of duty and not as something self-sacrificing and noble.

F. SOME GENERAL COMMENTS

Professor R. C. Lodge has pointed out that the traditional and classical educationist will probably find in Plato everything that has ever had any lasting influence upon education; the progressive educationist, on the other hand, will put most of this down to wishful thinking and exaggeration or misapplication. The truth of the matter probably lies somewhere between the two extremes.

When Rousseau made his claim that *The Republic* was the finest treatise on education ever written, it is clear that, however Rousseau himself may be classified, the influence of Plato was still being felt in the latter part of the eighteenth century.

It is perhaps impossible to say whether Plato was directly, or even indirectly, responsible for a particular line of philosophical or educational thought, or for a particular educational practice; or whether Plato was, in many instances, so much in advance of his time that our own present theory and practice, though often similar to that suggested in *The Republic*, are quite unconnected with Plato's teaching itself. Professor R. C. Lodge makes the point that

"The child-psychology and infant-pedagogy of our day do not change, but endorse the traditional lessons inculcated by Plato. . . . As far as infant education is concerned, then, there is no fundamental difference in principle between what Plato teaches and what we find in our most modern practice"[36].

This, of course, may be perfectly true without there being any connexion between modern psychology and pedagogy and what Plato taught; but at least it bears out the fundamental accuracy of some of Plato's approaches to the problems of education. He believed that education should begin from birth and in the home; that education was, in fact, growth and that the early years were all-important; that the environment of the child influences his character, and that all true education involves balance and harmony[37]. E. B. Castle finds, to give another example, that in the education of women for impending motherhood we depart little from the suggested practice of Plato:

"We are not surprised, therefore, to find that Plato begins education in the pre-natal clinic where advice is given to young parents"[38].

It is, however, the general ethos of Plato's idealism that has influenced western educational thought and practice rather than specific or isolated ideas. It is the "archaic principle" itself, the tendency to look back to the best in the past—very often with starry-eyed, romanticized views of some "Golden Age"—which has so strongly affected our education for hundreds of years. Benjamin Jowett remarks that

"The Republic of Plato is also the first treatise upon education, of which the writings of Milton and Locke, Rousseau, Jean Paul, and Goethe are the legitimate descendants"[39].

He might have also added the names of Quintilian (*Institutes of the Orator*), More (*Utopia*), Campanella (*City of the Sun*), and many others. The debt is certainly there, in general spirit if not in any detail.

Plato was concerned with the development of the individual mind and character, and for him Gymnastic and Music, in his definition of those terms, were jointly directed towards the evocation of sound character—"mens sana in corpore sano". The essential purpose of such education was to turn the "inner eye" towards the Light, so that it might see for itself. The great Oxford scholar, Sir Walter Raleigh, used to say to his students, "Don't look at me, look at where I am going"[40]; and it was the purpose of Plato to provide for his educands a "Vision of Goodness" at which they might perpetually aim. And there are educators who have strongly felt this to be one, if not the chief, of the aims of education[41]. The aim seems vast, remote, unattainable; and yet in a sense present and realizable. For, says Plato, the world of sense-objects and shadows participates in the "Form of the Good", and so the knowledge of the Good is possible since it is already partially known. The ideal is already present in the actual.

Plato considered nursery and infant education, primary and secondary education, and finally higher education. Plato's Academy was really the first University in Euope, and its general concept and plan of education permeated European universities for a very long time. In the third and fourth centuries A.D. the philosophy of Neo-Platonism developed—an attempt by Plotinus and the Alexandrian School to blend Platonic and Christian elements. This had a strong appeal for the thinkers of the Renaissance, and its basic principles could be seen in the writings of both the Italian philosophers and the Cambridge Platonists. The Mediaeval curriculum was almost entirely Platonist—he may have neglected grammar and rhetoric in the *Trivium*, but to him dialectic was the queen of studies; the *Quadrivium*, comprising music, arithmetic, geometry and astronomy, was entirely his own.

R. R. Rusk has said of Rousseau that "he is manifestly an idealist"[42], and much of Rousseau's apparently revolutionary writing smacks of Plato's idealism. In *The Timaeus* Plato remarks that

"no man is voluntarily bad; but the bad become bad by reason of an ill disposition of the body, and bad education"[43].

All this Rousseau accepted and suggested that man's *nature* was good in itself, that a feeble body made a feeble mind, and that the current educative processes of society were deleterious, making man evil.

Much more could be said with reference to Plato's influence both within the theoretical and the practical realms. It is natural to look at any ancient book through modern eyes—the thousands of commentaries on the Christian gospels alone testify to man's incredible and incurable ability to transmute the sayings of the wise into current areas of thought and belief. It is popular today to speak of Plato's "totalitarianism" both in his political and educational processes, and K. R. Popper has outlined Plato's "totalitarian programme" in some detail[44]. But one wonders how far any sort of comparison between a Greek City-State in the fourth century B.C. can be made with, say, the Stalinist Communist régime or the Hitlerite Nazi régime of the twentieth century A.D. Because he linked up his theory of leadership with his theory and practice of education, Plato, so Popper maintains, "utterly corrupted and confused" the latter[45]; and he further argues that Plato's educational aim was not "the awakening of self-criticism and of critical thought in general" but rather "indoctrination"[46].

Plato lived in a time of insecurity and instability; it was natural that he should look for something stable, lasting and unchangeable. He was persuaded that the best in everything could be ascertained and used; or, if we accept Popper's "historicist" thesis that Plato was looking into the past, he believed that there had been such a state of stability and that we must return to it. It never occurred to Plato that there was "no return to a harmonious state of nature", that such a return was ultimately a "return to the beasts"[47], or at least that it was in "danger of decay from stagnation"[48]. Yet in a sense the problem that faced Plato is no different from ours, or from that of any society that has ever existed; it is the problem of translating the best that we "know" in terms of the society in which we live. Many of the questions raised in *The Republic*—those of education for leadership, the intellectual *élite*, indoctrination, social adaptation, perfect self-development or self-realization, equal opportunities for both sexes, moral and religious education, social education—are the questions we still discuss and debate[49]. It is, therefore, not surprising that the cynic has said that you can find in Plato whatever you are looking for: and whatever you are looking at you can find in Plato.

REFERENCES

1. *Vide* Castle, E. B.: *Ancient Education and Today.* Penguin Books (Pelican), 1961, pp. 11–105; Boyd, W.: *The History of Western Education.* A. & C. Black, 7th Edition, 1964, pp. 1–42; Taylor, A. E.: *Plato.* Methuen, Univ. Paperback, 1960, pp. 1–9.
2. Popper, K. R.: *The Open Society and its Enemies: Volume I— The Spell of Plato.* Routledge, 5th Edition (Revised), 1966, p. 178.
3. Barker, E.: *Greek Political Theory.* Methuen, Univ. Paperback, 1960 (Reprinted 1964), *vide* Chapter V, pp. 99–125.
4. Lee, H. D. P. (tr.): *Plato: The Republic.* Penguin Books (Pelican), 1955 (Reprinted 1964), p. 13. The whole of the translator's Introduction is a lively and valuable summary of the background and content of *The Republic.*
5. *Op. cit.*, pp. 189–94.
6. Jowett, B. (tr.): *The Republic of Plato.* O.U.P., 1908 (Third Edition 1927–8), Vol. I, 473 D–E. This translation has been used mainly throughout.
7. Castle, E. B.: *op. cit.*, pp. 49–58.
8. Lee, H. D. P.: *op. cit.*, p. 15.
9. Ross, J. S.: *Groundwork of Educational Theory.* Harrap, 1942, p. 70.
10. *Op. Cit.*, pp. 31–2.
11. Curtis, S. J.: *An Introduction to the Philosophy of Education.* U.T.P., 1958 (Reprinted 1963), p. 59.
12. *The Republic*, 433 A.
13. Urwick, E. J.: *The Message of Plato.* Methuen, 1920.
14. *Op. cit.*, particularly pp. 107–19, and pp. 138–56.
15. *Ibid.* p. 107.
16. *Ibid.* p. 108.
17. *The Republic*, 389 B.
18. *Op. cit.*, pp. 86–119.

19. *Ibid.* p. 86.
20. *The Republic*, 420 B.
21. *Ibid.* 421 E.
22. Lodge, R. C.: *Plato's Theory of Education.* Routledge, 1950 (2nd Impression), pp. 245–6.
23. *Op. cit.*, p. 42.
24. *Vide* Burnham, J.: *The Managerial Revolution.* Penguin Books; Young, M.: *The Rise of the Meritocracy.* Thames & Hudson, 1958, also in Penguin Books (Pelican).
25. *Op. cit.*, p. 155.
26. *Op. cit.*, p. 67.
27. Thomas, Dylan: "Light Breaks where no Sun Shines."
28. *Vide* Barker, E.: *Op. cit.*, Chapter XVII, pp. 430–43.
29. *The Laws*, 808 D.
30. *Vide* Barker, E.: *Op. cit.*, p. 440.
31. *Vide Ibid.* Chapter X, pp. 209–38.
32. *The Republic*, 412 A.
33. *Ibid.* 401 C–D.
34. *Ibid.* 526 E.
35. *Ibid.* 540 A–B.
36. *Op. cit.*, p. 270.
37. *Vide* Castle, E. B.: *op. cit.* (In particular Chapter 6: "Old Wine in New Bottles", pp. 188–210).
38. *Ibid.* p. 87.
39. Jowett, B.: *Op. cit.*, Vol. I, p. 3.
40. Castle, E. B.: *Op cit.*, p. 198.
41. *Vide* Jeffreys, M. V. C.: *Glaucon.* Pitman, 1950, pp. 71–3.
42. Rusk, R. R.: *The Doctrines of the Great Educators.* Macmillan, 2nd Edition, 1954 (Reprinted 1962), pp. 150–1.
43. *The Timaeus*, 86.
44. *Op. cit.*, pp. 86–119.
45. *Ibid.* p. 127.
46. *Ibid.* pp. 131–2.
47. *Ibid.* pp. 200–1.
48. Adam, A. M.: *Plato: Moral and Political Ideals*, C.U.P., 1913 p. 121.
49. *Vide* Elvin, H. L.: *Education and Contemporary Society.* C. A. Watts, 1965, *passim.*

BIBLIOGRAPHY

A. BOOKS BY PLATO

The Republic. (a) Tr. by H. D. P. Lee. Penguin Books, 1955 (Reprinted 1964).
— (b) Tr. by A. D. Lindsay. Dent (Everyman Lib.).
— (c) Tr. by B. Jowett. O.U.P., 1908; 3rd Edition 1927–8.
The Last Days of Socrates. Tr. by H. Tredennick. Penguin Books, 1959 (Reprinted 1964). (This contains *Euthyphro, The Apology, Crito,* & *Phaedo*).
Protagoras & Meno. Tr. by W. K. C. Guthrie, Penguin Books, 1956 (Reprinted 1964).
The Symposium. Tr. by W. Hamilton. Penguin Books, 1951 (Reprinted 1962).

B. OTHER BOOKS OF REFERENCE

Adam, A. M.: *Plato: Moral and Political Ideals.* C.U.P., 1913.
Barclay, W.: *Educational Ideals in the Ancient World.* Collins, 1959.
Barker, E.: *Greek Political Theory.* Methuen, Univ. Paperback, 1960 (Reprinted 1964).
Bluck, R. S.: *Plato's Life and Thought.* Routledge, 1949.
Bosanquet, B.: *Companion to Plato's Republic.* Rivington, 1895.
—: *The Education of the Young in the Republic of Plato.* C.U.P., 1904.
Boyd, W.: *Plato's Republic for Today.* Heinemann, 1962.
— *An Introduction to the Republic of Plato.* Allen and Unwin, 1922.
Castle, E. B.: *Ancient Education and Today.* Penguin Books (Pelican), 1961 (Reprinted 1964).
Crossman, R. H. S.: *Plato Today.* Allen and Unwin, 1959, 2nd Edition.
Curtis, S. J. & Boultwood, M. E. A.: *A Short History of Educational Ideas.* U.T.P., 4th Edition, 1965 (Chapter I, pp. 1–29).
Field, G. C.: *Plato and his Contemporaries.* Methuen, 1930.
Livingstone, R.: *Portrait of Socrates.* O.U.P., 1938.
—: *Plato and Modern Education.* C.U.P., 1944.
Lodge, R. C.: *Plato's Theory of Education.* Routledge, 1950 (2nd Impression).
Lowes Dickinson, G.: *The Greek View of Life.* Methuen, 1945 (20th Edition).

Marrou, H. I.: *A History of Education in Antiquity.* Sheed and Ward, 1956.

Moberley, W.: *Plato's Conception of Education and its Meaning Today.* O.U.P., 1944.

Nettleship, R. L.: *Lectures on the Republic of Plato.* Macmillan, 1901; 2nd Edition (Reprinted 1958).

Popper, K. R.: *The Open Society and its Enemies: Volume I—The Spell of Plato.* Routledge, 1966, 5th Edition (Revised).

Rusk, R. R.: *The Doctrines of the Great Educators.* Macmillan, 1954 (Reprinted 1962); (Chapter 1, pp. 1–37).

Taylor, A. E.: *Plato: The Man and His Work.* Methuen, Univ. Paperback, 4th Edition, 1960 (Reprinted 1963).

Urwick, E. J.: *The Message of Plato.* Methuen, 1920.

CHAPTER 4

JEAN-JACQUES ROUSSEAU (1712–1778)

A. HIS LIFE AND WORK

Jean-Jacques Rousseau was born in Geneva in 1712. His mother died at his birth and Rousseau was brought up by his father, who was also responsible for his early education. When he was ten years old he was sent to a tutor for two years and was taught some Latin "and all the useless stuff that goes along with it". From then on he lived a most unsettled life, being among other things apprenticed to an engraver from whom he ran away. He later tried his hand at tutoring but was equally unsuccessful in this.

It seems clear that many of the later attitudes of Rousseau, both to education and to life in general, may be attributed to these early experiences of his. He suffered from a sense of frustration, of unfulfilment and even inadequacy. He also felt strongly, even bitterly, about the society in which he lived. In his *Confessions* he tells of an experience he had when he was on a journey to Lyons[1]. He was desperately hungry and sought food at a peasant's cottage, at the same time offering to pay for it. The peasant gave him a few scraps of coarse bread and some skimmed milk, maintaining that this was all that he had. He relented, however, when he saw how famished Rousseau was and produced some wine and a white loaf, refusing to take any payment. The reason given by the peasant for his pretence of poverty was that this was the only way to escape from the rapacity of the tax-collector.

Rousseau's life reached a crisis when, in 1737, he had a serious illness during which he began to read a wide variety of books on literature, philosophy and science. Among the French writers that he read were Fénelon, Pascal, Voltaire, Montaigne and Descartes; whilst the English writers who most affected him were Hobbes, Addison, Pope, and Locke. Rousseau was by now convinced that his own *métier* was writing, and in 1750 he won a prize for a

Discourse on the Arts and Sciences—adjudged the best essay by the Academy of Dijon on the topic, "Has the progress of sciences and arts contributed to corrupt or purify morals?" After this effort he produced a number of essays and articles on such general topics as human inequality and political economy. He then went on to write the main works of his literary career: *The New Héloïse* in 1761, which was a romance of love and domestic life; *The Social Contract* in 1762, which, says Dr W. Boyd, with the *Discourse on Inequality* provided "the leaders of the French Revolution with their main ideas about government"[2]; and *Emile*, also in 1762, which was his chief work on education.

There was an immediate *furore* over the book *Emile*. It offended the Encyclopaedists and the Church, particularly the section referred to as "The Savoyard Priest's Confession of Faith"; and it was condemned by both Catholic and Protestant alike and ordered to be burnt in public. An order for Rousseau's arrest was issued, so he fled to the canton of Neuchâtel, where he was welcomed by the governor, himself an exiled Scottish Jacobite. Rousseau, however, suffered so much from persecution-mania that he could not remain in one place, or with one person, for any length of time. From Neuchâtel he fled to Berne; from Berne to Wooton in Derbyshire, England, where he started to write his *Confessions*; and from England he pursued a wandering life on the Continent, settling finally in Paris, where he completed the *Confessions* and some minor works, such as the *Dialogues* and *Rêveries*. He died, alone and poverty-stricken in 1778.

One incident in the life of Rousseau is of particular interest. Rousseau was obviously concerned, theoretically at least, with the reconstruction of society, since only in this way could the right sort of environment be provided for the proper education of children. In 1772, ten years after the publication of *Emile* and just before the partition of Poland, a Polish nobleman asked Rousseau for some advice concerning the reform of the Polish government. Rousseau characteristically replied with a treatise entitled *Considerations on the Government of Poland*. In this work he underlined the need for a national form of education.

"It is the national institutions which form the genius, the character, the tastes and the morals of a people and render it different from every other people"[3].

Apparently this result could be effected only by giving the children the right sort of education which should be entrusted to high-ranking magistrates, in a somewhat Platonic manner. These magistrates would ensure that young Poles would acquire all that knowledge required to make them good patriots, and would make them undergo gymnastic exercises and participate in all sorts of games that would encourage them to co-operate for a common purpose. In broader terms, Rousseau saw the ideal education as taking place in an Ideal State, in which inclination and duty, self-realization and good citizenship would never be in conflict. There is certainly an idealistic note about it all.

B. ROUSSEAU'S PHILOSOPHY: NATURALISM

In his *Doctrines of the Great Educators* R. R. Rusk has maintained that Rousseau was the "most maligned and most misunderstood figure in the history of education"[4], and that for this he has himself chiefly to blame. It is true that Rousseau's works are full of paradoxes and contradictions—but any great man who has had the temerity to say anything worth saying could certainly be accused of the same thing. Rusk is equally critical of the type of philosophy to which the thinking of Rousseau has generally and traditionally been assigned; he says that

"Rousseau is almost universally regarded as a naturalist in philosophy, the result of a superficial rendering of 'living according to nature' whereas ... he is manifestly an idealist. He serves as a bridge between the Stoics and Kant"[5].

One hesitates to disagree with this judgement by Rusk, a judgement which he also supports in *The Philosophical Bases of Education*[6]. But this is largely a question of precise nomenclature and word-juggling. It raises several issues, such as whether our divorce of thought and thinkers generally into strictly segregated types and brands has, ultimately, any real significance or validity; or whether, in the final analysis, words ever retain their original connotation. Sometimes the closer we seek to define things or ideas the less "meaning" they seem to have for us. Indeed, the "utilitarian" and practical content of *Emile* is so strong that one might perhaps have grounds for arguing that Rousseau was a "pragmatist" before Pragmatism. In his *Education and Values* G. H.

Bantock has said that "If anyone deserves to be termed the father of progressivism, it is he"[7], and he makes a very acute analysis of the four or more different meanings of the words "nature" and "natural" as employed by Rousseau.

Rousseau wrote things as he felt, and he could be sickeningly sentimental. Madame de Staël once said that Rousseau invented nothing; he set everything on fire. Voltaire remarked of the *Discourse on the Origin and Foundation of Inequality among Men* that it made him long to walk on all fours; and of *Emile* that it was a "hodge podge of silly wet nurse in four parts". Professor A. E. Meyer maintains that

"Rousseau was neither a man of science nor one of logic, but something of an evangelist and poet; and true to the licence of their ancient office, he allowed himself a frequent holiday from plain sense"[8].

Perhaps in a way Rousseau equated the "natural" with the "ideal", and considered that a reconstituted society would provide an ideal environment for "natural" man to grow and develop. Certainly there are elements of idealism in Rousseau's thought; there is also a considerable amount of progressiveness in his teaching, and most commentators who have been anxious to classify him as something have been satisfied to regard him as the apostle of Naturalism.

Rousseau's opening words in *The Social Contract* are that

"Man is born free; and everywhere he is in chains. One thinks himself the master of others, and still remains a greater slave than they"[9].

This is his "naturalism"—by birth, man is free. It is also the result of very narrow observation: any creature less free than man by birth, or at birth, one cannot imagine. There is not merely illogicality in the thinking of Rousseau, there is also a certain innate perversity about it; and it is this perversity which has resulted in the extreme difficulty of classifying him philosophically. As a philosophical principle one may say that "man *ought* to be free", or that he "*ought* to be born free"; but as a sociological observation it is obvious that man is certainly not born free by nature.

The first sentence of *Emile* reads:

"Everything is good as it comes from the hands of the Creator of things (*des choses*): everything degenerates in the hands of man."

This, again, is a provocative opening, but it is equally perverse; no one could possibly imagine that everything in Nature is "good", and only a myopic misanthrope could possibly conceive that man causes all that is naturally good to degenerate. To Rousseau, society was not a "natural" but an artificial production, the outcome of a contract; in consequence, Nature and society were opposed, and what was natural was "good", and what was artificial or conventional, was evil. This is another element in his "naturalism". To "live according to Nature" is to live according to the rational principle or Reason; and "he who obeys his conscience" is following Nature[10]. Again, in the *Emile*, Rousseau says:

"Let us lay it down as incontrovertible that the first impulses of nature are always right"[11].

It is hardly surprising that Professor Bantock refers to the "Rousseauesque self-complacency", that he "failed to come to any real understanding of his environment"[12], and that he had an "outsider" mentality[13]. There is certainly something very unrealistic (though not necessarily "idealistic") in Rousseau's picture of the child "naturally" obeying the rational laws of conscience, and "naturally" being right on impulse.

But, to some extent, this is linked up with his denial of the dogma of Original Sin. Man is by nature good, man is by nature free; it is society that has corrupted all the good things that God has created; through its meddling it has made man evil. It is perhaps not irrelevant to ask how it has come about that a being who is so basically good and perfect has contrived, in consort with other beings equally good and perfect, to create a society which is so devastatingly degenerate. Rousseau seems to have a view of "Society" which is virtually that of a created organism separate from its constituent members, and imposing its "unnatural" and evil will upon them, as if they were its slaves. But whilst man may not be "originally evil", he is not, *ipso facto*, "originally good" either. The revolt against the Doctrine of Original Sin and the Fall may have a sound and reasonable basis, but it is quite unsound to see in man something basically perfect. Nor is this in reality idealism, although it has a certain idealistic flavour about it. Rousseau was not, in fact, emphasizing any ultimate Form of the Good, but rather the essential goodness of Nature itself.

Rousseau stresses throughout the necessity to grant freedom and opportunity so that each individual may have the possibility of eliciting his innate goodness; and so, by a "natural" progress and by self-development and improvement, discover the higher spiritual values. For the natural Universe is also a spiritual one. This is a statement of naturalism, progressivism and idealism all rolled into one. And ultimately the false conventions and standards of our society would be transmuted by free man, living naturally, that is, according to his innermost nature. R. R. Rusk concludes that

"Rousseau's aim was to refute the materialistic philosophy of his age, to re-establish the validity of the concepts, God, freedom and immortality, and to re-affirm the principles of right conduct"[14].

On the other hand Professor J. Adams has maintained that

"Without doubt Naturalism in education came to its zenith in the reaction associated with the name of Jean Jacques Rousseau"[15].

C. EMILE (1762)

There may be a great deal of disagreement about the precise designation which should be given to the philosophy of Rousseau, but there seems to be considerable agreement concerning the value of *Emile* as a controversial work on education, provoking people to thought as well as practical application. In his biography of Rousseau, Lord Morley wrote an assessment of *Emile* in the following terms: it is

"one of the seminal books in the history of literature, and of such books the worth resides less in the parts than in the whole. It touched the deeper things of character. . . . It cleared away the accumulation of clogging prejudices and obscure inveterate usage, which made education one of the dark formalistic arts. . . . It effected the substitution of growth for mechanism . . . it was the charter of youthful deliverance"[16].

At a first reading such a eulogy seems a trifle unbalanced and
uncritical, and almost as sentimental as some of Rousseau's own
utterances. And we are perhaps inclined to think that there was
something inexpert and amateur about the judgement, however
great the biographer may have been. Yet when we turn to Dr
William Boyd, who has made one of the most complete studies of
Rousseau during the present century, we find something very akin
to Morley's judgement.

"Among the multitude of writings about education in the modern
world the *Emile* of Jean Jacques Rousseau is the one which has
exercised the greatest influence on the course of educational
thought and practice"[17].

   Emile was really the third book in a trilogy seeking to develop
the same general theme. *The New Héloïse* described in rather
idealistic terms a society functioning as a family unit in accordance with the principle of nature and with justice; *The Social
Contract* sought, in the language of the Law, to achieve the same
sort of thing; finally, *Emile* attempted to show how the "natural
man" can be formed and educated. The book is divided into five
main sections or "books", and the following is a very brief analysis on the basis of those divisions[18].

I. Infancy (Birth to 2 years)
Education should begin immediately after birth, and it should
start with the satisfaction of the physical wants because these are
natural. There should be no restraint of natural, physical liberty,
but the keynote should be a well-regulated freedom. Habits are
autonomous.

II. Boyhood (2–12 years)
This period commences with the development of speech through
simple, childish games. The child must be allowed to gratify its
wishes, suitable to its age, without any forcing. Since it is clear
that boys are different, by nature, from girls they will require a
different form of education; "natural education" is education
that takes full account of the pupil's nature in its differing aspects.
   The basic principle of education is the perfect balance of freedom and happiness. This, in turn, depends upon the equilibrium

of "will" and "can". We can supply the principle in a *positive* way by granting the pupil the necessary strength for freedom; we can apply it in a *negative* way by showing that nature is commanded only by being obeyed.

At this stage Emile has no true ideas since he lacks any ability to compare and relate data. Actual instruction must be confined to practical and sensory methods; that is, through drawing, speaking, measuring and singing. Rousseau regards the boy as a "noble savage" who learns through *direct experience* in the varied practical activities connected with his interests and needs.

The motive of self-love (*amour de soi*) dominates Emile in the sphere of personal conduct. Self-esteem (*amour-propre*) is of little significance to him in this "pre-social" stage. The sole way of keeping a child "natural" or true to his nature is to withdraw him from the artificial life of society. He must, therefore, be brought up by a tutor.

Emile should have no direct moral instruction. It is much more important to protect him from the error and vice of his society than to seek to inculcate truth and virtue. Books are harmful, and the less Emile learns about verbal studies and the deleterious facts of social life the better.

III. Early Adolescence (12–15 years)
Emile is now beginning to develop a greater capacity for sustained attention, and the urge to activity now becomes *mental*. He is able to compare and reason about data and phenomena within his own experience, and he is beginning to be able to predict and show foresight.

Still no moral instruction or observations are employed since Emile still lacks aesthetic and moral insight, and he possesses only a very elementary understanding of social relations.

Actions are the objects of instruction, and the general principle of "utility" and "learning by doing" is employed. Emile learns from his own observations, not from those of his tutor, or from other people or from written authorities. He must deal with *problems* as they arise; he must learn from his experience with nature and through observation.

During this period Emile should be introduced to science and handicraft and he should be taught a trade. He is still not permitted to read books, with the sole exception of Defoe's *Robinson*

Crusoe—the story of a solitary man, who learns to be self-suffi-
cient and to use his native intelligence and abilities in order to discover practical solutions for the problems of his island world. But
Emile's island is the world, and if he is left to his own resources he
will explore it intelligently.

IV. Adolescence (15–20 years)

In infancy Emile's life was characterized by the development of
habit and the training of emotions; in boyhood he discovered
the need to train his senses; in early adolescence his life was
marked by utility and intellectual training; the final stage of
adolescence, "the crown and coping-stone of education", is the
stage of *morality*, and of moral, religious, aesthetic and social
emotion.

Now passions are aroused which should not be clouded in
mystery. Self-love, which may degenerate into selfishness, is the
origin of all passions. Now Emile is acquainted with the life of
society, and with the fact that men seek to deceive themselves and
one another. He will learn to despise some and show compassion
for others. Gradually self-love will give way to self-esteem.

The study of history is now introduced because its portrayal of
men is realistic; this, in turn, will form a means of moral instruction. In religion, Emile is to be instructed in the most general facts
of religious evolution and distribution. He is not to be indoctrin-
ated for any particular sect.

Now Emile is introduced to the polite society of a great city,
and through literature and drama he will acquire good taste. He
will travel, and through the contact made with other peoples he
will learn more of society itself. There will be greater stress than
before on social studies, politics and the problems of government
so that he may become a well-equipped and intelligent citizen and
head of a household.

The section entitled "The Creed of the Savoyard Priest" has
been held by some critics to be suspect. R. R. Rusk, however,
accepted it as genuine, and Dr W. Boyd maintained in *The History of Western Education* that

"The *Emile* was immediately condemned both by Catholic Paris
and Protestant Geneva on account of a deistic treatise (*The
Savoyard Vicar's Confession of Faith*), which it included"[19];

although in his *Emile for Today* Boyd seems to regard it as an interpolation which is not worth including. The leading idea in Rousseau's ethical teaching is that nature is good, but that it has been spoilt by the work of man. Without some concept of a Fall this doctrine seems somewhat contradictory, for man is a part of nature. The remedy, however, is to go back to nature, for he who "obeys his conscience is following nature"[20], and the Inner Light of conscience is man's intuitive guide. Rousseau held that this Inner Light was in itself sufficient to give all the direction that man needs in religion and morals in matters of practical significance. "The Creed of the Savoyard Priest" was an attempt at a minimum hypothesis of religious belief in order to present a starting-point for further thought; it was not far removed, in fact, from Kant's basic and axiomatic "categories" of the mind— God, Freedom and Immortality. The Creed accepted:

(a) The Intrinsic Goodness of Nature.
(b) Man's Existence.
(c) The Inner Light of Conscience, as an intuitive guide.
(d) The Universal Will in Nature (God).
(e) Free Will.
(f) Immortality—infinite time will be required to redress the inequalities of this life.

V. Marriage

Finally, Rousseau accepted that men and women have different biological functions and vocations; and that, therefore, their education must be different. Sophie is the ideal woman, who is to be educated for no purpose other than to be suited to, and to please man: to be useful to him; to make herself loved by him; to bring him up when he is young; to care for him; and generally to make his life agreeable. Sophie is to learn her religion from her mother; she must pay special attention to housekeeping, and she must at all times appear charming. This is the education of the natural woman who is the only fit mate for natural man, her master. And the final task of the tutor is to give instruction to Emile and Sophie on matters of sex and on their marital duties and rights. Lord Morley characterized this final development as "the oriental conception of Women"[21].

D. ROUSSEAU'S MAIN EDUCATIONAL IDEAS AND INFLUENCE

The "seminal" nature of Rousseau's book may be more clearly seen if we attempt to reduce the ideas scattered about *Emile* to a number of general propositions, and then try and see how later developments in education have expanded his ideas. It is not suggested that all these influences were necessarily conscious ones, but as H. C. Barnard has pointed out,

"the mere fact that Rousseau was so provocative and original a writer secured him a wide audience and stirred people to think seriously about the questions which he raised"[22].

Rousseau was undoubtedly provocative and paradoxical at times, and frequently he obviously merely sought to shock. He himself suggested on more than one occasion that his ideas had been misunderstood or misapplied; and one enthusiastic admirer, who prided himself on the fact that he was educating his son on the lines outlined in *Emile*, received the following reply: "Good heavens! So much the worse for you, sir! and so much worse still for your son!"

1. *Education is Growth; it should be a natural process:* Rousseau complained that we had not in our society followed nature; in fact, our society had deliberately perverted the order of nature. "Nature wants children to be children before they are men"[23], but in our methods of education we treated the child as if he were a little man, and tried to force upon him levels of intellectual development for which he was not yet ready. In consequence, the fruits which we harvested "were neither ripe nor well flavoured", but already in decay. To Rousseau education was growth, it was a natural process, and this meant that education should be in accordance with the nature of the child, that is, its natural endowment. As we have said, he opposed any concept of Original Sin: the child was by nature good; it was his social environment which tended to make him evil. There was an initial equality among pupils: inequalities derived from intercourse with a perverted society. Children should be allowed to *grow*, for this was the very essence of education.

This is all very much like Chapter IV ("Education as Growth") in Dewey's *Democracy and Education*, where he insists that immaturity is the ability to develop, the power to grow; that habits are the expressions of growth, and finally that

"Since in reality there is nothing to which growth is relative save more growth, there is nothing to which education is subordinate save more education"[24].

Rousseau insisted that children had ways of thinking, seeing, and feeling which were peculiar to themselves, and that nothing could be more foolish than to substitute our ways for theirs. This was the adoption of a psychological standpoint in education, and Rousseau proceeded to try and delineate the different and successive stages of growth in the life of the child and adolescent. As always, when such a framework is attempted, there is a tendency to draw the lines too sharply and to make the various stages of human development too defined. But even more recent attempts at the analysis of child development have been found guilty of the same defect. As H. C. Barnard says, "it is the spirit rather than the letter of *Emile* which gave life"[25], and it was the *fact* of child growth and development rather than its precise delineation to which Rousseau eventually drew attention. As R. R. Rusk has pointed out:

"A consequence of the psychological standpoint was the acceptance of the 'participation' as opposed to the 'preparation' view of education. Rousseau argued that the possibilities of each stage of life should be fully exploited before proceeding to the next stage, a principle assumed by Froebel and Montessori, although generally associated with the name of Dewey"[26].

2. *Education should be Paedocentric:* This follows quite conclusively from the previous proposition. Education must be directed primarily to the child and our teaching adapted to his needs. Rousseau argues that "there is a time for every kind of teaching"[27], and that we ought to recognize it, for each has its own peculiar dangers to be avoided. We must consider the *utility* of what is being taught, for "nothing is useful and good for him which is unbefitting his age"[28]. This is almost Dewey's pragmatic test. We must "beware of anticipating teaching which demands more maturity of mind"[29]; in fact, we must have a thorough understanding of the child mind in all its stages, and at all levels.

It is the *child* who is important, not the subject, or the curriculum, or the examination.

"Begin thus by making a more careful study of your scholars, for it is clear that you know nothing about them"[30].

How often has it been said in our own time that the child is the *datum* in the educational process. And it was the general principle that Dewey was to adopt in his University Laboratory School.

3. *Education is for the Liberty and Happiness of the Child:* The freedom of the individual is the most precious ideal, according to Rousseau. Education is a necessary evil, but liberty and restraint must not be regarded as completely incompatible. Liberty does not mean licence or power, and there is always the "heavy yoke of necessity". Rousseau believed that there was a discipline in the very nature of things, "the discipline of natural consequences". If the child is permitted to suffer the consequences of his free activity he will learn, from experience, what makes for his own happiness as well as that of his fellows. He will, in fact, put a self-restraint upon his own liberty and thereby bring about his own happiness. This is, of course, a negative method—no positive guidance, moral or otherwise, will be given. It could also have disastrous results. A child, surely, does not need to recapitulate the whole history of human experience in order to discover, contrary to some more extreme contemporary views, that the child is *not* always right. There are some experiences that are best mediated to a child in a second-hand way, lest he destroy himself in the process of learning.

The "discipline of natural consequences" is, however, practised in some of our more progressive schools; and when the Head of one of these schools was questioned on the detail of "natural consequences" in his community (a very expensive one for the parents) he gave two interesting examples. A child was allowed to do any damage he liked in the school—but he had to pay for it; he was also allowed to kick the Head in the shins if he really felt the need for the experience—but the Head could kick him back, on the same principle, and he was likely to have bigger boots! These may seem to be odd ways of achieving the "heavy yoke of necessity", but no doubt a satiation point is reached very quickly—one hopes before too much damage is done.

Rousseau, however, honestly believed that the seeds of happiness were within us, and that given the right environment for the evocation of liberty we should find our happiness. In his earliest literary effort of all, written in 1750, he had said that we should not build our happiness on the opinions of others "when we can find it in our own hearts"[31]. But the Kingdom of Heaven may indeed be within us, and we may possess some strange "inner light" to guide us to it, yet

"To follow the 'inner light' ('the most untrustworthy and deceitful guide that ever offered itself to wandering humanity', as T. S. Eliot has called it) with any hope of success requires a self-honesty, an ability to learn from experience and to face the deeper implications of the self which Rousseau nowhere displays"[32].

4. *Education should be through Experience:* This cannot, of course, be separated from the previous proposition, and one grows out of the other. Children are to learn nothing from books which they can learn from experience[33]. Children, says Rousseau, are to learn by doing, they are to learn through activity, through first-hand experience. Nearly all the modern clichés, which seem to have reached us through Deweyism, pragmatism and modern progressivism, are to be found in *Emile*. Rousseau would have no predetermined curriculum, for "work and play are all one" to Emile; his games are his work and he cannot tell the difference[34]. It was the Hadow Report, in relation to the Primary School, which solemnly declared, one hundred and sixty-nine years later, that

"the curriculum is to be thought of in terms of activity and experience rather than of knowledge to be acquired and facts to be stored"[35].

Words were to be resorted to only when doing was out of the question—"Teach by doing whenever you can"[36]. The Play Way, the Project Method and Activity Methods generally are all previsioned here. In Dewey's Problem Method the question is posed, "What is your immediate problem? You must state it to your self, examine it in detail and practically, and then begin to formulate some hypothesis about it, finally testing it". Rousseau says that Emile must, in the stage of early adolescence, deal with his own problems and learn by his own efforts through a close observation of Nature. He is to educate himself by the method of discovery and experiment (cf. the Heuristic Method), for it is not the function of the tutor to teach him truths so much as to show him how to set about discovering them for himself. His experiences must be guided and his interest aroused, for "the art of teaching consists in making the pupil wish to learn"[37]; "let him not be taught science, let him discover it"[38].

We realize today, of course, how important interest and the creation, or evocation, of interest are in the class-room situation. And in the Project Method, for example, a practical, concrete problem is presented in its natural setting (or as near natural as possible) so that the child feels, first of all, that it really *is* his problem and that it is within his competence to solve it. Throughout, however, the only satisfying motive of learning is the interest shown at the child's level and derived from a realized need. The emphasis throughout, said Rousseau (and the Realists), must be upon "things not words". This is a plea for the planning of the right sort of environment, and environmental situations, for the child, and for the predominance of factors which are environmental rather than hereditarian. Even in the realm of morals, according to Rousseau, the most effective teacher is the planned environment —not the planned curriculum. And how are we to judge the value of any situation or experience? "What is the *use* of this? This is the sacred formula"[39]. Whether this is idealism, naturalism, pragmatism or progressivism may be meat for the pundits, or just apples for children—but it is a typically Rousseauian reply.

5. *Education is for Individual Development:* Rousseau maintained that the only really useful habit for children was to be accustomed to submit without difficulty to necessity; and that the only useful habit for men was to submit without difficulty to reason. All other habits, according to him, constituted vice. Our lives must be guided by necessity and reason, which would in turn evoke the ultimately good, individual character. Rousseau underlines, during the various stages of the pupil's development, the need to develop the physical condition, to train the emotions and the senses, and ultimately to maximize the mental, moral, aesthetic and social consciousness. Of course this is idealistic; it could equally be argued that it is realist and pragmatic—to Rousseau it

happens to be just "natural". Man's natural educational aim is the fullest development of himself as a person, with the right amount of *amour-propre*. In this personal development, the "Inner Light" is always the chief moral and religious guide. Indoctrination is, for Rousseau, always wrong; and children must be allowed to think and act as persons and individuals in their own right if they are ever to achieve full development.

"That man is truly free who desires what he is able to perform, and does what he desires. This is my fundamental maxim. Apply it to childhood, and all the rules of education spring from it"[40].

The "naturalism" of Sir Percy Nunn, if it may so be called, reflected in his writing, seems almost to echo these words of Rousseau:

"Nothing good enters into the human world except in and through the free activities of individual men and women ... educational practice must be shaped in accord with that truth"[41].

6. *Education is for Society, or at least for Social Awareness:* This may at first sight seem a strange proposition regarding the teaching of a man who saw nature and society eternally at strife with each other, and who claimed that the evils of contemporary society were the cause of man's condition. And yet there is intrinsically a desire on the part of Rousseau to reconcile natural and social training. The social implications of Emile's education may be delayed until later adolescence, but they are very much there. The whole purpose of the exercise seems to be that Emile may finally be equipped for intelligent citizenship, and that he may become the head of a household. He is no savage "to be banished to the desert; he is a savage who has to live in town"[42]. Through the observation of natural phenomena ("geography" and "local studies") he will have learned something of his physical environment; through the learning of a trade he will achieve a vocation in society; through his introduction to "polite society", through the study of the problems of government during his travels, and through a closer attention to "social studies", Emile will derive his knowledge of his social duties, and will become cognizant of his

D

civic, social and political environment. When he is finally ready he will be instructed in matters of sex and sex relationships, and in his marital duties and responsibilities. The aim of education is, therefore, to make a man, a husband, and a citizen.

This all sounds strangely modern; and in the increasing demands for accurate and intelligent sex education, for the preparation of girls for motherhood and of both boys and girls for social awareness, we are doing little more than echoing the *principle* which Rousseau enunciated, even if he did not reach in practice the more detailed approach of a Newsom Report.

E. SOME GENERAL COMMENTS

Rousseau was disgusted with the traditional methods of education, and as a result he tended to express himself in extremes. He once said, "Reverse the usual practice and you will almost always be right". This typical, provocative and unconsidered judgement was merely an expression of his ingrained contempt for society at large. Rousseau, however, has always had his supporters, and no one could deny that his influence has been considerable. In Geneva, a great admirer, Madame Necker de Saussure (1765–1841), became a pioneer of systematic child-study, and she kept a detailed diary of the progress and development of her own children. But a close examination of the work of Pestalozzi, Froebel and Montessori (to name only a few outstanding educators) will reveal more and more of the influence of Rousseau at work.

Rousseau's "charter of youthful deliverance" emphasized very clearly that we must study the child's development in all its aspects if our education is to be relevant. His own psychological characterization of the successive ages is based chiefly on the emerging "faculties", on sensations in infancy, sense-judgements in childhood, practical thought in adolescence, and finally abstraction in later adolescence. This all smacks very much of the now discredited Faculty-Psychology, but it was a beginning and Rousseau revealed the vital importance of psychological analysis and child-study generally.

Rousseau emphasized also the relevance of natural and unfettered physical growth. From the biological as well as from the psychological point of view, the educator must consider the child as a little human animal destined ultimately for the moral and spiritual life: and this animal develops according to certain laws of progression. Rousseau laid stress, at quite an early stage in the history of education, upon the importance of physical education[43], and upon the link between successful education and what today we more familiarly call "maturation". Moreover, Rousseau, in perceiving the connexion between mental and physical energy, anticipated something of later psychology. It must be said in general criticism, however, that growth *per se* cannot produce any sort of criterion for life; too often Rousseau confuses progress with process; and of itself growth, or process, does not provide canons for living.

Rousseau's emphasis throughout on experience and activity, on "things" rather than upon books and words, has served a very useful purpose in making us realize that children learn through observation and through play; through action, drama, and their own immediate environment. And this all, undoubtedly, makes an excellent starting-point. But to leave the child with nothing of a written nature (save some modern equivalent of *Robinson Crusoe*) would be quite unrealistic; and, again one wonders whether this is just another example of Rousseau's sometimes perverse love of extremism and exaggeration—a Rousseauesque joke. He does, however, make a point: one from which we are still learning; but there are limits to a child's (or adult's) first-hand experience. We must all learn from words and from books; and the world of a child who reads widely (and, in some cases, even voraciously) is fuller, richer and replete with adventure and enchantment. Such a child has enlarged his environment, even though he cannot see or touch it; and he has augmented his experience—which, today, can come through a great variety of media and channels. Rousseau's concept of experience was itself limited and narrow.

In a complex society it is this mediation of experience which is now so important. Up to a point there is something in Rousseau's doctrine of "discipline of natural consequences". But only up to a point. Must a child really burn itself on a hot stove in order to learn that fire and heat have deleterious consequences? Must a youth really smoke marijuana in order to discover that drug-addiction can have most unpleasant "natural consequences"? The great lessons of history—physical, mental, moral and spiritual—do not have to be repeated in every single individual's life in order to establish their continuing validity. And this is not idealistic indoctrination; this is the pragmatic mediation of experiential truth; it is practical politics as well as sound, utilitarian (even "natural" in one sense) education.

Rousseau, like most enthusiastic pioneers, overstated his case; and, as Dr W. Boyd has emphasized in his criticism of Rousseau, every adult capacity has its origin in childhood. The finely-balanced judgement, the critical discernment, the aesthetic appreciation, the moral and spiritual awareness of the grown man must all be nurtured by the appropriate culture and methods from the very beginning of life—they don't just suddenly happen. But they must, of course, all be developed, *pari passu*, with the maturation of the child.

Again, if man really is a "social animal", then there must be schools in which it is possible for children to develop with a sense of freedom, with "well-regulated freedom and liberty"[44], and yet with a realization of community and initiation into the larger society[45]. And poor, solitary, "noble savage" Emile, with social contact delayed until the last possible moment, must indeed have suffered a life which was dreary, dull and unexciting compared with that of most of our children today, with their Froebel and Montessori schools, their progressive kindergartens, and even their enlightened State Infant and Junior Departments (which all owe much to Rousseau), to say nothing of the great variety (at present) of Secondary Schools.

Finally, Rousseau's treatment of the education of women was largely an embarrassed acknowledgement of his own mystification. He obviously knew that Sophie was different biologically, but this seemed to be the extent of his knowledge of women. As to whether there are deep mental, moral and spiritual differences between men and women which they will need to express in different forms of education altogether was not a question that he debated. Whether the psychological and intellectual differences between the sexes were themselves due to social training, he never questioned. And so it is that Rousseau's "natural" scheme of things left Sophie literally holding the baby and presenting herself as little more than a pleasant plaything for her lord and master, Emile.

G. H. Bantock has admirably summed up the defects of Rousseau in his essay "*Emile* Reconsidered", where he says,

"Like many 'progressive' educationalists Rousseau is too taken up with physical activity to appreciate the full value of mental exercise. Rousseau's emphasis on the 'natural' man leads, in fact, to a misconception of man's nature; what was 'natural' to man, as an older view made clear, was precisely his capacity for complex development, his ability to respond to training and nurture, his building up on an assimilation of previous knowledge and wisdom; this most obviously marks him off from the animals"[46].

REFERENCES

1. Curtis, S. J. & Boultwood, M. E. A.: *A Short History of Educational Ideas*. U.T.P., 4th Edition, 1965, p. 268. Reference to Rousseau's *Confessions*. J. B. Lippincott Co., 1891, Vol. I, p. 169.
2. Boyd, W.: *The History of Western Education*. A. & C. Black, 7th Edition, 1964, p. 292.
3. Boyd, W.: *The Minor Educational Writings of Jean-Jacques Rousseau*. Blackie, 1911, p. 139.
4. Rusk, R. R.: *Doctrines of the Great Educators*. Macmillan, 2nd Edition, 1954 (Reprinted 1962), pp. 135–85.
5. *Op. cit.*, pp. 150–1.
6. Rusk, R. R.: *The Philosophical Bases of Education*. U.L.P., 1928, p. 148.
7. Bantock, G. H.: *Education and Values*. Faber, 1965, p. 13.
8. Meyer, A. E.: *An Educational History of the Western World*. McGraw-Hill, 1965, p. 340.
9. Rousseau, J.-J.: *The Social Contract and Discourses*. J. M. Dent (Everyman Lib.), 1913 (Reprinted 1930), p. 5.
10. Rousseau, J.-J.: *Emile*. J. M. Dent (Everyman Lib.), p. 250.
11. *Ibid.* p. 56.
12. *Op. cit.*, p. 56.
13. *Ibid.* p. 59.
14. *The Doctrines of the Great Educators*, p. 175.
15. Adams, J.: *The Evolution of Educational Theory*. Macmillan, 1912, p. 252.
16. Lord Morley: *Rousseau*. Chapman and Hall, 1883, pp. 391–2.
17. Boyd, W.: *Emile for Today*. W. Heinemann, 1956, p. 1.
18. *Vide Emile for Today, passim.* The summary that follows owes much to Dr Boyd's book.
19. *Op. cit.*, p. 292.

20. *Emile*, p. 250.
21. *Op. cit.*, pp. 387–8.
22. Barnard, H. C.: *A History of English Education from 1760.* U.L.P., 2nd Edition, 1961, p. 34.
23. *Emile*, p. 54.
24. Dewey, J.: *Democracy and Education.* Macmillan, 1916 (Reprinted 1955), p. 60.
25. *Op. cit.*, p. 37.
26. *The Doctrines of the Great Educators*, p. 156.
27. *Emile*, p. 293.
28. *Ibid.* p. 212.
29. *Ibid.* p. 165.
30. *Ibid.* p. 54.
31. Rousseau, J-J.: *The Social Contract and Discourses.* J. M. Dent (Everyman Lib.), 1913 (Reprinted 1930); *Discourse on the Moral Effects of the Arts and the Sciences*, p. 153.
32. Bantock, G. H.: *op. cit.*, p. 58.
33. *Emile*, p. 214.
34. *Ibid.* p. 126.
35. Hadow Report: *The Primary School.* 1931 (Reprinted 1946), p. 93.
36. *Emile*, p. 144.
37. *Ibid.* p. 210.
38. *Ibid.* p. 131.
39. *Ibid.* p. 131.
40. *Ibid.* p. 48.
41. Nunn, T. P.: *Education: Its Data and First Principles.* E. Arnold, 3rd Edition, 1945, p. 12.
42. *Emile*, p. 167.
43. *Ibid.* p. 58; "Exercise his body, his limbs, his senses, his strength, but keep his mind idle as long as you can."
44. *Ibid.* p. 43.
45. *Vide* Peters, R. S.: *Education as Initiation.* Evans Bros., 1964. (Especially pp. 33–48.)
46. Bantock, G. H.: *op cit.*, p. 82.

BIBLIOGRAPHY

A. BOOKS BY JEAN-JACQUES ROUSSEAU

The Social Contract & Discourses. J. M. Dent (Everyman Lib.).
Emile. J. M. Dent (Everyman Lib.).
Confessions. J. B. Lippincott Co., 1891; also Penguin Books.

B. OTHER BOOKS OF REFERENCE

Archer, R. L.: *Rousseau on Education*. Arnold, 2nd Impression, 1928.

Bantock, G. H.: *Education and Values*. Faber, 1965. (Essay on "*Emile* Reconsidered", pp. 53–84).

Boyd, W.: *The History of Western Education*. A. & C. Black, 1964, 7th Edition (pp. 291–301).

—: *Emile for Today*. Heinemann, 1956.

—: *The Educational Theory of Jean-Jacques Rousseau*. Longmans, 1911.

—: *The Minor Educational Writings of Jean-Jacques Rousseau*. Blackie, 1911.

Curtis, S. J.: *An Introduction to the Philosophy of Education*. U.T.P., 1963.

Curtis, S. J. & Boultwood, M. E. A.: *A Short History of Educational Ideas*. U.T.P., 4th Edition, 1965, (Chapter XI, pp. 262–89).

Morley, Lord: *Rousseau*. Chapman & Hall, 1883.

Quick, R. H.: *Educational Reformers*. Longmans, 1902 (Chapter 14).

Rusk, R. R.: *The Doctrines of the Great Educators*. Macmillan, 2nd Edition, 1954, (pp. 135–85).

CHAPTER 5

JOHN DEWEY (1859–1952)

A. HIS LIFE AND WORK

John Dewey was born and grew up in the New England State of Vermont where his father was a shopkeeper in a small village. He early became aware, from village gossip in the shop and from the general compactness of the rural community, that there was considerable strength in the group consciousness of such a society. The authors of *A Short History of Educational Ideas* suggest in their chapter on Dewey that

"It is not too much to say that the experience of those early years brought John Dewey the two outstanding convictions which directed the whole course of his educational work—a conviction that traditional methods of schooling were futile and fruitless, and an even firmer conviction that the human contacts of everyday life provide unlimited natural, dynamic 'learning situations'"[1].

Dewey proceeded to the University of Vermont where he graduated in 1879, and in 1880 he went on to Johns Hopkins University to read philosophy, psychology and history. In 1882 he received his Ph.D. and accepted an appointment at the University of Michigan to lecture in philosophy. His very wide abilities and his energetic approach to all current problems led to his appointment as Professor of Philosophy at the University of Minnesota, and then subsequently at the University of Michigan.

At the age of thirty-five, in 1894, Dewey received a position in the academic world which provided scope for all his interests; he became Chairman of the Department of Philosophy, Psychology and Pedagogy at the University of Chicago. Here in 1896 he founded the University Laboratory School, which he hoped would provide the raw material for experimentation in order to "prepare the way for the school of the future"[2]. Dewey had observed that the old simple village life and village community were breaking down, and that, whilst social structures were rapidly changing, the institutions of school and church had done little or nothing to make the child aware of the new society growing up around him. Whilst the village child had always been fully aware of the context of his daily and social life, and participated considerably in it, the town child of the newly developed and more complicated communities made use of amenities that he had never seen constructed, and that he was never really able to "internalize". He wore clothes, but knew nothing of their manufacture; he lit the gas but knew little or nothing about its preparation or about the principles of combustion.

✓ Dewey's experimental school aimed at taking into consideration the new environment of the child, and it sought to experiment and research in new ideas and methods. Children were accepted for the school between the ages of four and thirteen or fourteen, and specially trained teachers were appointed over groups of no more than ten pupils each. Dewey had been strongly influenced by Froebelian aims, and he regarded his school largely as an exercise in fulfilling those aims. Its purpose was to promote a social spirit of co-operation and mutual aid; the problem was to provide within the classroom living situations in which such co-operation might be evoked.

In one of his earliest works, *The School and Society*, Dewey posed four questions, which he held that it was the purpose of a sound educational system to answer:

(1) What can be done to bring the school into closer relation with the home and neighbourhood life?

(2) What can be done in the way of introducing subject-matter in history and science and art that shall have a positive value and real significance in the child's own life?

(3) How can instruction in reading, writing and arithmetic, the formal subjects, be carried on with everyday experience and occupation as the background, and made interesting by relating them to other studies of more inherent content?

(4) How can adequate attention be paid to individual powers and needs?[3]

The school must be another home; it must be a good home in which the sense of community, of common interests, pursuits and hopes could all find a high place in Dewey's Laboratory School. Practical activities and manual skills naturally had a premium, and all the pupils were encouraged to engage in creative work in the school shop where all sorts of tools and materials were available; they were all taught how to sew and weave, and how to cook. Dewey held that the school was a miniature community, an embryonic society, and that they must conceive of work in wood and metal, of weaving, sewing and cooking, "as methods of living and learning, not as distinct studies"[4].

Dewey was not a crank; he had thought deeply about the problems of educational content and method before he inaugurated his Laboratory School. But he had no precisely conceived plans which *had*, at all costs, to succeed. He wanted to experiment, to find out what was ultimately in the best interests of the child. On the other hand, it was not a policy of laissez-faire; there was no suggestion that children should not do things unless they wanted to, or unless it had first occurred to them. Dewey accepted that if the school was a microsociety it also required leadership, control and direction.

"There is no ground for holding that the teacher should not suggest anything to the child until he has *consciously* expressed a want in that direction. A sympathetic teacher is quite likely to know more clearly than the child himself what his own instincts are and mean"[5].

Nothing was neglected, and basic skills, such as the three R's, would find double acceptance with pupils because they would appreciate their necessity for the living of a full community life, and for the development of their other work.

Dewey was appointed Professor of Philosophy at Columbia University, New York, in 1904, a position which he held until his retirement in 1930 at the age of seventy-one; he was still writing books nineteen years later. He was a most prolific writer, and his works ranged the whole field of education, aesthetics, ethics, psychology, history, politics and philosophy. The titles of many of these books reveal that this was no ivory-tower academic; he was concerned with the public and its problems, with characters and events, with experience and nature, with man's quest for certainty —"compensatory perversion" though it might be—and with social action[6].

B. DEWEY'S PHILOSOPHY: PRAGMATISM

The term "pragmatism" is popularly associated with the names of John Dewey and of the American philosopher and psychologist, William James (1842–1910), but in more recent years it has become evident that the actual term "pragmatism", used in a technical and philosophical sense, was first employed by the logician and applied mathematician, C. S. Peirce (1839–1914). To Peirce "pragmatism" was a logical *method* for ascertaining the meaning of a formula or an abstract idea. His illustrations of the method reveal his preoccupation with mathematics and the experimental sciences rather than with any philosophical approach to life itself.

The word "pragmatism" itself is derived from the Greek πρᾶγμα (pragma), meaning "an action, deed, or thing which is right or fit to be done". James, who was a realist and pluralist philosophically seized on the word and in his book entitled *Pragmatism* he defined the pragmatic method as

"primarily a method of settling metaphysical disputes that might otherwise be interminable ... to try to interpret each notion by tracing its respective practical consequences"[7].

James went on to claim that ideas *become* true insofar as they assist us to get into a satisfactory relation with all other parts of our personal experience. There was, in fact, a general *pragmatic test* which could be applied to all our so-called truths—"true ideas are those which we can assimilate, validate, corroborate and verify. False ideas are those that we can not"[8].

Peirce did not accept at all this interpretation of his own use of the term; as a logician and mathematician he had an intellectual and analytical approach to problems, and James's pragmatic principle seemed to him to be thoroughly anti-intellectual, if not irrational. James appeared to give to the "coherence" theory of truth a very personal and individual interpretation; so individual that, in the last analysis, what might be "true" in the experience of one person might equally appear to be "untrue" in the experience of another. Peirce surrendered to James the right to use the term "pragmatism" for his particular brand of philosophy, and coined the term "pragmaticism" for his own original principle[9]. It is not germane to the discussion of Dewey's philosophy to examine precisely what Peirce meant by his "pragmaticism", and the reader is recommended to examine W. B. Gallie's important analysis in *Peirce and Pragmatism*; but in very general terms Peirce was considering more precisely the relationship between our conception of an object and its practical effects; and he saw in our conception of these effects the whole of our conception of the object. This was not a pragmatic test of truth, it was more in the way of an analysis of subject-object relation; it was a logical method whereby we could ascertain the *meaning* of an abstract conception from its practical effects.

Dewey was particularly interested in the teachings of C. S. Peirce and William James. It was the business of living and the solution of practical problems that appealed to him throughout his long career, which was itself both academic and practical. He saw the possibility of defending in rational terms many opposing metaphysical theories, and he also saw it partly as his mission to resolve these oppositions by means of a "pragmatic" solution. R. R. Rusk has said that

"Hegelianism . . . left 'a permanent deposit' in Dewey's thinking. Hegel's synthesis of opposites—of subject and object, spirit and matter, the divine and the human—had a special attraction for him, and throughout his later writings we find him constantly contesting all dualisms"[10].

In his own thinking Dewey began to abolish the distinction between ends and means. After all, what, in fact, was the "end"? It was simply a name which we gave to a series of acts taken collectively; the "means" was a name which we gave to the same series taken distributively. Indeed, it was not the "end" that mattered, since in absolute terms it could never be reached; in relative terms, each means was equally an "end". It all depended upon the point of view. But, again, it was not some distinct "end" that mattered, it was the practical effects along the way; and it was in these practical, moment by moment effects that we had our present and immediate involvement.

If we were to enter effectively into any sort of detailed criticism of Dewey's position at this point, we would have to question very seriously his definition of an "end". Words have a habit of doing the work we want them to do. But one thing is clear, and that is that no idealist would define an "end" as "a name which we give to a series of acts taken collectively".

For Dewey, however, there were no absolute truths and there was no Realm of Ends. Dewey had grown up in the exciting period of biological theory and discovery, and he sought quite enthusiastically to explain, or describe, everything in terms of "growth" and "evolution". But although to him nothing was ultimate, all was provisional, there was nothing inconsequential in his somewhat relativist view. He saw its dangers as well as its exciting possibilities; he saw equally that a relativist view of truth could lead to a popular laissez-faire in thought and behaviour. His belief in his doctrines and his personal integrity would not permit him to change his fundamental acceptance of "pragmatism" simply because of this possibility of abuse. He uttered a warning, in 1910, to the effect that the increased control of, and power over, means did not in itself guarantee happiness. We had carefully to examine and weigh the means we used, because the means was an end-in-itself. If the Realm of Ends, in an absolute sense, had been dismissed we had not thereby made life a shallower or more care-free experience; on the contrary, it should mean a greater involvement in all we do and a deeper consideration of the values of the means we employ.

"With the tremendous increase in our control of nature, in our ability to use nature for human use and satisfaction, we find the actual realization of ends, the enjoyment of values, growing unassured and precarious"[11].

One might perhaps add that, whatever our philosophy in life, whether pragmatist, idealist, realist, Christian or whatever, this statement still has a ring of "truth" about it, and current religious discussions about the nature of God, the Universe and Morality[12] only help to underline the fact that even those who accept a Realm of Ends are not quite so sure as formerly of its nature and content.

Thus Dewey emphasized the personal and variable element in things; and the truth or falsity of human inquiry depended upon its success or failure, in its results for the individual himself. Dewey's theory of Truth is usually referred to as Instrumentalism. Knowledge is never an end-in-itself, it is always a means; it is a personal matter, and each individual uses it for the purpose of adapting himself to new problems, new situations and new involvements. The meaning of any concept depends upon its relationship to the individual, and so the latter uses thoughts, concepts and "truths" in order to find personal solutions to his daily problems. The criterion of truth in any situation thus becomes the pragmatic test—is the result satisfactory or unsatisfactory? The authors of *A Short History of Educational Ideas* point out that on the basis of Dewey's Instrumental Theory of Truth

"even scientific laws are but generalizations which may be modified again and again—they remain true only as long as they summarize truly the current state of human knowledge"[13].

But this is a view which such scientists as Ernst Mach and Karl Pearson have expressed—that what we are pleased to call scientific laws are, in fact, no more than current descriptions of observed "statistical averages"; and that as our experience of the Universe increases and our observations are tabled and analysed, so the statement of our scientific laws is modified. Scientific laws are held to be "true" because they square with all the known evidence; but they are "true" only so long as they conform, and when new evidence is discovered with which a law does not conform, that law is modified, or an entirely new law may be substituted.

Dewey appears to have reduced all "truths" to the scientific level of causation; a thing is "true" if it "furthers our purpose", i.e. if it causes or brings about the consequence we want. But there are several objections to this doctrine. R. R. Rusk points out, for example, that

"If we accept Dewey's statements that the test of truth lies in the consequences to which it leads, and that we can never know what these consequences are, we are convicted of pure scepticism"[14].

We certainly don't always know the consequences of our actions, whether immediately or mediately, and we certainly cannot know them finally; so that the pragmatic test itself seems to depend upon something further and outside itself.

But can we accept that Dewey's pragmatic idea of "furthering our purpose" really *means* Truth? There is a sense in which something may be true for us at any particular moment, because it furthers our purpose and is emotionally satisfying, but this is to deny to the word "truth" any meaning other than a "provisional utility" or a "passing emotion of satisfaction". It may be "useful" at one particular moment in a man's life to embezzle five thousand pounds, and emotionally satisfying at another to cosh an old lady on the head, but these events, thus stated, are little more than biographical data lacking any evaluation in real terms of what is "true" for any really workable or viable society. If the pragmatic theory of truth claims that we tend to hold beliefs to be true which are emotionally satisfying, this is a psychological fact which might include anything from fanaticism to fantasy; if it claims that we persist in holding beliefs to be true when the consequences of their adoption are found to be satisfactory, then it is saying little more than the fact that we are all open to self-deception, and that when the consequences of the adoption of these beliefs cease to be satisfactory, the beliefs will automatically cease to be true. But if pragmatism claims that the properties of "emotional satisfaction" and "satisfactory consequences" are the same thing as the *truth* of a belief, then we are left with a chaotic and anarchic world in which a perfectly successful criminal posseses as much of the "truth" as a perfectly honest citizen; and perhaps more if the latter finds his life lacking in satisfaction. And if even here the validity of the pragmatic test is held, it must be argued that it is self-limiting since not all citizens could be perfectly successful criminals, however emotionally satisfying it might be individually.

Dewey accepted in broad terms the general theory of evolution, of development, change and mutation. He saw no end to the possibilities and potentialities of such process, and of the influences and interrelations of environment and the individual. Dewey saw things "whole".

"Dewey's reference to a 'unified whole' is an instance of his concern for the oneness of the world. If it dared be said that he had an aim, it was to see the world become a more organic, smoothly-functioning whole"[15].

Any vision of the possibilities of the future by an educational philosopher must, in a sense, be regarded as an aim; and Dewey saw his philosophy as a basis for a *progressive* form of education, which will be considered in greater detail later. Education was for him a realistic training in the breaking down of existing social barriers and in the developing of ever new links within the whole framework of society. The *function* of education, if not its aim, was, like that of inquiry generally, to act as a process of reconciliation of opposites (cf. Hegel), whether in the make-up of the individual or in that of the group, the community or the macrosociety. In his *Reconstruction in Philosophy*, Dewey stated that the time had arrived

"for a pragmatism which shall be emphatically idealistic, proclaiming the essential connexion of intelligence with the un-achieved future"[16].

There is an implicit perfectionism about this that even Dewey himself could not deny. The evolution of man was not merely a *process*; by the application of his intelligence to his living in the present, by refining his works, by maturing and perfecting, he could achieve *progress* for the future. It is, perhaps, not surprising that R. R. Rusk described pragmatism as a combination of the methods of naturalism and the conclusions of idealism[17].

Dewey undoubtedly wanted "the best" in life, whatever the best might be, and he wanted to maximize each moment of living. It is rather as if he said, "Don't let's have any preconceived ideas of what the best is, and then proceed to subordinate all our activity towards that—we may be wrong, and each moment of our life may well be a disappointment. Rather let us accept that the best is in the process of development itself; and then let us proceed to distil everything of value that we can from the process of living." He believed, with Rousseau, that education was a natural development, a steady growth through experience and experiment, and it is perhaps noteworthy that the first chapter of *Schools of Tomorrow* is largely a series of quotations from Rousseau's *Emile*. Schools

"take the accumulated learning of adults, material that is quite unrelated to the exigencies of growth, and try to force it upon the children, instead of finding out what these children need as they go along"[18].

Dewey's philosophy needs careful examination, and some of the chief questions still remain for deeper consideration. Is the "pragmatic test" a sufficient, or even valid, criterion for finding Truth, or even a truth? Is success or failure, judged contextually, a sound basis for discovering Reality? Can we really partake of the "ever enduring process of perfecting, maturing, refining"[19] without some concept of perfection, without some idea of the end towards which we are maturing? Is "growth", *per se*, a sufficient philosophy without a further and detailed definition of "growth"? Growth is not always pleasant—it may be a cancerous dissemination and proliferation of destructive cells; process is certainly not always progress—even a crab progresses, sideways. Dewey believed that all values are relative, all truths subjective, and all living experiential. He may, of course, be "right", but, firstly, on his own criterion he can never positively *know* this, even if in pragmatism such a statement is meaningful; and, secondly, on this criterion there is no way of evaluating a "good" or "bad" life. Life is simply "emotionally satisfying" or productive of "satisfactory consequences". And both "satisfying" and "satisfactory" imply further standards of comparison and judgement.

C. DEWEY'S PSYCHOLOGY

Dewey read psychology under G. Stanley Hall (1846–1924), who was particularly interested in the study of the child, and who produced his outstanding work *Adolescence* in 1904[20]. Through the efforts of Hall and his colleagues the scientific study of the child mind had become a serious and essential part of educational activity. Hall used prepared *questionnaires* for a great deal of his material, but much of the psychological work in America at this time was of the anecdotal type and non-statistical. Of Hall Dr William Boyd says:

"Hall was first and foremost an evolutionist. His prime interest was in psychic rather than in biological evolution, but he did not put the two in opposition. For him, 'mind is almost, possibly quite, co-extensive with life, at least animal life'; and in introducing evolutionary thought into the field of the human soul, he claimed to be making a necessary and inevitable extension of Darwinism"[21].

In *The School and Society*[22] Dewey made the following points about the psychology of elementary education. He said that earlier psychology had regarded mind as a purely individual affair in direct and naked contact with an external world; educational practice had exhibited an unconscious adaptation to and harmony with the prevailing psychology; the older psychology was a psychology of knowledge, of intellect; and, finally, the modern conception of mind was essentially one of a *process of growth*, not a fixed thing. Thus Dewey took up the theme of G. Stanley Hall and developed it. In the process of evolution man has gradually acquired a brain, a mind and an intelligence which are all superior to those of other animals. Gradually man has evolved through adjustment to environment, and through the adjustment of the environment to himself, and he has now acquired a measure of intelligent control over his own evolution. Dewey opposed the mechanistic psychology of behaviourism, and accepted that all persons had basic individual differences. The problems and difficulties, which he observed in the various children of his experimental school, demanded some special help and attention, and he found part of the solution in the psycho-analytic methods of Freud. He did not reject the then current tendency

"to conceive individual mind as a function of social life, as not capable of operating by itself, but as requiring continuous stimulus from social agencies and finding its nutrition in social supplies"[23].

Mind was, it is true, essentially social, but children, according to Dewey, were still very much individuals and should be allowed to develop and grow in an atmosphere of freedom. This did not mean, however, that he supported the more *popular* interpretation of Freudian psychology, namely, that no restraint whatsoever should at any time be used in the upbringing and education of children. Indeed, in this respect, Dewey seemed to change very little in his views, for as early as 1900 he had said that a really sympathetic teacher was likely to know much more clearly than the child himself what his own instincts were and meant, and that the teacher was there to suggest and direct the child who might not consciously know what his needs were[24]. Thirty-eight years later, in 1938, he said:

"Some teachers seem to be afraid even to make suggestions to the members of a group as to what they should do. I have heard of cases in which children are surrounded with objects and materials and then left entirely to themselves, the teacher being loath to suggest even what might be done with the materials lest freedom be infringed upon"[25].

In his chapter on "The Psychology of Elementary Education"[26] Dewey gave an outline of elementary school life on a psychological basis. There are, according to him, three main types of growth: from four to eight years of age, from eight to twelve, and from twelve onwards. Briefly, the first period, from four to eight years, is one of *play*, in which the child has left the narrowness and the limitations of the home and begins to make his first contacts with the social world beyond. In this new atmosphere, in which ends and means are not distinguished, he is untroubled by problems. The main concern of his first studies is the life and occupations of the home, followed by the larger social activities upon which the home itself is dependent—mainly farm life. Finally, he learns about the development of various occupations and vital inventions through an experimental reconstruction of the various phases of human evolution and life. Reading and writing are now introduced, and a systematic approach to geography is embarked upon.

The second period, from eight to twelve years, is one of *spontaneous attention* and the development of technique. The child is now able, and also ready, to acquire skills because he is becoming increasingly aware of the possibility of objective results which may also be permanent. In ordinary affairs and in the solution of practical problems, the child begins to develop the ability to analyse details, and to act according to general rules of behaviour and thought. Because of these developments in the child there is a need for changes both in matter and in method of school pursuits. Special studies now find a place in the curriculum quite independent of one another.

The third period, from twelve years onwards, is one of *reflective attention* in which the child has mastered sufficiently the methods of activity, inquiry and thought appropriate to the various phases of experience, in order to be able to specialize in particular studies for technical and intellectual aims. Dewey seems to admit that in this stage there is a sense of more remote ends, and the child is able to raise problems and look for solutions.

Compared with the work of other educational psychologists concerned with child development, such as Piaget, this outline seems perhaps a little thin, but we must not forget that when Dewey first made this study Piaget, for example, was barely four years old.

Dewey emphasized very strongly, in a discussion of "The Psychology of Occupations" and the "Development of Attention"[27], the place of interest in school work and of learning through interest. To Dewey, an interest was "an outgoing of the self" which was "imperiously demanded" if the individual were to develop his natural growth[28]. But "imperious" or not, it was not just "interests" as such which were important, but the organization and canalizing of interests.

"It is necessary to decide between interests that are really important and those that are trivial; between those that are helpful and those that are harmful; between those that are transitory or mark immediate excitement, and those which endure and are permanently influential"[29].

It is the control and direction of interests which Dewey regards as important in the ensuing discourse, and when we somewhat loosely talk about "arousing interest" in our teaching, it would be well to consider whether it is the right sort of interest that we are arousing, and whether it can be permanently related to something of value.

In his *Democracy and Education*, in which Dewey discusses at some length the various theories of education, he considers education as a formal discipline. Older views of psychology had held that the mind possessed, or comprised, a series of faculties concerned with certain mental operations, such as memory, judgement, inference and so forth. Some of these were "keyed-in" as it were at a later stage than others, though memory was considered to operate from the beginning. There were, of course, quantitative differences between individuals, and between the individual as child and the individual as an adult. Dewey's belief in evolutionary growth would not permit him to accept this view of the mind, nor the view that education was the training of faculties. He says that

"another influential but defective theory is that which conceives that mind has, at birth, certain mental faculties or powers, such as perceiving, remembering, willing, judging, generalizing, attending, etc., and that education is the training of these faculties through repeated exercise"[30].

D. DEWEY AND EDUCATION

Dewey said that philosophy might be defined as the general theory of education, or as the theory of education "in its most general phases"[31]. His philosophical position was that of pragmatism; his educational principles were pragmatic. The very installation of the Laboratory School at Chicago, in 1896, was a brave attempt to demonstrate that he had the courage of his convictions. It is true that he had ideal conditions; it is also true that he left it all eight years later to become Professor of Philosophy at Columbia University, New York; but H. H. Horne's criticism of Dewey, to the effect that he used the literary and dialectic methods which he decried rather than the experimental view which he praised, in advocating his own views, seems a trifle harsh. Dewey *did* go into the laboratory and experiment, and continually made use of the experimental method. But it is a trifle naïve to suggest that one cannot afterwards write about it even dialectically, or, for that matter outline the experiment before the laboratory is entered. Dewey's work in the educational field is not to be dismissed by verbal legerdemain, although of course H. H. Horne has adduced much weightier and more damaging arguments against Dewey's educational theory and practice[32].

Dewey obviously owed a great deal to Friedrich Froebel (1782–1852). Froebel saw the problems of education in their social setting, and he visualized the school as a nursery for the citizens of the future. His central theme for all child education was *Darstellung*—a concept of creative self-expression, in which children lived out their experiences in all their activities. In *The School and Society*, Dewey summarizes the main educational principles of Froebel in the following terms[33]:

1. The primary business of the school is to train children in co-operative and mutually helpful living; to foster in them the consciousness of mutual interdependence; and to help them practically in making the adjustments that will carry this spirit into overt deeds.
2. The primary root of all educative activity is in the instinctive, impulsive attitudes and activities of the child, and not in the presentation and application of external material, whether through the ideas of others or through the senses—the

spontaneous activities of children are capable of educational use.

3. These individual tendencies and activities are organized and directed through the uses made of them in keeping up the co-operative living already spoken of, taking advantage of them to reproduce on the child's plane the typical doings and occupations of the larger, maturer, society into which he is finally to go forth.

The sort of school that Dewey envisaged was one capable of producing people for complete living in the world of today; and he regarded the ideal home as the model for the ideal school (cf. Pestalozzi at Yverdun). The school was a large family, a living community involved in a variety of pursuits which were of interest to the pupils, and which made them fully alive to the fact that they were all partners in a common effort. Each had something of importance to contribute to the success of the whole.

The Discipline of Experience and Experimentalism: For Dewey the school was a place for living, working citizens; it was a place where each individual could learn to discipline himself through experience, and in consequence there must be room to experiment. For example, Dewey saw history as dynamic and moving:

"The question of how human beings live, indeed, represents the dominant interest with which the child approaches historic material"[34].

To him the whole history of mankind could be concentrated into the evolution of flax, cotton and wool fibres into clothing, and into the "re-invention" of both materials and machines. In this way, from the examination and manipulation of raw materials to the construction of machines, and the final production of clothing, the child was able to recapitulate the history of his race and its culture epochs, and to participate in its discoveries and manufactures.

Such a method, of course, has its limitations. We can, in practice, import only to a very limited extent into the microcosm of the school the economic life and conditions of the macrocosm of society. Moreover, as Dewey himself admitted[35], experience *per se* is not necessarily educative; it depends upon the sort of experience and the ability of the experiencer—to use the terminology of Spearman—to apprehend his experience, and to make the right eduction of relations and correlates. Some experiences, indeed, may be termed *miseducative*. And again, despite Dewey's denial of ends, the Deweyan teacher has a great responsibility for helping the young to *evaluate* experience, and to see the direction in which their experience is leading them. Dewey himself said that

"The suggestion upon which pupils act must in any case come from somewhere. It is impossible to understand why a suggestion from one who has a larger experience and a wider horizon should not be at least as valid as a suggestion arising from some more or less accidental source"[36].

It is clear from the foregoing that Dewey accepted the need for a teacher fully to understand his individual pupils so that he might be in a position to provide the right suggestion at the right time. He must also realize that the influences and contacts experienced by a child are all-important. Dewey has said that meaning arises through communication[37]; if, therefore, children are to apprehend the meaning of experience they must be able to communicate, and he suggests that the teacher should engineer situations and arrange experiences wherein such communication is possible, and so that there may be continuity, expansion, development, progress and growth. Dewey saw, further, that within the context of the relative freedom of the atmosphere of experimentalism there was also the need for the discipline of group experience. All human life is lived in groups, and an essential part of individual development is the acceptance of social controls, and the intellectual and disciplined participation in the creation and formulation of such controls as may be both acceptable and socially desirable.

The Five General Features of Reflective Experience: Because Dewey has so often been pictured in the more popular mind as the initiator of "progressive" forms of education, with children milling around engaged in noisy and messy projects without purpose or completion, it is perhaps a sobering corrective to look at his five steps in the thinking process, which he applied to the educational process. These are frequently compared with Herbart's famous "Five Formal Steps" of preparation, presentation, association, generalization and application. In *How We Think*[38] Dewey posed the question, "How does a child get to know his world?" And he answers, "Through reflective experience." In all experience there must exist a cause-effect relation, and the causal connexion is made by thought or reflection. This is, of course, a psychological analysis, but it is included here rather than under the section on Psychology because it is very closely related to Dewey's pedagogical thought and practice. Dewey stated that there were the five following steps in the thinking process:

1. There existed first of all a state of confusion, doubt and general perplexity due to the fact that the individual was involved in an incomplete situation whose full nature and significance were not yet ascertained. In terms of education the pupil must have a *problem*, which should be his own.

2. The second step was an attempt at a conjecture, a tentative interpretation of the given data, attributing to them a tendency to produce certain consequences. In terms of the pupil once more, his problem must be a *real* one, that is, real to himself, and a *stimulus* to further thought.

3. The third step was a careful exploration, examination, inspection, analysis and survey of every available consideration that would help to clarify and further define the problem under consideration. Here the pupil must have the necessary *information* and make the *observations* required to deal with the problem.

4. There next followed an elaboration of the tentative hypothesis to make it more precise and more consistent as it began to square with a wider range of available elements and data. Here the pupil was in the position of the *researcher*, developing his ideas and seeking his own solution.

5. Finally, the hypothesis was tested; one took a stand upon the projected hypothesis as an organized plan of action to be applied to the existing state of affairs. The pupil must be allowed to try out and *test the validity* of his own conclusions.

This may all, at first blush, seem a far cry from the Play Way and the Project Method, but in fact, rightly conceived and conducted, and one may add concluded, these would involve, just as any formal scientific experiment, the five general features of reflective thinking. This, said Dewey, is how we think when faced with the task of solving a problem; this is the Problem Method.

The Child and the Curriculum: Paedocentricism: Dewey objected strongly to the subject-based curriculum as the logical summary of the experience of the adult. He maintained that subjects were nothing but summaries of human activities, and therefore children should reach them by making a summary of their own experiences. To adults all these subjects were useful compartments for the convenient storage of knowledge, but young children were not yet ready for this analytical approach to their world. The abstractions made by geography and history, for example, in terms of space and time were not meaningful to them. Out of this belief Dewey developed his paedocentric view of education and the curriculum, and the influence which his ideas have had upon our modern school curriculum has been considerable. The child is the starting-point; he is the centre; and he is the end. His development and growth are, in fact, the only "ideal" that Dewey will allow; these are the considerations that furnish the standard[39].

Dewey goes on to say that we should begin with the child's present experience before entering that represented by the organized bodies of truth which we refer to as "studies". The present world of the child is a total, integral one—for him: to us it may seem narrow, limited and small, but it is his personal world. There is a unity about this world of the child; an almost complete lack of differentiation which leads to a wholehearted interest in all things—from worms to cloud-formations—without any specializations or divisions of the curriculum. And because, in this paedocentric approach the subject-matter is always related to the child's personal experience, it leads ultimately to an enrichment of the subject-matter itself. In this view the task of the teacher is to organize learning situations and contexts of experience. But experiences have no final value—they are of passing value only, and are specifically related to the growth of the child at some particular time and place. Dewey warned as early as 1906 that

"it is the danger of the 'new education' that it regards the child's present powers and interests as something finally significant in themselves"[40].

The pragmatic test, it would seem, does not validate any experience *in vacuo*, nor in any final or absolute sense; the child's experience is useful, significant, satisfactory, even "true" only contextually. There are no absolutes; and there are no ends, whether immediate or remote; the educational process has no end beyond itself. It is its own end and it is a process "of continual reorganizing, reconstructing, transforming"[41]. Education is growth, and its purpose is to encourage growth—mental, moral and physical.

Thus, theoretically and philosophically, Dewey denies the existence of ultimate and eternal values; practically, he rejects ends and anything in the way of ready-made solutions. Subject divisions are an attempt to present such a solution, and therefore subjects, as such, should not, at least at first, appear on the curriculum.

Moral and Religious Aspects of Education: Although strongly influenced in his early years by the philosophy of Hegel, Dewey gradually divorced himself from idealism and the realm of absolute values. In this he also rejected any idea that morals should be regarded as a special department of education requiring special lessons. Morality was not a fixed or final achievement, but a continuing process; it was all one with growing itself;

"in the largest sense of the word, morals is education. It is learning the meaning of what we are about and employing the meaning in action"[42].

In view of this Dewey naturally disapproved very strongly of any separation of moral or religious education from any other form of educational experience; morality grows out of specific empirical facts; morality is social. Thus, in the realms of morality and religion, experience and empirical facts must be the real teacher; the teacher as a person may be a guide, counsellor and friend, but he may do no more than indicate short cuts to his pupils, and encourage them to spare themselves miseducative experiences. But ultimately, the moral significance of a personal, disciplined and organized life can come only through the free and purposive judgement of each individual. This is the way that human progress is made; this is the way that communication is assured between people.

Dewey maintained that the young must become the regenerating force in our future society, since education itself was a process of reconstitution or reconstruction of experience "giving it a more socialized value through the medium of increased individual efficiency"[43]. It was this innate desire for increased *efficiency* which eventually led to discipline. But self-discipline and group-discipline develop through the will of the pupils themselves in order that their progress may be attained with an absolute minimum obstruction or disorganization. Morality and discipline are thus seen as utilitarian and as promoting "efficiency". And insofar as they achieve this they possess pragmatic sanction. In all this the educator's part is to achieve and to furnish the type of environment which will stimulate responses and direct the learner's course, for

"In the last analysis, *all* that the educator can do is modify stimuli so that response will surely as is possible result in the formation of desirable intellectual and emotional dispositions"[44].

The word "desirable" immediately conjures up the equation which John Stuart Mill made between "desirable" and "able to be desired"; and all sorts of "emotional dispositions" are capable of being desired. If, however, Dewey means by "desirable" that which "*ought* to be desired" we are entitled to ask what dispositions of an intellectual and emotional nature ought to be desired—and this brings us back once more to a realm of values or ends.

E. SOME DEVELOPMENTS OF DEWEYISM

The Project Method: The methods employed by Dewey in his Laboratory School grew quite naturally out of his pragmatic philosophy and his psychological theories. In *The School and Society* he discusses the psychology of occupations[45], and he there states that the fundamental point in the psychology of an occupation is that it maintains a balance between the practical and the intellectual phases of experience. We have already mentioned that Dewey was concerned with the processes involved in all human activity, particularly those involving man's basic needs for food, clothing and reasonable comfort. He, therefore, set about "re-inventing" and rediscovering the means for the fulfilment of these needs. This involved the posing of certain "problems" which arose naturally in the pupils' minds, and others which were cunningly contrived by the teacher so that they appeared to originate from the children. This was known as the Problem Method.

Whilst Dewey does not appear to have invented the term "Project Method" he was certainly responsible for the idea, and in Chapter XV ("Play and Work in the Curriculum") of *Democracy and Education* he refers to "projects". It was Professor W. H. Kilpatrick of Columbia University who developed the Project Method from about 1918 onwards, and who, in 1925, published an account of it in his *Foundations of Method*[46]. Kilpatrick regarded the project as wholehearted and purposeful activity proceeding in a social environment; he said that pupils must propose what they actually wish to do; that they should be permitted to do only those things which would build up certain attitudes; that all learning should be done only if it were necessary for what the pupils had actually proposed; and that what pupils were allowed to do should be guided so as to enrich the subsequent stream of experience. Kilpatrick's detailed analysis of the different types of project—producer, consumer, problem and drill—may be read in Chapter XXI of his *Foundations of Method*.

The Dalton Plan: The 'Contract Plan'', which Helen Parkhurst developed at Dalton in Massachusetts, has been described by her in her book *Education on the Dalton Plan*. The Plan was a "contract" between the pupil and the teacher to allow the independence of the pupil to work at his own rate on his particular assignment, and to permit the teacher to serve in a consultative capacity. The Dalton Laboratory Plan emphasized in particular the value of the *heuristic* method—a method of "finding out" by the pupil, but not on any haphazard basis. The assignment was fully organized and planned in collaboration with the teacher, and procedures were to some extent programmed: then the pupil was allowed to go off to his "cubicle" to search for the solutions, and the teacher was always available to give guidance when necessary. The hall-marks of the Plan were freedom and co-operation. The restrictions of time-tables, curricula, syllabuses, bells, rooms and so forth are often incredibly frustrating to the teacher and pupil alike; the Dalton Plan sought to eliminate all these as formal limitations. But the Plan was not a "free for all"; there must exist freedom within co-operation. In the words of Helen Parkhurst:

"The Dalton Plan lays emphasis upon the importance of the child's living while he does his work, and the manner in which he acts as a member of society rather than upon the subjects of his curriculum. It is the sum-total of these twin experiences which determine his character and his knowledge"[47].

The Play Way: In his *Democracy and Education* Dewey emphasized that play and work were not mutually exclusive, and that plays, games, and constructive "occupations" were not merely agreeable diversions. Play is not amusement or aimlessness, nor is work necessarily arduous and without enjoyment. Indeed, work which remains "permeated with the play attitude is art—in quality if not in conventional designation"[48]. Writing only a year later, in 1917, Caldwell Cook maintained in *The Play Way*[49] that play methods were simply an active way of learning, not a relaxation or diversion from real study.

Many schools, and many individual teachers, make use today of various aspects of the pragmatic approach, including problem and project methods, assignments and play methods, without seeing the necessity to discard a more formal framework as the general setting and organization of the work.

F. SOME GENERAL CONSIDERATIONS

Most of the more serious criticisms of Deweyism may be found in R. R. Rusk's *The Doctrines of the Great Educators* and in H. H. Horne's *The Democratic Philosophy of Education.* A world in which there are no ideals, in which there is no Realm of Ends, can become a world in which life is aimless. A world in which all knowledge is merely a means, an instrument, can become a cultureless world. The doctrine of Instrumentalism, taken to its logical conclusion, could result in a society of pragmatic opportunists without consideration or compassion. But to Dewey there was no real antithesis between culture and utility—when knowledge ceased to be "useful" it also ceased to be "cultural"; and if it were really "cultural" it would also be "useful"[50]. It is interesting to note that in this connexion Dewey was quoted cheek by jowl with Professor A. N. Whitehead in an Appendix to the

Spens Report. Whitehead regarded the antithesis between a technical and a liberal education as fallacious as Dewey regarded the antithesis between utility and culture[51]. In the world of Dewey knowledge and practice were always interacting and both must be used as a means of making "good" realizable and secure in experienced existence. As he saw it, the real problem of education in a democratic society was to do away with the dualism and begin to construct a course of studies which would make thought "a guide of free practice for all", and which would make "leisure a reward of accepting responsibility for service rather than a state of exemption from it"[52].

One of the great objections to pragmatism, as also to hedonism, is that we can be wise only after the event, since we can never really fully foresee the final outcome of our activity. This could, as Rusk has pointed out, lead to sheer scepticism. Rusk further argues that pragmatism is not so much a philosophy as a way of trying to do without a philosophy: the pragmatist, as such, is uninterested in motives, he is concerned only with consequences. Even the view that practice takes pride of place over theory in the educational sphere is highly suspect—almost all the great educators have been philosophers first; indeed, Dewey was himself a philosopher first and last, in spite of himself.

Dewey's unqualified support for experimentalism is equally without foundation, since many of the great discoveries of our Universe, from planets and comets to man's Unconscious have been made largely at the theoretical level. Dewey, so Rusk has argued, was more interested, in his experimentalism, in the means or instrumentality of attaining knowledge than in testing its validity. Even methods tend to become ends in themselves.

During a long life of ninety-three years, in which he was always mentally alert and active, Dewey had examined most of these criticisms, and had accepted the validity of some of them. In a typically "pragmatic" way he modified many of his ideas, theories and practices. Dewey accepted that not *all* experiences were genuinely or equally educative, that interests and desires can be acquired as well as knowledge, and that it is the duty of the educator to stimulate their development. He also agreed that some systematic teaching was from time to time necessary, indeed inevitable, to fill up the gaps in pupils' knowledge. And, finally, he disapproved very strongly of some of the "progressive" schools, which, very often in the name of Deweyism, provided an arena for almost unlimited freedom without control, direction, guidance or even advice.

REFERENCES

1. Curtis, S. J. & Boultwood, M. E. A.: *A Short History of Educational Ideas.* U.T.P., 4th Edition, 1965, p. 463.
2. *Vide* Boyd, W.: *The History of Western Education.* A. & C. Black, 7th Edition, 1964, pp. 398f.
3. Dewey, J.: *The School and Society.* Univ. of Chicago Press, 1900, p. 116.
4. *Ibid.* p. 11.
5. *Ibid.* p. 125.
6. *Vide The Public and its Problems.* Holt, 1927; *Problems of Men.* New York Philosophical Lib., 1946; *Characters and Events.* Holt, 1929; *Experience and Nature.* Open Court, 1925; *The Quest for Certainty.* Minton, Balch, 1929; *A Common Faith.* Yale U.P., 1934; *Liberalism and Social Action.* Putnam, 1939.
7. James, W.: *Pragmatism.* Longmans, 1907, pp. 45–6.
8. *Ibid.* p. 200.
9. Gallie, W. B.: *Peirce and Pragmatism.* Penguin Books (Pelican), 1952, p. 22.
10. Rusk, R. R.: *The Doctrines of the Great Educators.* Macmillan, 2nd Edition, 1954, p. 285.
11. Dewey, J.: *The Influence of Darwin in Philosophy.* N.Y., 1910, p. 71. Quoted in Curtis & Boultwood (*vide supra*), p. 492.
12. *Vide* Robinson, J. A. T.: *Honest to God.* S.C.M. Press, 1963; Robinson, J. A. T. & Edwards, D. L.: *The Honest to God Debate* S.C.M. Press, 1963; Robinson, J. A. T.: *The New Reformation?* S.C.M. Press, 1965; Vidler, A. R. (ed.): *Objections to Christian Belief.* Constable, 1963; Tillich, P.: *The Shaking of the Foundations.* S.C.M. Press, 1949.
13. *Op. cit.,* p. 471.
14. Rusk, R. R., *op. cit.,* p. 293.
15. Curtis, S. J. & Boultwood, M. E. A., *op. cit.,* p. 473.
16. Dewey, J.: *Reconstruction in Philosophy.* Holt, 1920, p. 177.
17. Curtis, S. J.: *An Introduction to the Philosophy of Education.* U.T.P., 1958, p. 75.

18. Dewey, J. & E.: *Schools of Tomorrow*. J. M. Dent, 1915, p. 3.
19. Dewey, J.: *Reconstruction in Philosophy*, p. 177.
20. Hall, G. S.: *Adolescence*. Appleton, 1904.
21. Boyd, W., *op cit.*, pp. 395–6.
22. Dewey, J.: *The School and the Society*, Chapter IV *passim*.
23. *Ibid.* p. 90.
24. *Ibid.* p. 125.
25. Dewey, J.: *Experience and Education*. Macmillan, 1938, p. 84.
26. *The School and Society*, Chapter IV.
27. *Ibid.* Chapters VI and VII.
28. Dewey, J.: "Interest as Related to the Training of the Will". Article in the *National Herbart Society Yearbook*, 1895, p. 15. Quoted in Curtis & Boultwood (*vide supra*), p. 479.
29. *The School and Society*, p. 134.
30. *Op. cit.*, p. 80.
31. Dewey, J.: *Democracy and Education*. Macmillan, 1916 (Reprinted 1955), Chapter XXIV.
32. Horne, H. H.: *The Democratic Philosophy of Education*. Macmillan, 1932, p. 483 *et passim*.
33. *The School and Society*, Chapter V.
34. *Ibid.* p. 157.
35. *Experience and Education*, p. 13.
36. *Ibid.* pp. 84–5.
37. Mead, G. H.: *Mind, Self and Society*. Univ. of Chicago Press, 1934, p. 79. Quoted from Dewey, J.: *Experience and Nature*. Open Court, 1925, Chapter V.
38. Dewey, J.: *How We Think*. Harrap, 1910; Revised Edition, 1933.
39. Dewey, J.: *The School and the Child*. Blackie, 1906, pp. 22f.
40. *Ibid.* p. 29.
41. Dewey J.: *Democracy and Education*, p. 59.
42. Dewey, J.: *Human Nature and Conduct*, Holt, 1922, p. 280.
43. Curtis, S. J. & Boultwood, M. E. A., *op cit.*, p. 485.
44. *Democracy and Education*, p. 212.
45. *Op. cit.*, Chapter VI.
46. Kilpatrick, W. H.: *Foundations of Method*. Macmillan, 1925.
47. Parkhurst, H.: *The Dalton Plan*. Bell, 1922, p.12.
48. *Op. cit.*, pp. 241–2.
49. Cook, C.: *The Play Way*. Heinemann, 1917.
50. *Democracy and Education*, p. 305.
51. The Spens Report: *Secondary Education*. H.M.S.O., 1938 (Reprinted 1959), pp. 413–14; Whitehead, A. N.: *Aims of Education*. Williams & Norgate, 1929, p. 74.
52. *Democracy and Education*, p. 305.

BIBLIOGRAPHY

A. BOOKS BY JOHN DEWEY

The School and Society. Univ. of Chicago Press, 1900.
The School and the Child. Blackie, 1906.
How We Think. Harrap, 1910 (Revised Edition, 1933).
Democracy and Education. Macmillan, 1916 (Reprinted 1955).
Reconstruction in Philosophy. Holt, 1920.
Human Nature and Conduct. Holt, 1922.
Experience and Education. Macmillan, 1938 (19th Printing, 1955).
Dewey, J. & Dewey, E.: *Schools of Tomorrow.* J. M. Dent, 1915.

B. OTHER BOOKS OF REFERENCE

Boyd, W.: *The History of Western Education.* A. & C. Black, 7th
    Edition, 1964. (Especially pp. 398–407).
Cook, Caldwell: *The Play Way.* Heinemann, 1917.
Curtis, S. J.: *An Introduction to the Philosophy of Education.*
    U.T.P., 1958, *passim.*
Curtis, S. J. & Boultwood, M. E. A.: *A Short History of Educational
    Ideas.* U.T.P., 4th Edition, 1965. (Especially Chapters XVII
    and XX).
Dewey, E.: *The Dalton Laboratory Plan.* J. M. Dent, 1922.
Gallie, W. B.: *Peirce and Pragmatism.* Penguin Books (Pelican),
    1952.
Gull, H. K. F.: *Projects in the Education of Young Children.*
    McDougall, 1926.
Horne, H. H.: *The Democratic Philosophy of Education.* Macmillan,
    1932.
James, W.: *Pragmatism.* Longmans, 1907.
Kilpatrick, W. H.: *Foundations of Method.* Macmillan, 1925.
—: *Education for a Changing Civilization.* Macmillan, 1926.
Mayhew, K. C. & Edwards, A. C.: *The Dewey School.* Appleton-
    Century, 1936.
Nathanson, J.: *John Dewey, The Reconstruction of a Democratic
    Life.* Scribner, 1951.
Parkhurst, H.: *Education on the Dalton Plan.* Bell, 1930.
Roth, R. J.: *John Dewey and Self-Realization.* Prentice-Hall, 1962.
Rusk, R. R.: *Doctrines of the Great Educators.* Macmillan, 2nd
    Edition, 1954. (Pages 284–303).

E

Thomson, G. H.: *A Modern Philosophy of Education*. Allen &
Unwin, 1929. (Chapter V on John Dewey).
White, M. G.: *The Origin of Dewey's Instrumentalism*. Columbia
Univ. Press, N.Y., 1943.

PART TWO

Psychological

CHAPTER 6

PSYCHOLOGY AND EDUCATION

A. PSYCHOLOGY, ITS NATURE AND DEVELOPMENT

The word "psychology" is derived from the Greek ψυχή (psyche), meaning "mind" or "soul", and R. and M. Knight define "psychology" as

"the systematic study of thought and behaviour—human and animal, normal and abnormal, individual and social"[1].

From this definition it would appear that psychology is concerned with the nature and working of the mind and its aberrations, and with behaviour generally. Dr C. J. Adcock, however, maintains that psychologists themselves prefer to avoid any assumptions about the nature of the mind, and that most of them would prefer a definition in terms of behaviour rather than of mind.

"Behaviour is objective and observable; mind is an assumption and, even if a justifiable assumption, not the primary object of our study"[2].

This seems fair enough if psychology is to be regarded as a science, since mind, or soul, or even consciousness are not in themselves objects of observation; they are abstractions or assumptions—or just inferences. We can observe overt behaviour, and to some extent measure it, however inexact such measurement may be. But behaviour must ultimately involve mental processes, such as motivation, which cannot be directly observed. In his *Educational Psychology and Children*, Dr K. Lovell states that psychology may be defined as a branch of that science "which studies the activities of the organism (human and animal)"[3], since activities will also include the thinking process. This definition seems far less objectionable than many others which concentrate exclusively on overt behaviour or, on the other hand, on processes of mentation.

Psychology began as a speculative branch of philosophy and was primarily concerned with ways of talking about mental facts; it was theoretical and abstract, and not much concerned with any practical application of its theories, or with any experimentation to establish a scientific basis for them. The chief source of information about the mind was *introspection*, or the process of "looking inwards", in order to observe our own mental operations. Having observed these in a systematic way, it was argued, we could proceed to make generalizations about our observations.

There are, however, limitations to the introspective method; we can introspect so much and no more. We can introspect our sensations, but just get into a rage and you will soon see how incapable you are of observing, examining, and recording your emotive experience. Emotions and motives are well-nigh impossible to introspect; even when our motives are fully conscious we cannot view them with any real impartiality; but if they are unconscious, then, by definition, we cannot introspect them. Even within the cognitive field, where we may feel that we are reasonably safe, we find that sensation and perception "play tricks" on us, and we cannot satisfactorily measure, in numerical terms, their relative strength or persistence. Indeed, the whole of introspective data are private to the observer, and there is no way of generalizing from them in a scientific manner.

The second main method in the earlier days of the development of psychology was the *anecdotal* one. There are fields, such as animal psychology, where introspection is impossible. Here the pioneers in animal psychology had to rely largely on anecdote, a word used for

"an account of an observation from which no conclusion can be drawn either because the observation is badly controlled with perhaps an unreliable observer or because it is a single observation made under conditions in which numerous similar observations would be necessary for the drawing of a valid conclusion"[4].

Dr R. H. Thouless goes on to say that anecdotalism becomes a vice when it is mistaken for scientific method.

Towards the end of the nineteenth century, psychologists such as William James, William McDougall, G. F. Stout and W. Wundt began to approach the whole subject in a much more critical and experimental way. In 1879 W. Wundt established the first Psychological Laboratory at Leipzig, where, in fact, his prime aim was to secure the best possible conditions for introspection; but his development of experimental psychology began, in itself, to open up the whole subject in all sorts of fascinating ways, and gradually there was a movement away from the method of introspection. Through experimentation it became clear that behaviour could become an objective study, and could to some extent be measured under controlled conditions. Behaviourism now developed as an objective science, and almost as a branch of physiology. Many of the conditions of the psychological laboratory, however, are artificial and it seems clear that in a more natural environment reactions might be different.

New schools of psychology have arisen from time to time, and emphasis has changed from one aspect of mind and behaviour to another. Gestalt ("form", "pattern", "whole-made-of-related-parts") psychology in Germany developed the theory of configuration, or organized wholes, as a revolt against the methods of Wundt. It also opposed the analysis of associationism, according to which association is the basic process from which all the higher processes of thought are built up.

In a consideration of purpose and conation, in fact of all experienced mental activity, we find at least two opposed schools of psychology. On the one hand, there is the Behaviourist School already referred to, and on the other, the Hormic School, the most famous proponent of which was Dr William McDougall. The latter made purpose and conation central features of his psychology, and asserted that these could not be the effects of purely physiological causes. Hormic psychology emphasized feeling and conative urge, and also the importance of instinctive impulses and *purposive* striving.

The psychology of the Unconscious, or Subconscious, is certainly older than the work of Freud, or of the other psychoanalytical schools of Adler and Jung. It was the use of hypnotism which first revealed mental processes below the level of consciousness. Hypnotism is a technique for inducing the state of hypnosis, or trance, which is characterized by considerably heightened suggestibility, and by the reduction of censorship, or the repressing force which prevents memories and ideas from entering into consciousness. This technique was first practised extensively in more modern times, about 1880, by the French psychologists Janet and Charcot, who used it for the recovery of buried memories, and for the removal of symptoms by hypnotic and post-hypnotic suggestion. Through Freud, and those associated with his work, a new world was opened up—the subcontinent of the Unconscious Mind, which Jung took a stage further into the realms of the Collective Unconscious.

In psychological discussion, particularly in the field of education, we frequently find ourselves using the term "intelligence", although we are aware that there is no final or absolutely adequate definition of it. It has been defined as

"(1) the capacity to meet novel situations, or to learn to do so, by adaptive responses, and
(2) the ability to perform tests or tasks, involving the grasping of relationships, the degree of intelligence being proportional to the complexity, or the abstractness, or both, of the relationships"[5].

In 1904 C. Spearman produced evidence of a mathematical nature to demonstrate that all mental abilities are related, or correlated, in a positive way. Spearman argued that if an individual possesses one type of mental ability, then there is a degree of probability that he possesses another; and that this probability, demonstrated by his experiments, statistical analyses and correlation factors[6], could be accounted for only on the basis that there is a common factor in all mental abilities, which he termed g (or general factor). A second factor was specific, or s, to each ability. Spearman's theory was termed the "Two-Factor Theory", and the general factor g was regarded as the capacity for relational thinking. Spearman evolved what he termed "noegenetic principles", i.e. the principles upon which the human mind worked. They were:

1. *The Apprehension of Experience:* This was the ability to observe one's own mental processes, and to grasp quickly any situation, or set of actions, which became a part of one's experience.

2. *The Eduction of Relations:* This was the ability to discover essential relationships between different data or items of knowledge. Thus the relation between "left" and "right" is "opposite".

3. *The Eduction of Correlates:* This was the ability to discover a correlate when provided with a datum and a relation. Thus, when given the word "left" and the relation "opposite", the correlate would be "right".

Other psychologists, such as Burt[7], have demonstrated quite conclusively that there are, in addition to a general ability, group abilities involved in a group of subjects, and that these group abilities are not specific in the way that Spearman thought. Such group abilities are verbal, numerical, practical and spatial.

This analytical approach towards the "factors" of the mind, (or factorial analysis), has led to a further development in experimental psychology in an attempt to evolve more and more accurate methods of testing and measurement. And so statistical methods have become increasingly important in experimental and applied psychology[8]. Statistical analysis has stressed, in turn, individual differences, and this has contributed to the development of a psychology of *personality*, which attempts to establish a list of discoverable traits of personality, with suitable scales and tests for their measurement[9]. Personality "profiles" are constructed which help to provide assistance in matters of vocational guidance and employment. It is important, however, to note that this type of assessment is still in its infancy, and that whilst we have put the dividers over everything, from muons to moon craters, we still find certain intractable and irreducible elements in the personality of man. As R. and M. Knight have said:

"in spite of all that is being done, and of the increasing recognition that tests of personality are not impracticable (although the same tests are not all equally suited to selection, experimentation, and diagnosis or guidance), we must not suppose that the assessment of personality has reached the same level of precision as the assessment of abilities or attainments"[10].

This is not to derogate from or to depreciate the work of the psychologists who are interested, and involved, in the scientific analysis and measurement of human personality. E. L. Thorn-dike's dictum, that "whatever exists, exists in some quantity and can (in principle) be measured"[11], may possibly be applied to behaviour, though not to consciousness, as Professor R. B. Cattell points out; but this leaves a very large field of human mental activity (and therefore personality) quite untouched. Some of the finer and more cultural elements in human personality are (so far) quite unamenable to measurement in any absolute, or even in any significantly relative, terms. Professor R. B. Cattell's own "multi-variate experimental approach", by means of handling many variables at once, seems more likely to succeed in studying human behaviour and personality in a natural way, than the older Wundt-Pavlovian univariate, and highly artificial, methods. But the most detailed differentiation of human personality, or the most elaborated profile, may at present be little more than a caricature of the total, integrated being. The information amassed, however, in producing the profile, may be invaluable in problems of vocational guidance, educational failure, and mental sick-ness.

B. THE SCOPE AND TECHNIQUES OF PSYCHOLOGY

Today the ramifications, divisions and sub-divisions of psychology are manifold. *Pure* psychology is a term used for the increase in psychological information and knowledge, whilst *applied* psy-chology is concerned with the application of this body of acquired knowledge to every branch of behaviour, and to every department of society where human behaviour is involved. Thus "applied psychology" simply means psychology applied to any problem, whether in industry, mental health, social pathology, advertising, design, military operations, vocational guidance, propaganda or education. These two general divisions are fairly clear-cut, but the subject-matter of psychology itself is classified in a number of different ways by different psychologists. Dr K. Lovell[12] divides psychological studies into (a) Normal psychology, (b) Abnormal psychology, (c) Child psychology, (d) Animal psychology, and (e) Social psychology. R. and M. Knight, however, consider that there are six main areas: physiological psychology, psychology of cognition, psychometry, animal psychology, psychology of moti-vation and social psychology[13]. There are obvious overlaps here, but the lists indicate that the division of the subject-matter is a somewhat arbitrary one, and that it varies according to the predilections of the writers. Lovell's terms are self-explanatory, but some of those used by the Knights require a little further elaboration.

1. *Physiological psychology:* This concerns those aspects of the body most closely involved in our mental life, such as the physiology of the brain, the nervous system, and the sense organs.

2. *The psychology of cognition:* This covers the activities of the mind concerned with *knowledge* as distinct from emotions and desires—perception, attention, learning, memory and reasoning.

3. *Psychometry* involves the measurement of mental and behavioural qualities, with the testing and measurement of intelligence, special and group abilities, and the assessment of personality traits.

4. *The psychology of motivation* is concerned with innate and acquired motives, whether conscious or unconscious, which impel us to action.

The Knights point out that the change of emphasis from that on the psychology of cognition to psychometry, motivation and social psychology has led to a rapid advance in technique from anecdotalism to controlled experiment and observation[14].

Today the methods and techniques of psychology are basically the same as those of any other science. Certain facts are observed as accurately as possible, and a generalization or hypothesis is formed. The hypothesis is then tested on the basis of its capacity for prediction. Dr Lovell[15] outlines three main techniques used in psychology today—the designed experiment, the developmental method, and the case-history method. It is obvious that the designed experiment in psychology is much more difficult to control than, say, the designed experiment in physics; the real-life situations with which psychology and social psychology are concerned cannot be artificially controlled, nor can human motives be observed or explored in a mechanical or objective way. The desire to eliminate certain causal factors has led to the univariate type of laboratory experiment. R. B. Cattell says of this type of experiment:

"The univariate, laboratory method, with its isolation of the single process, has worked well in the older sciences, but where total organisms have to be studied, the theoretical possibility must be faced that one can sometimes hope to find a law only if *the total organism* is included in the observations and experiences—not just a bit of its behaviour"[16].

The multivariate method, like the clinical method, emphasizes "wholeness", but unlike the clinician the multivariate experimenter actually *measures* all the variables and makes use of the electronic computer to abstract any regularities that exist.

The developmental method is concerned with the psychosomatic development of the individual from birth to old age, and with the interaction that occurs between the individual and his environment. The developmental and observational method is being pursued only as long as environmental conditions are not manipulated in any way; when any part of the total situation is deliberately varied, the observer is taking part in a designed experiment. Using the developmental method, such psychologists as Susan Isaacs, Gesell and Piaget have pursued systematic studies of children in an attempt to establish norms and patterns of behaviour at certain ages, or at specific phases of development. Piaget has, of course, also designed many controlled experiments as well.

Finally, there is the case-history method in which much or all of the past behaviour of the individual under consideration has been unobserved by the clinician or social worker. The method cannot hope to be exact, or "scientific", since it deals largely with a group of people who are deviant, delinquent, neurotic, or abnormal in some way, and there is no means of establishing a comparative "norm". The method must be largely anecdotal and retrospective, and it depends very much upon the subjective interpretation of the clinician or investigator. This does not mean, however, that it cannot be highly successful, but obviously a great deal depends upon the human factor.

C. PSYCHOLOGY AND EDUCATION

The value of psychology to the teacher becomes more obvious every year as the subject develops its many facets. In the first place, psychology enables the teacher to understand *himself* and the manner in which his own mind works; and no one would deny the importance of understanding oneself before seeking to understand or to teach others. But, secondly, psychology assists the teacher in understanding the *child*. Through the techniques of psychology and psychometry, the teacher is made aware of the endowment of the individual child, his general level of intelligence, his special abilities, and something of his general personality. Through the work of developmental psychologists the teacher may learn something of the laws and phases of child development, the effect upon the child of environmental changes, and the processes of character development and mental maturation. It is very important for the teacher to understand as fully as possible the way in which one personality acts upon another, the extent to which group life may modify the individual, and the manner in which the life of the school may help, in a corporate way, to develop the child. And, in general, the techniques examined by psychology in an experimental way can guide the teacher in the skills and craft of teaching itself, as well as indicating the way in which knowledge systems are developed, how fresh knowledge is gained, and how we observe, learn, remember, and reason.

We shall see, in Chapter 7, that Freud, in his general theory of the Unconscious, maintained that our mental processes are predominantly unconscious, and that this "realm of the Unconscious" is the real determinant of conduct. Within the Unconscious are stored up all the evil as well as the good effects of our experience, and these can lead to conflict in our mind. It is important for the teacher to comprehend as fully as possible the means by which mental conflict may be resolved or prevented, and in particular to understand the processes of suppression, repression, and sublimation and deflection. The value of such knowledge to the teacher is not that he may become an amateur psycho-analyst, but that he may with deeper understanding appreciate the type of problem with which the child is faced, and the various ways in which the latter may deal with his problems. By *regression*, for example, the individual may revert to an earlier stage in childhood, and to childhood ideas and memories. In this way he may find a somewhat primitive and infantile escape from the tendencies within himself which are being frustrated and baulked. Or he may seek, unconsciously, to deny his inferiority by an over-emphasis on the opposite of the characteristic which he seeks to conceal—this is the process of *compensation*. When he finds that some of his motives are not in harmony with the totality of his personality, the individual may seek to adopt a mechanism termed *rationalization*, whereby conflicts between moral sentiments and impulses are avoided or resolved. But, as Professor R. S. Peters points out, it would be "logically absurd" to suggest that *all* reasons were rationalizations:

"It is only because people sometimes give genuine reasons for what they do, and because they sometimes change their course of action in the light of considerations that are logically relevant to the end that they have in mind, that it makes sense to talk of rationalizations as distinct from reasons. The term "rationalization" is a parasite. It flourishes because common experience has provided hosts in the form of genuine reasons for action"[17].

But the term "rationalization" is not different, in this respect, from many other terms used in psycho-analysis. Just as we may give right reasons for activity, "which satisfy certain obvious common-sense standards"[18], and may pursue that activity with sound results, so also we may "compensate" (another parasitic term) in a conscious, deliberate, logical and sensible way, for deficiencies that we know we possess. It is clear that all our activity does not take the form of unconscious "compensation" any more than all our thinking takes the form of "rationalization", and we should naturally be on our guard against hasty judgements and imputations of false motives, when referring to the activity of other people, whether children or adult. In true reasoning, as distinct from rationalization, the action *follows* the thought, even though the reasoning itself may be faulty, and, like Thomas à Becket[19], we may be tempted to do "the right deed for the wrong reason"; in rationalization specious excuses and "reasons" are produced to justify a decision or an action already completed. Thus, when an individual under hypnosis is told that ten minutes after being released from hypnotic trance he will go and poke the fire, when no fire exists in the fire-place, the subject will do what has been suggested; and when asked why he has performed this somewhat odd action he will provide, in an embarrassed way, a "reason".

The psychoanalytic schools of Freud, Adler and Jung provided theories concerning mental disturbances and aberrations, manifestations of maladjustment and neuroses, as well as methods and techniques for dealing with sufferers. We are becoming increasingly concerned with individual deviations from the norm, and with methods of preventive and curative treatment in the home, the school, the clinic, and in society at large. In the general mental health concept, and in the implications for education, the dynamics of parent-child, teacher-child and teacher-parent relationships are becoming progressively more important. More than ever before we are concerned to consider how pupils may be helped to solve their problems in and through their face-to-face relationships with their teachers and with other pupils. In all this, of course, the County psychological services and the Child Guidance Clinics have an invaluable part to play. The aim of psychoanalytic therapy, whether the subject be child or adult, is not directly to solve all the problems of the individual for the rest of his life, and to render life devoid of all conflicts or risks, but, as Karen Horney maintains,

"to enable an individual eventually to solve his problems himself. . . . The end is to help him to regain his spontaneity, and to find his measurements of value in himself, in short, to give him courage to be himself"[20].

And this, surely, is as much an educational aim as a psychotherapeutic one—to help the child to develop the capacity and initiative to solve his problems for himself; to assist him to maintain, or regain, a spontaneity in his approach to life, to living, and to all his problems; and, perhaps, above all to give him "the courage to be" in the great "Waste Land" of contemporary anxiety and despair. Merely to help a child, or any individual, to adapt himself or adjust himself to social norms is not enough, however important initially this may be. True liberation, as Alan W. Watts has indicated[21], is attained not by accepting uncritically the forms of conditioning imposed upon us by social institutions, but by the "transformation of consciousness" and by the "inner feeling of one's own existence".

As we have already indicated, psychologists such as Jean Piaget and Susan Isaacs have done much to help the educator comprehend more fully the psychosomatic development of the child. Through these, and other educational psychologists, we have been given a fairly comprehensive view of the emotional, intellectual and social development of the child from infancy to adolescence. Moreover, an examination and elucidation of some of the more complex problems of maturation have helped the educationist, *qua* educationist, to evolve the right sort of curricula and syllabuses at the right time. Professor G. H. Bantock, in his essay on "Fact and Value in Education", states that the psychologist, in his function as a psychologist, is not concerned to make value-judgements, but only factual-judgements. It is not, he avers, the function of the psychologist to say whether such-and-such a thing *ought* to be learnt—

"In other words, from the empirical fact that children are capable of learning certain things it does not logically follow that they *ought* to learn them. The psychological is a factual situation, the educative an evaluative or moral one; the combination of the two, without a clear-sighted realization of what is implied, is almost invariably fraught with grave dangers, and discrimination between them, in the present state of the educational world, a matter of the most important consequence"[22].

This is, of course, very true, but it is the factual-judgements of the psychologist which prevent the educationist from making the mistake of giving what may be the right material at the wrong time: in other words, the psychologist (or educational psychologist) is concerned with curriculum building and syllabus development in terms of *when*, if not in terms of *what*. The educational psychologist is, however, both psychologist and educationist, and the recent work of Dr Ronald Goldman is a striking example of the production of a teaching programme out of an acute understanding of the child mind. In his *Religious Thinking from Childhood to Adolescence*[23], Dr Goldman presents a systematic account of the religious thinking of the child from the age of six years to seventeen years. To say that Dr Goldman has caused a major ripple of disturbance in our general attitude to religious education is to underestimate what he has achieved; he has, in fact, added "a new dimension to our insights into child development"[24]. In his subsequent book[25], Dr Goldman outlines a programme of religious education which he considers, as both psychologist and educationist, to be consistent with the intellectual and emotional development of the growing child. Thus the educational psychologist, with training in the disciplines of psychology and education, is in a reasonably good position (with Bantock's proviso of "a clear-sighted realization of what is implied") to know what a child is *capable* of learning at a certain time, as well as to judge what *ought* to be taught. This assumes, of course, that (in the example quoted) some form of religious teaching *ought* to be given—but there are clearly many educationists who would not accept this.

The educationist is interested not only in what ought to be taught, and when it should be taught, but also in how the subject-matter may best be learnt, i.e. he is interested in the processes of learning, learning theory generally, and learning techniques. The psychologists have in turn proposed a variety of theories (e.g. Thorndike, Tolman, Piaget, Skinner, etc.). We shall not elaborate on these learning theories here, but in Chapter 8 we shall consider the "schematic learning" of Piaget, and in Chapter 9 the problem-solving and programmed learning of Skinner. It is perhaps unnecessary to emphasize the vital importance of the theory of learning to the teacher, and also the possibilities of positive and negative transfer of training. Learning is being studied at various levels of complexity, but the fundamental principles of learning still remain rather obscure, despite all the laboratory experiments with rats, mice, monkeys, chicken and pigeons in Skinner and other boxes. The problems of learning and memory are undoubtedly some of the most fascinating and difficult in psychology. Professor D. O. Hebb maintains that

"It appears generally true that learning is a function of earlier learning, an influence referred to as transfer of training. Transfer may be positive (promoting the present learning) or negative (hindering it). Learning set is a form of positive transfer, a 'learning how to learn' which must be an important part of what the student gets from the formal educational process"[26].

This psychological support for what the practising teacher has so often claimed, that the important feature in education is not so much the actual material learned but the process of "learning how to learn", is very welcome. And the development of learning sets is clearly one of the most important features of the educational process.

Every teacher is involved in the intelligence of his pupils, and it is through the investigations and field work of psychologists that he is in a far better position than ever before to know something of the nature of intelligence, the structure of abilities, and the individual mental differences among his educands. The educator is now in possession of psychological information which will assist in dealing with special types of children, such as the gifted, the dull, the backward, the handicapped and the E.S.N.

There is today a far greater emphasis upon the environment of the child and its effects upon both intelligence and learning. It is becoming, therefore, important to observe, to examine, and to analyse the social behaviour of children, and to understand the nature of adolescent groups, as well as the "unattached" both within and outside the school. All this involves an appreciation and understanding of how groups arise and form, develop leadership, organize action, define roles, assign status, discipline members, create mores, and generally maintain rules, standards and morals. Many of our social problems today must be regarded as educational problems: many of our educational problems are basically social in origin. We are all of us involved, in society, in the prevention of the development of deviant and delinquent groups, in the understanding and control, or absorption, of subcultures, and in questions of mass communication, social pressures and propaganda. All this involves both an interest in, and study of, social psychology.

When all has been said, however, psychology remains a discipline, a technique and a tool. The educationist, educator or teacher must listen to, and learn from, everything that the psychologist has to say, and must do his best to evaluate the psychologist's findings. But, as G. H. Bantock has underlined, he must never allow the psychologist *qua* psychologist to dictate the values which it still remains the province and function of the educationist to establish, and to mediate to others.

REFERENCES

1. Knight, R. & Knight, M.: *A Modern Introduction to Psychology.* U.T.P., 1959 (6th Edition, Reprinted 1964), p. 1.
2. Adcock, C. J.: *Fundamentals of Psychology.* Penguin Books (Pelican), 1964 (Revised Edition), p. 15.

3. Lovell, K.: *Educational Psychology and Children.* U.L.P., 1960 (4th Edition), p. 1.
4. Thouless, R. H.: *General and Social Psychology.* U.T.P., 1958 (4th Edition; Reprinted 1963), p. 10.
5. *Vide* Drever, J.: *A Dictionary of Psychology.* Penguin Books, 1964 (Revised Edition), p. 141.
6. *Vide* Thouless, R. H.: *Op. cit.*, pp. 393–405, for a detailed examination of Spearman's theory.
7. Burt, C.: *The Distribution and Relations of Educational Abilities.* King, 1917.
8. *Vide* in particular Thouless, R. H.: *Op cit.*, pp. 336–418. For a very succinct account, *vide* Lovell, K.: *Op. cit.*, pp. 31–65.
9. *Vide* Lovell, K.: *Op. cit.*, pp. 68–80.
10. Knight, R. & Knight, M.: *Op. cit.*, p. 212.
11. Quoted by Cattell, R. B.: *The Scientific Analysis of Personality.* Penguin Books (Pelican), 1965, p. 12.
12. Lovell, K.: *Op. cit.*, p. 12.
13. Knight, R. & Knight, M.: *Op. cit.*, pp. 1–2.
14. *Ibid.* pp. 1–2.
15. Lovell, K.: *Op. cit.*, pp. 14–16.
16. Cattell, R. B.: *Op. cit.*, p. 21.
17. Peters, R. S.: *The Concept of Motivation.* Routledge, 1960 (2nd Edition; Reprinted 1965), p. 60.
18. *Ibid.* p. 59.
19. Eliot, T. S.: *Murder in the Cathedral.* Faber, 1935 (Reprinted 1948), p. 44.
20. Horney, K.: *New Ways in Psychoanalysis.* Routledge, 1961 (4th Impression), p. 305.
21. *Vide* Watts, A. W.: *Psychotherapy East and West.* Mentor. New American Lib., 1963, p. 18.
22. Bantock, G. H.: *Education and Values.* Faber, 1965, pp. 115–116.
23. Goldman, R.: *Religious Thinking from Childhood to Adolescence.* Routledge, 1964.
24. *Vide* dust-cover synopsis.
25. Goldman, R.: *Readiness for Religion.* Routledge, 1965.
26. Hebb, D. O.: *A Textbook of Psychology.* W. B. Saunders Coy., 1958 (Reprinted 1961), p. 153.

BIBLIOGRAPHY

A. BOOKS ON GENERAL PSYCHOLOGY

Adcock, C. J.: *Fundamentals of Psychology*. Penguin Books (Pelican) 1964 (Revised Edition).

Bartlett, F. C.: *Remembering*. C.U.P., 1933.

—: *Thinking*. Allen and Unwin, 1958.

Blackburn, J.: *Psychology and the Social Pattern*, Routledge, 1945 (6th Impression, 1961).

Brown, J. A. C.: *The Social Psychology of Industry*. Penguin Books (Pelican), 1954.

Cattell, R. B.: *An Introduction to Personality Study*. Hutchinson's Univ. Lib., 1950.

—: *Personality and Motivation Structure and Measurement*. Harrap, 1958.

—: *The Scientific Analysis of Personality*. Penguin Books (Pelican), 1965.

Eysenck, H. J.: *Dimensions of Personality*. Routledge, 1947.

—: *The Structure of Human Personality*. Methuen, 1960 (2nd Edition).

—: *Handbook of Abnormal Psychology*. Pitman, 1960.

—: *Fact and Fiction in Psychology*. Penguin Books (Pelican), 1965.

—: *The Uses and Abuses of Psychology*. Penguin Books (Pelican), 1953.

—: *Sense and Nonsense in Psychology*. Penguin Books (Pelican), 1962.

Flugel, J. C.: *A Hundred Years of Psychology*. Duckworth, 1951.

Guilford, J. P.: *Personality*. McGraw-Hill, 1959.

Hadfield, J. A.: *Psychology and Mental Health*. Allen & Unwin, 1950.

Hebb, D. O.: *A Textbook of Psychology*. W. B. Saunders Coy., 1958.

—: *The Organization of Behaviour*. Wiley, 1949.

Hull, C. L.: *Principles of Behaviour*. Appleton-Century, 1943.

Hunter, I. M. L. *Memory, Facts and Fallacies*. Penguin Books (Pelican), 1963 (2nd Edition).

Knight, R. & Knight, M.: *A Modern Introduction to Psychology*. U.T.P., 1959 (6th Edition; Reprinted 1964).

Koffka, K.: *Principles of Gestalt Psychology*. Kegan Paul, 1935.

Krech, D. & Crutchfield, R. S.: *Elements of Psychology*. A. A. Knopf, 1958.

Mace, C. A.: *Current Trends in British Psychology*. Methuen, 1953.

Mowrer, O. H.: *Learning Theory and Behaviour*. Chapman & Hall, 1960.

Peters, R. S.: *The Concept of Motivation*. Routledge, 1960 (2nd Edition; Reprinted 1965).

Spearman, C.: *The Nature of Intelligence and the Principles of Cognition*. Macmillan, 1923.

Stafford-Clark, D.: *Psychiatry Today*. Penguin Books (Pelican), 1952.

Storr, A.: *The Integrity of the Personality*. Penguin Books (Pelican), 1963 (Reprinted 1964).

Thouless, R. H.: *General and Social Psychology*. U.T.P., 1958 (4th Edition; Reprinted 1963).

Tolman, E. C.: *Purposive Behaviour in Animals and Men*. Appleton-Century, 1932.

Valentine, C. W.: *Introduction to Experimental Psychology*. U.T.P., 1953 (5th Edition).

Vernon, M. D.: *The Psychology of Perception*. Penguin Books (Pelican), 1962.

Vygotsky, L. S.: *Thought and Language*. The M.I.T. Press, 1962.

Woodworth, R. S. & Marquis, D. G.: *Psychology*. Methuen, 1949 (20th Edition).

Young, P. T.: *Motivation and Emotion*. Wiley, 1961.

Zangwill, O. L.: *An Introduction to Modern Psychology*. Methuen, 1950.

B. BOOKS ON EDUCATIONAL AND CHILD PSYCHOLOGY

Bowlby, J.: *Child Care and the Growth of Love*. Penguin Books (Pelican), 1965 (2nd Edition).

Burt, C.: *The Causes and Treatment of Backwardness*. U.L.P., 1953 (2nd Edition).

Cleugh, M. F.: *Psychology in the Service of the School*. Methuen, 1951.

Erikson, E.: *Childhood and Society*. Penguin Books (Pelican), 1965.

Fleming, C. M.: *The Social Psychology of Education*. Routledge, 1959 (2nd Edition, Revised).

Fleming, C. M.: *Adolescence: Its Social Psychology*. Routledge, 1962 (2nd Edition).

Gesell, A. & Ilg, F. L.: *The Child from Five to Ten*. Hamish Hamilton, 1946.

Goldman, R.: *Religious Thinking from Childhood to Adolescence*. Routledge, 1964.

Hadfield, J. A.: *Childhood and Adolescence.* Penguin Books (Pelican), 1962.
Hughes, A. G. & Hughes, E. H.: *Learning and Teaching.* Longmans, 1946 (2nd Edition, Revised).
Isaacs, S.: *Intellectual Growth of Young Children.* Routledge, 1930 (8th Impression, 1963).
—: *Social Development in Young Children.* Routledge, 1933 (9th Impression, 1964)
Jersild, A. T.: *Child Psychology.* Staples Press, 1955 (4th Edition).
—: *The Psychology of Adolescence.* Staples Press, 1957.
Lovell, K.: *Educational Psychology and Children.* U.L.P., 1960 (4th Edition).
Peel, E. A.: *The Psychological Basis of Education.* Oliver & Boyd, 1956.
—: *The Pupil's Thinking.* Oldbourne Press, 1960.
Simon, B. & Simon, J. (ed.): *Educational Psychology in U.S.S.R.* Routledge, 1963.
Valentine, C. W.: *The Normal Child.* Penguin Books (Pelican), 1956 (Reprinted 1962).
—: *The Psychology of Early Childhood.* Methuen, 1946 (3rd Edition).
—: *The Difficult Child and the Problem of Discipline.* Methuen, 1947 (4th Edition).
Wall, W. D.: *The Adolescent Child.* Methuen, 1948.
—: *Child of Our Times.* National Children's Home, 1962.
Wiseman, S.: *Education and Environment.* Manchester Univ. Press, 1964.

C. BOOKS ON INTELLIGENCE TESTING AND STATISTICAL ANALYSIS

Anastasi, A.: *Psychological Testing.* Macmillan, 1955.
Burt, C.: *Mental and Scholastic Tests.* Staples Press, 1947.
—: *Factors of the Mind.* U.L.P., 1940.
Daniels, J. C.: *Statistical Methods in Educational Research.* Univ. of Nottingham Inst. of Ed., 1953.
Garrett, H. E.: *Statistics in Psychology and Education.* Longmans, 1953 (4th Edition).
Guilford, J. P.: *Psychometric Methods.* McGraw-Hill, 1954 (2nd Edition).
Heim, A.: *The Appraisal of Intelligence.* Methuen, 1954.
Knight, R.: *Intelligence and Intelligence Tests.* 1948 (4th Revised Edition).
Rodger, R. S.: *Statistical Reasoning in Psychology.* U.T.P., 1967 (2nd Edition).

Thomson, G. H.: *How to Calculate Correlations*. Harrap, 1947.
—: *The Factorial Analysis of Human Ability*. U.L.P., 1951 (5th Edition).
Valentine, C. W.: *Intelligence Tests for Children*. Methuen, 1950 (4th Edition).
Vernon, P. E.: *The Structure of Human Abilities*. Methuen, 1951.
—: *Intelligence and Attainment Tests*. U.L.P., 1960.
—: *Measurement of Abilities*. U.L.P., 1940.
Watts, A. F.: *Can We Measure Ability?* U.L.P., 1953.

CHAPTER 7

SIGMUND FREUD (1856–1939)

A. FREUD'S LIFE AND WORK

Sigmund Freud was born in 1856 in the small town of Freiburg, in Moravia, which was then a part of Austria-Hungary. Freud was the eldest child of the second wife of his father, Jakob Freud, who was a middle-class wool merchant and a Jew. In 1860, as a result of his increasing financial difficulties Jakob decided to settle his family in Vienna; and although he faced perpetual monetary problems he determined to give Sigmund the best education possible. At the age of nine he went to the Gymnasium, where he was almost invariably head of the class until he left.

Despite the fact that his father must have been brought up as an orthodox Jew (although he certainly became liberal minded and progressive in his general views) Sigmund himself

"grew up devoid of any belief in God or immortality, and does not appear ever to have felt the need for it. The emotional needs that usually manifest themselves in adolescence found expression first in rather vague philosophical cogitations and, soon after, in an earnest adherence to the principles of science"[1].

At the age of seventeen, Freud graduated with the highest distinction at the Gymnasium. He now had to choose a profession, and his father, who seems to have been both generous and wise in his attitude to his son, did nothing to persuade him in any particular direction. Freud decided upon a scientific career and enrolled as a medical student at the University of Vienna in the autumn of 1873. During the first year or two he went to lectures mainly on anatomy, physiology and biology; and during his third year he completed his first piece of research on the anatomy of the eel, involving the dissection of something like four hundred specimens.

He now entered the Physiology Laboratory of Ernst Brücke

(1819–92) and for the next six years worked happily, but without much serious consideration for his future career. During this period he worked mainly on the anatomy of the central nervous system, and published some important papers in the learned journals. Under Brücke he imbibed an unrelentingly deterministic view of human behaviour. In 1881, facing at last the necessity for earning a living and for helping to support his parents and their family, he decided to take his medical degree, and passed with the grade "excellent".

In 1882 Freud entered the Vienna General Hospital where he worked in various departments, but became most interested in neuroanatomy and neuropathology. E. Jones tells us that

"He found no more interest in treating the sick patients in the wards than in studying their diseases. By now he must have been more convinced than ever that he was not born to be a doctor"[2].

He became engaged during this year to Martha Bernays, the daughter of a well-known Jew in Hamburg. During the next few years he saw her only rarely, but they maintained a regular and frequent correspondence.

After three years of uncertainty as to his future he was appointed in 1885 to the position of *Privatdozent*, a sort of honorary, unpaid lectureship, which was, nevertheless, highly prized as a necessary condition for any further university advancement. It indicated that Freud was regarded as a man of some considerable competence. During the autumn of this year he spent some months working under the great neurologist, Charcot, at the famous Paris hospital for nervous diseases, the Salpêtrière. Charcot was, at this time, mainly interested in the uses of hypnotism in cases of hysteria, and Freud became very absorbed in them as an entrée into the world of the mind.

He returned to Vienna in the spring of 1886 and married his Martha. Jones tells us that

"Freud's attitude toward the loved one was very far from being one of simple attraction. It was a veritable *grande passion*. He was to experience in his own person the full force of the terrible power of love with all its raptures, fears and torments. It aroused all the passions of which his intense nature was capable. If ever a fiery apprenticeship qualified a man to discourse authoritatively on love, that man was Freud"[3].

He set up in private practice and became a consultant in nervous diseases; he also became a leading authority on the cerebral palsies of children, and produced important papers on neuropathology, and a monograph on aphasia. In his treatment of neurotic patients, Freud began to use electro-therapy and then hypnotic suggestion, but he was still very unsatisfied with the results that he was obtaining and so he turned, in 1888, to the work of his friend Dr Joseph Breuer, a senior consultant in Vienna. Breuer had treated what has become the classic case of hysteria, that of Fraulein Anna O., a very intelligent girl of twenty-one who developed "a museum of symptoms in connexion with her father's fatal illness"[4]. She found that the relation of the details of the first appearance of a particular symptom resulted in its complete disappearance; this she termed "the talking cure" or "chimney sweeping", known more technically as catharsis or the cathartic method.

Psycho-analysis dates from the transition from the method of catharsis to that of free association. Jones considers that

"The devising of this method was one of the two great deeds of Freud's scientific life, the other being his self-analysis through which he learned to explore the child's early sexual life, including the famous Oedipus complex"[5].

In the process of free association there was an injunction to the patient to say anything that came into his head without any form of censorship whatsoever, to express every thought however, apparently, irrelevant or unimportant or unpleasant. The actual term "psycho-analysis" was first employed in a paper published in French on 30 March 1896. Quite early in his practice Freud found that there was an unmistakable unwillingness on the part of many of his patients to disclose memories that were unwelcome or in any way painful to them. He termed the opposition which they expressed "resistance", and he connected it with the "repression" that caused symptoms to replace memories. He also noted that a large number of the significant memories involved sexual experiences; this gradually led him to the conclusion that the essential features in the aetiology of neuroses and psychoneuroses were disturbances in the sexual lives of his patients. And when later he propounded his theories of "infantile sexuality", he could not understand the hostile reception that his ideas incurred. He says:

"I understood from now onward I belonged to those who have 'troubled the sleep of the world' . . . and that I could not reckon upon objectivity and tolerance"[6].

From 1891, until Freud departed for London in 1938, he lived with his wife and family in the same house in Vienna, where he also had his consulting rooms. His marriage was a happy and productive one, with six children, and it provided that haven for him which he needed in a society which objected very strongly to many of his theories concerning sexual aetiology, and which, however unconsciously, resented the fact that he was a brilliant Jew. From 1897 he pursued a line in self-analysis which resulted in the discovery that he had deep within him a great passion for his mother and a jealousy of his father. He felt that his personal experience was one which could be universalized into a general human characteristic, and that it formed the basis for an understanding of the legend of Oedipus[7].

Freud's literary output was considerable, and every new book or monograph was calculated to shock a little more than its predecessor. *The Interpretation of Dreams*, published in 1900, was regarded as quite fantastic and risible; the *Three Essays on the Theory of Sexuality*, which appeared in 1905, was considered evil, shocking and obscene. But gradually the work of Freud was gaining international interest and support. Writers in English, such as F. W. H. Myers, Havelock Ellis, Wilfred Trotter and Dr Morton Prince, were all paying tribute to Freud's original research; whilst from about 1904 onwards Eugen Bleuler, Professor of Psychiatry at Zurich, and his chief assistant Carl G. Jung, were busily engaged in using psycho-analytic methods. Jung had devised some "Association Tests" to demonstrate experimentally the presence of repressed material in the form of "affective complexes"; this, he believed, had helped to confirm Freud's conclusions concerning the manner in which emotional factors may interfere with recollection.

In 1908 the first international congress of psychologists was held at Salzburg, when nine papers were read, four from Austria, two from Switzerland, and one each from Hungary, Germany and England. Forty-two analysts were present. In 1909 both Freud and Jung were invited to lecture in the United States and a strong friendship grew up between them. Jung had a great interest in mysticism and mythology, and his discussions with Freud on these topics led to a revival of interest for Freud in religion.

"They brought back opposite conclusions from their studies: Freud was more confirmed than ever in his views about the importance of incestuous impulses and the Oedipus Complex, whereas Jung tended more and more to regard these as not having the literal meaning they appeared to have, but as symbolizing more esoteric tendencies in the mind"[8].

In 1912–13 Freud published his *Totem and Taboo*, in which he discussed the parallels between the symptomatology of primitive taboos and that of obsessional neurotics. He found in both a complete lack of conscious motivation, an imperiousness arising from an inner need, the capacity of being displaced and of infecting other people, and the causation of ceremonial actions and commandments designed to undo the harm feared[9]. Thus Freud was led into the fields of anthropology and comparative religion in order to find parallels for neurotic symptoms and built-in fears.

In 1911 one of Freud's most prominent supporters, Alfred Adler, who had presented a paper at the 1908 Congress on "Sadism in Life and in Neurosis", broke away from him. Adler rejected most of Freud's aetiology of sex, and he regarded the boy's incestuous desires for intimacy with his mother as the male wish to conquer a female, masquerading as sexual desire. Adler interpreted everything in terms of aggressiveness and the will to power, and the concepts of the Unconscious, of repression, and of infantile sexuality were all discarded[10]. In 1912 there was a decisive separation between Freud and Jung.

Although the First World War interrupted the spread of psycho-analysis internationally, Freud himself continued with his clinical researches and his examination of hypotheses. In 1936 he was elected as a Corresponding Member of the Royal Society, and when Hitler invaded Austria two years later, in 1938, Freud left Vienna with some of his family and journeyed to London. He died on 23 September 1939 after having suffered from cancer of the jaw for sixteen years, and after having undergone thirty-three operations.

That Freud was a man of considerable affection, and very permissive in his attitude towards the upbringing of children, is well brought out by E. Jones in his biography. According to one

American author, Freud was a stern, patriarchal figure, lacking any simple, spontaneous affection and demanding obedience to his slightest whim; but

"On the contrary, it is perhaps possible to criticize Freud's education of his children on one point only—it was unusually lenient. To allow a child's personality to develop freely with the minimum of restraint or reprimand was in those days a very rare occurrence, and Freud may even have gone to the extreme in that direction—with, however, the happiest results in their later development"[11].

B. SOME OF FREUD'S BASIC IDEAS

In the first place the term "psycho-analysis", when strictly used, refers only to the theories of Sigmund Freud. The work of Alfred Adler is termed "Individual Psychology", and that of Carl Jung "Analytical Psychology"; whilst Horney, Fromm, Sullivan and Kardiner are referred to as the "Neo-Freudian school of analysts"[12]. James Strachey has said that Freud's discoveries may, in general, be grouped under three headings: the discovery of an instrument for research; the findings which were produced by this research instrument; and finally the theories and hypotheses which Freud inferred from these findings[13]. We have already mentioned the instrument of "free association" which Freud developed; and we shall be concerned more particularly in this and the next section with some of Freud's findings and theories.

1. *Determinism:* The starting-point for all Freud's scientific study was the acceptance of a certain determinism in all behaviour. He derived this thorough-going determinism from the great Ernst Brücke's lectures on physiology, but Freud applied it equally to the mind, thus producing a "psychic" determinism as well as a physiological one. In the mental world there was nothing "accidental" any more than in the physical world: there was a nexus in all our thinking however inconsequential, at first blush, it might appear. In his *Psychopathology of Everyday Life* Freud has given some really remarkable examples of how the mind can make connexions which, superficially, seem quite illogical and unrelated,

but which, on analysis, are demonstrated to have a logical continuity[14]. Freud deduced that there were certain operations or processes going on in the mind which produced a chain of association which resulted finally in all the mistakes we make in everyday life, our verbal *faux pas*, written and spoken, and which resulted also in the dreams that we have.

There is a difference, however, between "determinism" and "causation" or "determination". And Professor L. A. Reid has argued, in his *Philosophy and Education*[15], that the predictability of human action does not entail determinism but "causal determination". When we assert freedom of choice we are not implying any denial of causation of choice in *some* sense. My actions may be free, but they are not *un*caused by anything that may have gone before, or freedom would simply be "liberty of indifference", indeterminism and, in fact, utter chaos. When I make a choice, what I do in making the choice may "be called in *some* sense a cause of the resulting action"[16].

It is interesting to note that E. Jones briefly broaches this question in his *The Life and Work of Sigmund Freud*, where he says:

"Yet Brücke would have been astonished, to put it mildly, had he known that one of his favourite pupils, one apparently a convert to the strict faith, was later, in his famous wish theory of the mind, to bring back into science the ideas of 'purpose', 'intention', and 'aim' which had just been abolished from the universe. We know, however, that when Freud did bring them back he was able to reconcile them with the principles in which he had been brought up; he never abandoned determinism for teleology"[17].

No doubt this is so; but "purpose", "intention" and "aim"—if words mean anything at all—suggest an end in view, however immediately unconscious. And such an end in view, usually referred to as "teleological", is no less a *cause* of action simply because it seems to be in front rather than behind. And unless we deny any distinction between determinism and teleology, it is quite open to argue that Freud, for all his protestations, was not a complete determinist in the mental realm; indeed, his very injunction to his patients not to try and censor or evaluate in their free association seems to demonstrate that he tacitly accepted the possibility of an element other than purely "determinist". But whatever label Freud adopted for his belief in the matter of mental causation, one thing is certain, and that is that he did not present his findings or his arguments as a reason or excuse for denying responsibility for our actions. There is no room to develop this theme further here, but the whole question has been fully dealt with by Professor R. S. Peters in *Authority, Responsibility and Education*. In Part II of this book, which is concerned with "Freud, Marx and Responsibility", Professor Peters comments:

"Freud's aim as an analyst was to get people to stand on their own feet and to take more responsibility for their own lives, and not to escape it on pretexts dug out of their childhood reminiscences. The last thing he intended was a universal get-out"[18].

2. *The Unconscious:* All systems accept the hypothesis of the Unconscious in analysis, with the exception of the Adlerian system. As a concept the "Unconscious" was not new, nor the discovery of Freud himself. Eduard von Hartmann had written, in 1868, a book entitled *The Philosophy of the Unconscious*, whilst Johann Friedrich Herbart (1776–1834) made use of the concept in both his psychology and pedagogy. Freud had also observed Charcot, in Paris, produce states of "unconsciousness" by hypnotism, in order to remove the symptoms, if not the causes, of hysteria. Freud's "Unconscious" is sometimes represented as a sort of general refuse dump for all the unwanted, waste material of our life's experience. This is not quite how Freud saw it.

"From our present vantage point it now appears that what Freud was trying to accomplish during the thirty years between 1890 and 1920, when the unconscious mind reigned as the sovereign concept in his psychological system, was to discover those determining forces in personality that are not directly known to the observer"[19].

The Unconscious was, in fact, not a passive receptacle of memories but a dynamic force. Our behaviour is frequently motivated by unconscious forces; even an individual's accident may represent an unconscious desire to hurt himself.

Nevertheless, Freud felt that all our behaviour was capable of rational explanation. This obviously becomes very important in the realm of education when we realize that all children's behaviour has to be rightly understood before it can be judged, or before any real attempts can be made successfully to influence it. The child has a vast inner world of feeling and phantasy that needs to be explored before we can fully understand child behaviour. In a similar way, our own behaviour as parents and teachers towards children is motivated by dynamic and unconscious forces. Thus it becomes vitally necessary to understand ourselves, our desires and our infantile wish-fulfilments. It is interesting to note that Dr E. Jones cannot forbear a piece of psycho-analysis on Freud himself:

"The extreme dependence he displayed towards Fliess, though in diminishing degree, up to the age of forty-five has almost the appearance of a delayed adolescence"[20].

3. *All Behaviour is Motivated?:* One of the postulates of Freud, according to Dr J. A. C. Brown, was that "all behaviour is motivated and goal directed"[21]. There is within us the "pleasure-principle" which moves us towards the gratifications of drives. But this, in turn, is opposed by the "reality-principle" which is established largely by the standards and mores of our society. Attention has been drawn many times to Freud's "obstinate dualism": there had to be two opposite powers in all his thinking and classifications[22]. In the conflict between the pleasure-principle and the reality-principle the compromise solutions are frequently uncomfortable, painful and unrealistic; they serve to maintain the individual's self-esteem in "dangerous" situations. These solutions, however, keep him absorbed in primitive yearnings which produce fear, hatred and disgust. Under analysis the original conflict may be recalled, and less harmful solutions may be promoted.

In a close piece of analysis, Professor R. S. Peters discusses the concepts of "motive" and "motivation" and states that

"Theorists . . . are coming round to the view that it is misleading to say that *all* behaviour is motivated. Some make contrasts between 'drives' and 'habits'; others between sequences of acts characterized by effective arousal and sequences that are affectively neutral"[23].

Professor Peters goes on to provide a critique of Freud's pleasure-principle as an over-all postulate, and he concludes that it is inadequate because of the very limited range of phenomena which it really explained. He also concludes that the reason for the inadequacy of the theory is probably his "physiological orientation". Freud's theory of the nervous system, whereby activity is always occasioned by stimulation, is, says Peters, outmoded:

"nowadays it is held that the nervous system is in a constant state of activity and explanation is needed of the patterning of activity rather than of its initiation"[24].

It seems clear Freud did not believe that we had an unconscious motive for everything that we did, but rather that his postulate concerning such motivation applied to certain "inadequacies in our psychic functions" at specific times and in relation to particular forms of behaviour.

4. *The Importance of Early Relationships:* Throughout his writings Freud insisted on the tremendous importance of the periods of infancy and childhood. It was during this early time that the child's "undifferentiated psyche" was developed and shaped, the personality formed, and its general evolution directed. All our later relationships with people, all our emotional behaviour in society, were somehow regulated or coloured by our emotional experiences and relationships during these early years. A child deprived of love may be left with a sense of insecurity and even deep anxiety; he may mistrust everybody he meets, and later fail to fulfil himself adequately in any sort of love-life, sexuality or marriage.

The child, according to Freud, experiences powerful feelings of Love and Hate towards both its parents, and this ambivalence of feeling produces in him, in consequence, a deep and unconscious sense of guilt. This in turn is the internal source of his morality, and it is the function of the Super-Ego (*vide infra*) to pass judgement upon his activity. Ian Suttie rejected the Freudian view of regarding Love and Hate as wholly independent in their origin, and as conflicting in "ambivalence", and uniting in the perversions of masochism and sadism.

"I do not take this view, but regard hate as the *frustration aspect of love*, as 'tails' is the obverse of 'heads' on the same penny. I consider that the most true and *useful* way of regarding the infinitely varied forms of human emotion is as *incontrovertible forms of one and the same social feeling*"[25].

However the Love-Hate relationship is interpreted, the fact remains that a child very early on develops these feelings towards objects and individuals. Associations charged with emotion have a way of unconsciously controlling our lives and affecting our relationships with other people. Parents and educators generally, therefore, cannot afford to ignore these vital early years. In his book on *Child Care and the Growth of Love*, Dr John Bowlby has demonstrated some of the adverse and even disastrous effects upon the child of the deprivation of maternal love and care[26].

5. *Libido, or Drive Energy:* During his clinical observations Freud's attention became focused on the significance of sexuality in creating mental disturbances. He found that in some neuroses sexual difficulties are in the foreground, as in perversions and impotence; and he found generally that the majority of neurotic patients had sexual difficulties of one sort or another. As such, the libido theory contains two doctrines: one, the enlargement of the concept of sexuality, and the other, the concept of the transformation of instincts.

With regard to the enlargement of the concept of sexuality, Freud concluded that the heterosexual genital drive was merely one manifestation of a non-specific energy, the libido. Sexual strivings might be directed towards persons of the same sex, towards animals, or towards the self; they might be aimed at other organs besides the genitals, including the mouth and the anus. The libido might be excited by all sorts of practices, normally referred to as perverted, such as masochism, sadism, fellatio, voyeurism and exhibitionism. But Freud pointed out that some of these practices were not entirely restricted to perverts: sometimes signs of them were found in people who were otherwise healthy, whilst most people become involved in "libidinous" practices in their dreams. One cannot help recalling Plato's discussion of "unlawful appetites" which everyone dreamed about. When asked which appetites they were, he replied:

"I mean those which are awake when the reasoning and human and ruling power is asleep; then the wild beast within us, gorged with meat or drink, starts up and having shaken off sleep, goes forth to satisfy his desires; and there is no conceivable folly or crime—not excepting incest or any other unnatural union, or parricide, or the eating of forbidden food—which at such a time, when he has parted company with all shame and sense, a man may not be ready to commit"[27].

Freud considered that even the pleasure strivings of infants have a certain resemblance to strivings in perversions, such as intense interest in defaecation, in urination, in thumb-sucking, or in sexual curiosity and sadistic phantasies. Thus the libido could be concentrated or localized with the same sort of intensity at the genitals, the mouth, the anus, and the other erogenous zones. The extra-genital expressions of the libido occur, in normal people, in early childhood or the "pre-genital" stage; but, at about four or five, they are subordinated to the genital drives.

Disturbances occur in the forms of fixations or regression; in either case the individual returns to the pre-genital stage and follows paths of sexual satisfaction in immature or perverted ways. Even what most observers might regard as perfectly normal behaviour has been interpreted by Freud and Freudians as transformations of "pre-genital" drives into non-sexual activity. Thus the craving for oral libidinal performance may be transmuted into a general attitude of greed or acquisitiveness; sadistic urges may reappear in surgery or carping criticism; and the desire to retain the faeces may be deflected into a general stinginess. Dr J. A. C. Brown points out the serious danger involved in interpreting *all forms* of behaviour along these lines:

"If, for example, one accepts for the sake of argument the orthodox thesis that hoarding or collecting is a trait associated with a particular stage of libido development, the anal retentive phase, it seems absurd in the view of Neo-Freudians and many others that one should be further expected to believe that this is a complete and adequate explanation of collecting in general. . . . Experience suggests that for every stamp collector who is satisfying his libidinous needs at the anal level there are dozens who collect because it is profitable to do so, because their friends

F

collect too, or simply because they were given a stamp album as a present when they were wondering what hobby to adopt"[28].

C. SOME FURTHER DEVELOPMENT OF FREUD'S THEORIES

1. *Infantile Sexuality and the Oedipus Complex:* Nothing in the teaching of Freud aroused so much antipathy, disgust and anger as his hypothesis of infantile sexuality and the Oedipus Complex. We have already mentioned infantile sexuality under the concept of libido—the mouth, the anus, and the genitals, according to Freud, were associated with libidinal satisfaction, and the child's interest in them developed in a definite chronological sequence from the moment of birth onwards.

By Oedipus Complex, Freud meant the sexual attraction to a parent of the opposite sex with a sense of hostility, jealousy and rivalry towards the other. Freud regarded this as a universal experience in infancy, and considered it biologically conditioned. When he could find no trace of the complex in the majority of healthy adults, he assumed that the latter had successfully repressed it. When later he found many examples in which the major link occurred between son and father, daughter and mother, on the basis almost of "heads I win, tails you lose" Freud developed the concept of the inverted Oedipus. Now the inverted, or homosexual, Oedipus Complex was as important as the normal or heterosexual one; for example, the homosexual tie, in the case of the boy, is a normal precursor of a later attachment to the mother.

In both sexes, the Oedipus Complex (or Electra Complex in the case of the girl) comes as a climax of infantile sexuality, that is, at about the age of four or five, and in order to reach normality the strivings of this period must be overcome: the neurotic mind clings unconsciously to Oedipus tendencies, and as a result adult sexuality cannot be achieved.

In an interesting discussion on "Behaviour Tendencies of the Child in the Family", Dr R. H. Thouless concludes that Freud's general discussion of the emotional development of the child in the family is probably the best guide to the problem that we have at the moment although it "obviously still needs scientific verification"[29]. He objects to the terms used, such as "infantile sexuality" and "Oedipus Complex" since they may imply a maturity of sexual development in the child which no one supposes to exist. Thouless coins a new term for the child's early love tendencies which he calls *protosexuality*. He further points out that a study of comparative psychology reveals the fact that in the Tobriand Islands the father has only tender relations with his sons and the mother's brother is the disciplinarian. The Oedipus Complex, therefore, must inevitably take a different form, and hate reactions are directed against the mother's brother and not the father. It should be emphasized here that many psychologists and psychiatrists reject the Oedipus theory, some *in toto* and some on a universal scale.

2. *Castration Fear and Castration Complex:* In *The Question of Lay Analysis*[30] Freud discusses the question of castration fear and complex, which developed out of his theory of the Oedipus. The development of the Oedipus Complex creates a danger for the boy—if he continues to feel attracted to his mother he will run the risk of being physically harmed by the father, who will castrate him. This is castration fear or anxiety. According to Freud, the reality of the danger is brought home to the boy when he sees the female without the male penis. To the boy the girl is castrated, and he feels it may also happen to him. In consequence of his castration fear the boy resolves the Oedipus Complex by giving it up. On the other hand, when the girl discovers that she does not possess the male organ, she feels inferior, develops a "penis envy" and feels castrated. Because of her castration-complex she accepts that she has been punished, and this in turn produces in her the female counterpart of the Oedipus Complex, namely the Electra Complex. This complex does not disappear so quickly in the girl, but it weakens with maturation and with the impossibility of possessing the father.

3. *The Organization of the Personality: The Id, the Ego, and the Super-Ego:* In the organization of the Personality Freud recognized three major elements, or systems, the Id, the Ego, and the Super-Ego. When an individual was mentally healthy these three systems worked together harmoniously; but when the systems became disorganized, the individual became ill. Normally the three elements co-operated in order that the individual might cope with his environment and fulfil his basic needs and desires.

The Id (or the "It") begins as a reflex apparatus which discharges the excitatory sensations that reach it; it does this by various motor activities, such as sneezing, eye-watering and so on. Stimuli may also come from within the body itself, such as pressure on the bladder and the emptying of its contents. New developments take place in the Id through the blocking, or frustration, of primary needs and tensions; thus an individual may be hungry without possessing any means of satisfying his hunger and this results in tension. This new development in the Id is termed a primary process, and Freud believed that many of these tensions were released in *wish-fulfilment*. Through our perceptual and memory systems we form a mental image of the object that will reduce tension—our dreams, said Freud, are often of this order: we dream about the things we want and so release our tensions. But it is clear that the Id does not always satisfactorily rid the individual of tension: but it reduces through the pleasure-principle the amount of the tension to a low and fairly constant level. Tension results in pain, relief in satisfaction—and so the aim of the pleasure-principle is to give satisfaction or pleasure and to reduce pain.

Whilst the Id is the sum-total of crude and unmodified instinctual needs, the Ego is "the executive of the personality"[31]. Its essential characteristic, according to Karen Horney, is its weakness[32]. The sources of energy lie in the Id, and its preferences, goals, dislikes and decisions are determined by the interplay of the Id and the Super-Ego. The Ego is also very much concerned with the outside world, and it must ensure that the instinctual drives of the Id do not merely contravene the censorship of the Super-Ego, but also do not conflict too dangerously with the external world. Whilst it desires to submit to the pleasures of the Id, it also tends to submit to the prohibitions of the Super-Ego. When the Ego fulfils its executive functions with discrimination and wisdom, harmony and adjustment will prevail. Maladjustments in the personality occur when the Id, the Super-Ego or the external world exert too much power.

Just as the Id is controlled by the pleasure-principle, so the Ego is controlled by the reality-principle. It is through this principle, through the knowledge of Reality, or that which exists, that the Ego learns to postpone action and to tolerate tensions until pleasure may be attained at the "right" time, and in the "right", or most fulfilling, way. This development in the Ego is termed a secondary process; it is developed after the primary process of the Id.

"The secondary process accomplishes what the primary process is unable to do, namely, to separate the subjective world of the mind from the objective world of physical reality. The secondary process does not make the mistake, as the primary process does, of regarding the image of an object as though it were the object itself"[33].

The Ego is the product of an interaction with the external world, or the environment, but Freud held that its general development was also controlled by heredity and the process of maturation. We all have innate powers of reasoning, which we more fully understand through the processes of training, education and experience. Thus education itself is very much concerned with the development of the Ego in training it to think and make increasingly more effective judgements, in order to arrive at Truth or Reality.

If the Id is concerned with pleasure, the Ego with Reality, then the Super-Ego, the moral element in the personality, is concerned with the ideal. The Super-Ego represents the individual's moral code, which is largely the internalization of parental authority, and then gradually of the other traditional and external values and ideals of his society. It is an inner agency of a forbidding character, detecting any trends of impulses that are not allowed, and punishing the individual if they are present. The Super-Ego comprises the ego-ideal, which corresponds to what the individual considers, via his parents and society, to be morally good; and the conscience, which corresponds to what the individual has internalized as morally bad, and therefore requiring punishment. The Super-Ego rewards with feelings of pride and punishes with feelings of inferiority, shame and guilt. By these means it serves to regulate the impulses, such as sex and aggression, of the Id, whose uncontrolled expression would endanger our society.

4. *Defence Mechanisms of the Mind:* In its attempt to solve its problems, the Mind, and in particular the Ego, which has the executive function, devises all sorts of mechanisms and methods. Some of these methods are realistic and successful in a healthy

way, others are simply means of alleviating the situation by various forms of denial, distortion and falsification. A conflict in the mind may, first of all, be dealt with by *suppression*, which is a process whereby we deliberately and *consciously* refuse to permit an undesirable impulse to express itself. We thus consciously control such instinctive energies, which we will not allow to express themselves in the natural way. This process of self-control is a perfectly healthy one. R. H. Thouless says:

"If patterns of behaviour are socially undesirable, the first problem is to suppress these patterns of behaviour by building up attitudes incompatible with them. This is a task for education in the widest sense, not only education in school but also the social influence exerted in the home and by the social standards of those whom the individual meets and respects"[34].

Repression, on the other hand, is an *unconscious* process. When we feel that a particular impulse is socially unacceptable, or contrary to our ego-ideal or self-respect, we refuse to admit its existence and try to forget it by ignoring it. Thus we banish the impulse from our conscious mind and it is forced down into the Unconscious, where we have both forgotten it and lost control over it. The repressed impulse now becomes a *complex*; it struggles to gain entry to express itself in the conscious mind; nervous energy is wasted in the effort to keep it in the unconscious mind, and this in turn results in neurotic disturbance and other harmful effects. Repression is one of the root causes of mental maladjustment and mental disease, and if we hope to avoid or cure such maladjustment there must be a redirection or canalization of the instinctual energy of impulses into socially acceptable channels. Freud gave the term *sublimation* to the process of bringing under conscious control repressed tendencies and the redirecting of their energies into channels of permanent social or individual value. In his Fifth Lecture on Psycho-Analysis, delivered at Clark University, Worcester, Massachusetts, in 1909, Freud says:

"We know of a far more expedient process of development, called 'sublimation', in which the energy of the infantile wishful impulses is not cut off but remains ready for use—the unserviceable aim of the various impulses being replaced by one that is higher, and perhaps no longer sexual"[35].

Because of its value-judgement in the use of the word "higher" the word "sublimation" may perhaps be regarded as a special case of the more general process of finding a substitute outlet, which is usually termed *displacement* or *deflection*. This does not imply any moral judgement, but merely expresses the process[36].

When an object is unattainable, or a person fails to find a satisfactory substitute, the individual resorts to the process of *compensation*. This is, again, an unconscious mental process, and is found, for example, in the physically small person who has never really come to terms with his size but who must "act big", or by hook or by crook be "a big noise". Another defence mechanism is that of *projection*, in which the individual relieves his anxiety by attributing its cause to the external world. When a person has strong feelings of hatred, or jealousy, or aggression, he may well attribute these feelings to people in his outside environment. "He hates me" equals in all respects "I hate him". "I won't be pushed around by you" means "I'm going to push you around—or at least I'd like to". There is a denial that these feelings, which one finds in fact objectionable, proceed from one's own Id; such a thing is unthinkable—they must come from outside. Thus projection relieves anxiety, whilst at the same time presenting an excuse for one's own behaviour. This is closely associated with *rationalization*, whereby the individual distorts his motives, which may not be in harmony with his total personality or with the demands of society, by the elaboration of invented explanations that assume the place of the true motive. In the process of rationalization specious excuses are produced to justify a decision already made: in the process of reasoning the action follows the thought.

Normally an individual passes from one stage of physical and psychological development to another, from infancy to childhood, from childhood to adolescence, and from adolescence to adulthood. When the psychological development comes to a halt at any particular stage, there is, says Freud, a *fixation*. The fixation occurs because the individual is afraid of the next step in his development; he wants to remain the baby, or the teacher's pet, or mother's boy, or the eternal adolescent. There is a fear of separation from the security of the home, or the parent, or later even the school. And a mother-fixation may result in the individual's inability to marry. Finally, in *regression* the individual may have reached a certain stage of development, but some disturbance created by the external world, some hurt suffered, may result in flight from reality and regression into some previous state of security and happiness, or into a completely isolated and private world of phantasy.

D. SCHISMATICS AND OTHER ANALYTICAL SCHOOLS

Any discussion of Freud would be incomplete without some mention, however brief, of those who broke away from some of his main tenets, and of those who developed other and Neo-Freudian Schools of Analysis. Alfred Adler (1870–1937) eventually discarded most of the Freudian theory of the libido, infantile sexuality, the Oedipus and everything that went with it. To Adler it was aggressiveness, the striving for power and superiority that was all-important and the cause of most of our anxieties and neuroses. He also emphasized some of the social aspects of psychological theory; in particular he was concerned with the environmental conditions which would, he felt, inevitably affect the individual's character development, such as his own physique, his social position, his education, his position in the family, and so on. When the individual strove for superiority, he might make a successful compensation, he might overcompensate, or he might become seriously or permanently ill, and so seek power in this way. There is no great following of Adlerian Individual Psychology today, but in consequence of his work "Freudian theory began to pay more attention to the ego and non-sexual factors" in the causation of mental disturbance[37].

Wilhelm Stekel (1868–1940) was

"above all practical and empirical, but the most important difference between him and Adler was that he had a ready access to the unconscious whereas Adler had so little that he soon came to disbelieve in its existence"[38].

His ability for recalling "repressed" material was so outstanding that he came to believe that most of the patients' conflicts were not repressed in the sense of being beyond conscious recall or control, but that they were matters to which they chose to "turn a blind eye". This he referred to as *scotomization*. He considered that it was vital to understand the whole life-style of the patient, and everyone accepted that he was a brilliant analyst despite his "moral insanity", his lack of "an ego-ideal", and the fact that he was "an unbearable fellow"[39].

Carl Jung (1875–1961) was a man of wide culture and interests, as his writings reveal; but he was deeply absorbed in mythological researches, particularly in 1910–11, and Freud felt that this work interfered with his presidential duties in the beloved International Psycho-Analytical Association. Jung regarded the "libido" as simply a designation of general tension, not specifically sexual; it was a general psychic energy.

"The concept of libido must not be thought of as implying a force as such, any more than does the concept of energy in physics; it is simply a convenient way of describing the observed phenomena"[40].

The idea of incest was not to be taken literally but as a symbol of higher ideas. Jung's interest in mythology and comparative religion led eventually to his theory of the Archetypes of the Collective Unconscious[41], and to a development of the concept of the Unconscious Mind generally. The Unconscious, he said, contained both the primitive processes which are held repressed and refused entry into consciousness, and also aspects of mental life which have been neglected in the course of development. It contained forgotten personal experiences and ideas which have been lost because their dynamic and energic value has been destroyed. In addition to the personal Unconscious there was also the Collective or Racial Unconscious, which contained the collected memories of the individual's race or culture. In a deeper dimension of the Unconscious realm there was the Cosmic or Universal Unconscious, the very *fons et origo* of all thought and life, of all energy and intuition. For Jung regression represented a useful process, rather than a neurotic one, for reviewing the situation and for creative re-adaptation and restoration—*reculer pour mieux sauter*[42].

Belonging to the British Schools of Analysis have been such outstanding names as those of Dr Crichton Miller, Dr W. H. R. Rivers, Dr I. D. Suttie and Dr J. A. Hadfield. One of the interesting features of some of these men is their great width of study and depth. Rivers was both an anthropologist and psychologist, and was one of the first to indicate the great variety and variability of the nature of man in the different patterns of culture. Hadfield qualified widely in Arts, Theology, Anthropology, Psychology and Medicine and he brings this span of learning to individual human problems. Suttie argued very strongly in favour of the significance of cultural factors and the total environment in the attempt to solve mental problems; he also considered that the function of religion was that of a psycho-social therapy.

In his *Freud and the Post-Freudians*[43] Dr Brown gives a very clear analysis of the differences between the psycho-analytic approach of Anna Freud and that of Melanie Klein. For our immediate purposes the most noteworthy points are that Anna Freud accepts the great importance of such environmental factors as the parents' attitudes towards the child, whereas Melanie Klein considers that such factors are much less important than previously thought; Anna Freud believes that the Super-Ego arises about the fourth year, whereas Melanie Klein argues that the forerunners of the Super-Ego are demonstrable during the first two years of life, and that, in consequence, if problems of anxiety and aggression are to be resolved it is necessary to reach back to the infantile stage. For Anna Freud the sexual drives are the important ones, for Melanie Klein the aggressive ones; Melanie Klein would treat children of two and upwards, whilst Anna Freud would psycho-analyse children of three years and upwards. Other members of the British School include Susan Isaacs, Joan Rivière, D. W. Winnicott and T. E. Money-Kyrle.

In her *New Ways in Psychoanalysis*, Karen Horney provides a rigorous examination of some of the assumptions of Freudian psychology. Whilst she does not try and develop a new "school" of psychology, she does, however, indicate that psycho-analysis must rid itself of many of the dogmas, the unproved hypotheses, and the unjustifiable beliefs of the past. For her the fields of anthropology and sociology are not merely of value as separate disciplines, but they are important also for the light they shed on the radical differences to be found in both human cultures and "human nature" throughout the world. The psychiatrist, the sociologist and the anthropologist, she says, must work together[44]. Sometimes, of course, one finds such men as Dr Hadfield and Dr John Layard with qualifications in all three fields. Other Neo-Freudians include H. S. Sullivan, Erich Fromm and Abraham Kardiner.

E. THE IMPORTANCE OF PSYCHO-ANALYSIS FOR EDUCATION

Freud himself did very little direct work with children and he seems to have had practically nothing to say about education as such. It is interesting, however, to note that at the first International Psycho-Analytical Congress at Salzburg in 1908 (called modestly a "Meeting for Freudian Psychology"), one of the nine papers read was by Dr Sandor Ferenczi on "Psycho-Analysis and Pedagogy". Yet although Freud himself had little to say about the effects of his theories on educational thought and practice, it is evident that both he, and the various schools and schisms that have developed from his teaching, have all radically affected our notions of child development and education. As a result of the psycho-analytic approach there have been considerable changes in the early upbringing of children, and in the training of children in nursery and infant schools.

It is the view of psycho-analysis that really effective learning takes place only when a child's energies and drives are properly and fully employed. When this is not the case all sorts of problems arise, from discipline to difficulty in paying attention and a general failure to grasp and retain what is being taught.

In a view of education which lays all the stress upon the development of academic learning and purely intellectual pursuits, it has obviously been important to provide the right sort of curriculum, the most "desirable" subject-matter, and the most efficient methods of instruction to achieve this aim. If some examination, such as "O Levels", is the aim, then a detailed analysis of previous papers for favourite questions as well as the type of question is indicated. In the mediation of subject-matter there will be a pruning of all "irrelevant" material and the presentation of distilled, residual notes. Experimental psychology has been used to discover both what is the right matter and what is the right method to present that matter.

Although much of this approach is still with us, and even an increasing anxiety for certification—our children can now end up as "A" or "O" or "C.S.E." types—there is also an increasing emphasis upon flexibility of mind, adaptability to new situations, readiness to face and deal with problems, and a general mobility of mind and body. Professor Ben Morris says that "while the aims of education are traditionally largely intellectual, the analytic view offers us a philosophy of education which lays its stress on the acquisition of the arts of living and on the development of mature personalities"[45].

We have seen that psycho-analysis lays great stress upon early relationships; but it is concerned, of course, not merely with early but with *all* relationships. Just as there is a transference in the analyst-patient relationship, so also is there in the teacher-pupil relationship. The teacher's role is that of a parent substitute; it is very important, therefore, that he should be as fully realized a personality as possible himself, otherwise he may make a very poor substitute. It has often been said that the problems in the classroom are mainly the parents, and that when one has met the parents the diagnosis, and perhaps even the prognosis of the problem may be outlined. It is, however, equally true that many of the problems in the classroom may be summed up in the teacher himself. A little self-examination might reveal the unresolved child or adolescent in himself; and if his own emotional attitudes and face-to-face relationships are problematic he may well have a problem class.

Just as the child will tend to identify with the parent, so also will he tend to identify with his teacher. This fact alone may be the cause of conflict and anxiety in the mind of the child at times. Who is right? His parent or his teacher? And if his parent is also a teacher he may have further difficulties. And just as the parent forms a part of his Super-Ego in providing his ego-ideals, so the child will tend to internalize the values and standards of the teacher, and they, in turn, will become a part of his personality organization.

In Chapter 14 of *The Origins of Love and Hate*, by Ian D. Suttie, the author discusses the interpretation of Freudianism which he holds, and that is that (to give the title of the chapter) "Freudian Practice is 'Cure' by Love"[46]. This seems to be as good a summary statement of Freud's aims as any. For Freud the Ego, or executive member of the Personality, was slowly and often painfully reaching out towards freedom; that is, a freedom from the compulsions and authorities of the external world, as sometimes represented by the reality-principle in the Super-Ego, and also freedom from the urges and instinctual compulsions of the primitive levels of the Id, with its pleasure-principle. Once the Ego was liberated from these "alien" pressures, or had in some way satisfactorily resolved and organized them, it could proceed to utilize the "energized structures" and drives, generated in the Unconscious, for purposes which were consciously approved and creative. For Freud freedom represented *consciously* motivated activity; activity that was self-directed and usefully channelled. Maturity occurred when the individual had organized and controlled the constellation of instinctual drives and the external forces: such a man was prepared to give love without seeking a return.

It must be obvious that many of the so-called "free schools" that claimed to develop out of Freudian principles of no repression, were likely to be as harmful as many of the more traditional schools, based on a very strict and sometimes sadistic discipline. But Freud was not merely pointing the way of freedom from *external* compulsion; he was just as interested in man's (or the child's) freedom from *inner* compulsion, a compulsion which some of the "free schools" exemplified. A truly psycho-analytical approach would emphasize the need for self-discipline and self-analysis[47]; and also the need for the development of the integration or the wholeness of the individual, and of his capacity for health, happiness and love. More and more, in a world of international and racial conflict, these are the qualities that need emphasizing in education—not bigger and better brains. The works of Anna Freud, Melanie Klein and Susan Isaacs indicate the great importance of observing children, of understanding their problems, of seeking to help them to reorientate their ideas and values, and to develop the right sort of face-to-face relationships with them. And this, in turn, emphasizes the teacher's need to understand himself. In the words of Professor Ben Morris:

". . . it seems to me that, far from reducing man to an automaton, a passive victim of instinct, a puppet controlled by unconscious desires, or a creature of conditioned response, Freud's work enables us to put the concepts of an integrated personality and an autonomous self at the centre of educational theory"[48].

REFERENCES

1. Jones, E.: *The Life of Sigmund Freud*. (Edited and abridged by L. Trilling & S. Marcus), Penguin Books (Pelican), 1964, p. 48.
2. *Ibid*. p. 79.
3. *Ibid*. p. 115.
4. *Ibid*. pp. 202–3.
5. *Ibid*. p. 214.
6. *Ibid*. p. 238.
7. *Ibid*. p. 282.
8. *Ibid*. p. 367.
9. *Vide* Freud, S.: *Totem and Taboo*. Penguin Books (Pelican), 1938 (Reprinted 1940), p. 50.
10. Jones, E.: *Op. cit.*, p. 399.
11. *Ibid*. p. 455.
12. *Vide* Brown, J. A. C.: *Freud and the Post-Freudians*. Penguin Books (Pelican), 1964 (New Edition), p. 181.
13. *Vide* Freud, S.: *Two Short Accounts of Psycho-Analysis*. Penguin Books (Pelican), 1962; p. 17 of James Strachey's "Sigmund Freud: A Sketch of his Life and Ideas".
14. Freud, S.: *Psychopathology of Everyday Life*. E. Benn, 1960, 2nd Edition (5th Impression). *Vide* his example given on pp. 10–14.
15. Reid, L. A.: *Philosophy and Education*. Heinemann, 1962. *Vide* Chapter 8, "The Freedoms".
16. *Ibid*. p. 112.
17. *Op. cit.*, p. 65.
18. Peters, R. S.: *Authority, Responsibility and Education*. Allen & Unwin, 1959, p. 70.
19. Hall, C. S.: *A Primer of Freudian Psychology*. New English Lib. (Mentor Book), 1954 (15th Printing), p. 55.
20. *Op. cit.*, p. 255.
21. *Op. cit.*, p. 8.
22. Jones, E.: *Op. cit.*, p. 475.
23. Peters, R. S.: *The Concept of Motivation*. Routledge, 1960, 2nd Edition (Reprinted 1965), p. 50. Cf. also his *Authority, Responsibility and Education*, p. 55, where Professor Peters states: "Freud . . . did not claim, as is generally thought nowadays, that we have an unconscious motive for *everything* we do, any more than Marx thought that men were moved mainly by their desire for gain."
24. *The Concept of Motivation*, pp. 77–8. See Chapter 3, "Freud's Theory", *passim*.

25. Suttie, I. D.: *The Origins of Love and Hate*. Penguin Books (Pelican 1960 & Peregrine 1963), pp. 69–70.
26. Bowlby, J.: *Child Care and the Growth of Love*. Penguin Books (Pelican), 2nd Edition, 1965.
27. *The Republic*, 571 C–D.
28. *Op. cit.*, pp. 12–13.
29. Thouless, R. H.: *General and Social Psychology*. U.T.P., 1958, 4th Edition (Reprinted 1963), pp. 197–201.
30. *Vide* Freud, S.: *Two Short Accounts of Psycho-Analysis*, pp. 123–4.
31. Hall, C. S.: *Op. cit.*, p. 28.
32. Horney, K.: *New Ways in Psychoanalysis*. Routledge, 1961, 4th Impression, pp. 184–5.
33. Hall, C. S.: *Op. cit.*, p. 29.
34. Thouless, R. H.: *Op. cit.*, p. 296.
35. Freud, S.: *Two Short Accounts of Psycho-Analysis*, pp. 85–6.
36. *Vide* Thouless, R. H., *Op. cit.*, pp. 299–303.
37. Brown, J. A. C.: *Op. cit.*, p. 41.
38. Jones, E.: *Op. cit.*, p. 402.
39. *Ibid.* pp. 403–4, where Dr Jones quotes Freud's opinion of Stekel.
40. Fordham, F.: *An Introduction to Jung's Psychology*. Penguin Books (Pelican), 1959 (New Edition; Reprinted 1963), p. 17.
41. *Ibid.* Chapter 3, pp. 47–68.
42. *Ibid.* pp. 18–19.
43. Brown, J. A. C.: *Op. cit.*, pp. 77–9.
44. Horney, K.: *Op. cit.*, p. 172.
45. Judges, A. V. (ed.): *The Function of Teaching*. Chapter 5 on "Sigmund Freud" by Professor Ben Morris, *passim*. Faber, 1959.
46. Suttie, I. D.: *Op. cit.*, pp. 225–36.
47. *Vide* Horney, K.: *Self-Analysis*. Routledge, 1962 (Reprinted 1965).
48. Judges, A. V. (ed.): *Op. cit.*; my debt to Professor Ben Morris' essay is obvious throughout this section.

BIBLIOGRAPHY

A. BOOKS BY FREUD

The Interpretation of Dreams. (1900) Allen & Unwin, 1955.
The Psychopathology of Everyday Life. (1901) E. Benn, 1948, 2nd Edition (5th Impression 1960).

Jokes and their Relation to the Unconscious. (1905) Routledge, 1960.
Three Essays on the Theory of Sexuality. (1905) Hogarth, 1962.
Leonardo da Vinci. (1910) Penguin Books (Pelican), 1963.
Totem and Taboo. (1912–13) Routledge, 1950.
Introductory Essays on Psycho-Analysis. (1916–17) Allen & Unwin, 1929.
Beyond the Pleasure Principle. (1920) Hogarth, 1950.
Group Psychology and the Analysis of the Ego. (1921) Hogarth, 1959.
The Ego and the Id. (1923) Hogarth, 1962.
Inhibitions, Symptoms and Anxiety. (1926) Hogarth, 1961.
The Future of an Illusion. (1927) Hogarth, 1927.
Civilization and its Discontents. (1920) Hogarth, 1930.
Moses and Monotheism. (1938) Hogarth, 1939.
An Outline of Psycho-Analysis. (1938) Hogarth, 1949.
The Origins of Psycho-Analysis. Hogarth, 1954.
Two Short Accounts of Psycho-Analysis. (Edited by J. Strachey), Penguin Books (Pelican), 1962 (Reprinted 1963). This contains:
  1. Five Lectures on Psycho-Analysis. (1909)
  2. The Question of Lay Analysis. (1926).

B. OTHER BOOKS OF REFERENCE

Adler, A.: *The Practice and Theory of Individual Psychology.* Routledge, 1924.
—: *Understanding Human Nature.* Allen & Unwin, 1929.
—: *The Science of Living.* Allen & Unwin, 1930.
Brown, J. A. C.: *Freud and the Post-Freudians.* Penguin Books (Pelican), 1964 Edition.
Erikson, E. H.: *Childhood and Society.* Penguin Books (Pelican), 1965.
Fine, R.: *Freud: A Critical Re-Evaluation of his Theories.* Allen & Unwin, 1962.
Fordham, F.: *An Introduction to Jung's Psychology.* Penguin Books (Pelican), 1959, New Edition (Reprinted 1963).
Freud, A.: *An Introduction to Psycho-Analysis for Teachers.* Allen & Unwin.
—: *The Ego and the Mechanisms of Defence.* Hogarth, 1937.
Glover, E.: *Freud or Jung.* Allen & Unwin, 1950.
Hall, C. S.: *A Primer of Freudian Psychology.* New English Lib. (Mentor Book), 1954 (15th Printing).
Horney, K: *New Ways in Psychoanalysis.* Routledge, 1961 (4th Impression).

Horney, K.: *Self-Analysis*. Routledge, 1962 (Reprinted 1965).

Isaacs, S.: *Intellectual Growth in Young Children*. Routledge, 1930, (8th Impression, 1965).

—: *Social Development in Young Children*. Routledge, 1933, (9th Impression, 1964).

Jacobi, J.: *The Psychology of C. G. Jung*. Routledge, 1942 (6th Edition, Revised 1962).

Jones, E.: *The Life and Work of Sigmund Freud*. (Abridged by L. Trilling & S. Marcus), Penguin Books (Pelican), 1964.

—: *What is Psychoanalysis?* Allen & Unwin, 1949.

Judges, A. V. (ed.): *The Function of Teaching*. Faber, 1959. (Chapter 5 on "Sigmund Freud" by Professor Ben Morris).

Klein, M.: *The Psychoanalysis of Children*. Hogarth, 1937.

—: *Contributions to Psychoanalysis: 1921–1945*. Hogarth, 1948.

Peters, R. S.: *The Concept of Motivation*. Routledge, 1958 (Reprinted 1960). (Chapter 3—"Freud's Theory").

—: *Authority, Responsibility and Education*. Allen & Unwin, 1959. (Particularly Part II—"Freud, Marx and Responsibility").

Suttie, I. D.: *The Origins of Love and Hate*. Penguin Books (Peregrine), 1963.

CHAPTER 8

JEAN PIAGET (b. 1896)

A. HIS LIFE AND WORK

Jean Piaget showed signs of obvious genius when he was still a schoolboy. He had not merely an inquiring mind, but also a highly analytical one, and very early in his studies he was interested in problems of classification and analysis. He was born in Switzerland in 1896, and before he reached the age of fifteen he was already researching into problems in zoology; he began to contribute to some of the journals in this subject, both Swiss and foreign. Through the brilliance and perception of the articles that he wrote Piaget was soon offered various positions of some importance in the academic world, and he was engaged in quite considerable correspondence with learned zoologists who were apparently unaware that their colleague was a schoolboy.

Very soon Piaget began to see that the whole of life could be understood only in terms of "totalities" or "structures-of-the-whole", whether one was considering life at the minute level of the cell or life in the complex and highly organized human society —or, of course, life in the development of the child mind. He became particularly interested in the processes of the mind, and so he turned to psychology as his life interest.

His interest in children began quite early when he associated at the Sorbonne with Théodore Simon, co-author of the Binet-Simon Test, and in 1924 he published in Paris his first book *Le Jugement et le raisonnement chez l'enfant*, which was translated into English four years later. From that date there has been a steady stream of books and articles from the pen of Piaget, who has taught, lectured, experimented and researched with a group of colleagues on almost every aspect of the child mind.

Piaget was, early in his career, appointed Professor of Psychology at the University of Geneva and also Co-Director of the

Institut J. J. Rousseau, which is affiliated to the University; he is President of the Swiss Society of Psychology, a Co-editor of the *Revue Suisse de Psychologie*, and a member of the Executive Council of UNESCO. A married man, with three children, he has said that it was only when he had children of his own that certain elements of the operations of intelligence became clear to him[1].

Throughout his busy, prolific production, Piaget has retained this dominating interest in the way the child mind works, both as a means of understanding and of educating the child, and also as the clue to a number of problems of adult thought and ultimately scientific abstraction. His brief comments on genetic epistemology, and the problems of time, duration and velocity[2], indicate not merely the calibre of the mind of the man, but also the fact that the clue to the time-space structures of the Universe is already within the mind of man.

In order to develop and establish his theories concerning mental development, Piaget initiated a programme of experiments on children of varying ages. Among his brilliant team of researchers are Barbel Inhelder and Alina Szeminska, both of whom have collaborated with him in the production of some of his books. Of his clinical method we have two very different, and at first sight somewhat opposed views—those of L. S. Vygotsky and Professor E. Claparède. In his article, "Learning and Mental Development at School Age", written in 1934[3], Vygotsky has given a very brief account of Piaget's method, and aims, that would seem to imply that, because the process of development is considered as independent of the process of learning, there is no connexion between the two, and that *learning lags behind development*. This is somewhat in the nature of a caricature of Piaget's method and conclusions; it was, however, written thirty years ago, the year in which Vygotsky himself died, and was therefore unable to take into consideration the further thirty years of development in Piaget's own thought, experiment and procedure. On the other hand, Professor E. Claparède somewhat glowingly remarks:

"This clinical method, therefore, which is also an art, the art of questioning, does not confine itself to superficial observations, but aims at capturing what is hidden behind the immediate appearance of things. It analyses down to its ultimate constituents the least little remark made by the young subjects. It does not give up the struggle when the child gives incomprehensible or contradictory answers, but only follows closer in chase of the ever-receding thought, drives it from cover, pursues and tracks it down till it can seize it, dissect it and lay bare the secret of its composition"[4].

As we shall see, there have been many and rigorous criticisms of Piaget's work and methods, not least from the British School, but in his experiments and researches Piaget has engaged in conversations with hundreds of children, conducted in such a way as to elicit, as far as possible, their ideas, beliefs, thoughts, attitudes and imagination upon a large number of specified subjects under investigation. He has been accused of lack of "statistical sophistication", of bad sampling, of artificial and clinical situations, and of seeking simply to demonstrate by somewhat anecdotal data a theory he already firmly holds; but as he himself has said:

"As a rule I remain indifferent to criticism, for it is sometimes the case that the objectors do not fully grasp the meaning of a writer whose claims are not in line with accepted habits of thought, but criticism serves to make one more cautious and forces one to put the case more clearly"[5].

B. DEVELOPMENTAL PSYCHOLOGY

Developmental Psychology is concerned with the psychosomatic development of the child from birth to maturity; and it attempts to indicate how the child mind develops and matures as his body grows, and what particular phases or stages and peculiarities his thinking processes and his subsequent activity pass through. Developmental Psychology may be studied in the series of works by A. Gesell, such as *The First Five Years of Life, The Mental Life of the Pre-School Child, The Child from Five to Ten, The Child from Ten to Sixteen,* and so on; and in J. A. Hadfield's *Childhood and Adolescence*[6], in which he describes the phases of mental development, of maturation, and the patterns of behaviour of the child as he progresses from infancy to adulthood. Other psychologists, such as C. W. Valentine, have experimented with a similar sort of approach[7]. It must be pointed out, however, that although many psychologists have now carried out systematic studies of children in an attempt to determine how they behave and think at certain points of their development, such methods as they employ are not generally regarded as "rigorously scientific"; they produce results which are variable, results which vary with different selections of children, and results which are open to a great variety of interpretation.

One of the most popular schemes of psychosomatic development produced in this country was that outlined by Susan Isaacs in her *Intellectual Growth in Young Children*[8]. She found five most significant phases of development, which she regarded at no time as being completely discrete: they pass imperceptibly one into another. In addition, individual children differ widely and do not all make the transition from one phase to another at precisely the same chronological age. The first stage, that of Infancy, lasts from birth to twelve months, during which there is complete dependence, finally concluding with the emergence of some fundamental skills connected with feeding, walking and speech. Early Childhood now begins, and ends at the age of five years. This period is marked by the instinctual drives of love and aggression, and of ambivalent emotions generally. There occurs during this period a rapid growth of the major bodily skills, and of knowledge of the external environment, both in terms of the physical world and of the behaviour of other people. Children now rapidly develop a mastery of simple language.

In Later Childhood, from five to twelve years of age, the child's emotions undergo various changes and he begins to turn from his parents to other children. There is a considerable movement from phantasy to achievement and knowledge of the world of reality. The child's linguistic and manipulative skills increase, and in his general thinking and attitudes he becomes less individual. There is a marked increase in the child's ability to co-operate with others and in his sociality generally. At about the age of six or seven a transition period occurs, which is a time of rapid physical growth, and the child no longer remains satisfied with sheer activity, but begins to pursue goals and purposes. He is now passing from an interest in means to an interest in ends. From eight to twelve or thirteen years there is a relatively stable period when growth is not so great, and the child suffers far less from fatigue. Phantasy is more and more repressed and there is developing an increased sense of loyalty to others.

Early Adolescence begins at about thirteen years and continues until sixteen. This is a period of rapid growth followed by the appearance of the secondary sex characteristics. The sense of the group, of group feeling and group awareness is now considerably increased, and is gradually turned towards the world of the adult which the child is fast approaching. There is an increase in the community of interests, in emotional instability, and often a tendency towards deviancy and delinquency. The ability to reason in words and to deal in abstract relations is considerably increased.

The final period, that of Later Adolescence, from about seventeen years to maturity, is a phase of marked emotional instability which derives from a combination of physical reproductive maturity and social and emotional immaturity. Alternating moods of self-assertion and diffidence occur; and it is during this period that the individual reaches his upper limit in the maturation of intelligence and of verbal logic. At maturity these will operate maximally and will provide a new stability and integration of personality and behaviour.

Dr Susan Isaacs was a strong critic of Piaget at the time of writing her *Intellectual Growth in Young Children*, and it is therefore of no little importance to know her own scheme of child development, to analyse the differences between her outline and that of Piaget, and later to note some of the reasons for her criticism of the Piagetian scheme.

C. PIAGET'S THEORIES CONCERNING CHILD DEVELOPMENT

In discussing, analysing or criticizing the theories of Piaget, one has to remember the long period of time during which Piaget has been experimenting and developing his ideas. Such a lively mind is not likely to stand still, whether in methods of research, terminology, or even some of the final conclusions.

I. The Language and Thought of the Child

Piaget's first full description of child development will be found in *The Language and Thought of the Child*, published in Paris in 1924. He there described what he regarded as the three well-marked phases of mental life through which the child passed:

(a) *The Autistic Stage* (From 0 to 18 months): During this stage the infant is immersed in a world of sheer phantasy, and he has little, if any, contact with the world of reality. He is entirely controlled by his immediate desires.

(b) *The Egocentric Stage* (From 18 months to 7/8 years): The autistic phase is followed by a long phase of egocentrism, during which the child has a complete belief in his own ideas and experiences. These beliefs require no further proof or demonstration. To him all things are "alive", that is, everything that moves, such as the sun, the wind or the rain, appears to him as much alive as himself. Thus his concepts are quite unrelated to any principle of causality— they are *animistic*. The language he uses in this stage is not in order to communicate with others but simply in order to have a means of self-expression. Such conversations, according to Piaget, are "collective monologues", in which children do not enjoy the exchange of ideas with one another, but in fact almost ignore their fellows during this "monologuism".

(c) *The Social Stage* (From 7/8 to 16 years): During this phase real social behaviour begins and also genuine conversation, in which there is mutual understanding. At first there is still a great deal of egocentric activity, but the child is now commencing the first stages of criticism, both of others and also of himself. He makes his first attempts at reflective thought and logical unification, as well as his first efforts to avoid contradiction. He is not yet fully conscious of his own thought processes, and it is not until he reaches the age of about nine years that he is able to take up a reciprocal standpoint.

More detailed criticisms of some of the points in these stages will be taken up later; one or two general comments, however, may be made at this stage. As L. S. Vygotsky pointed out in 1934[9], and as G. H. Bantock has more recently remarked[10], Piaget was influenced by the psycho-analytic dualism or polarity of Freud. For Piaget there was a polarity between autistic, undirected and subconscious thought and the social, directed and conscious thought of the third or "social" stage. Egocentrism occupied an intermediate position between autistic and directed thought, "genetically, structurally, and functionally". Vygotsky. was very critical of this scheme. He did not in any way suggest that Piaget's data were wrong; he quotes Piaget's figures that 44–47 per cent of the total recorded talk of children in their seventh year was egocentric; and that when, at the age of seven or eight the desire to work with others manifested itself, the egocentric talk subsided. But

"In his description of egocentric speech and its developmental fate, Piaget emphasizes that it does not fulfil any realistically useful function in the child's behaviour, and that it simply atrophies as the child approaches school age. Our own experiments suggest a different conception. We believe that egocentric speech early assumes a very definite and important role in the activity of the child"[11].

Vygotsky then goes on to mention some experiments in which he organized children's activities in much the same way as Piaget did, but a series of obstacles, frustrations and difficulties were also presented to the child at the same time. Vygotsky found that in these difficult situations "the coefficient of egocentric speech almost doubled". The child would find that he had no pencil for the work he wanted to do, or it was the wrong colour, etc., and his monologuism would increase: "Where's the pencil? Oh, this is the wrong colour, I can't use this. Where's the red one?" And so on.

From these experiments Vygotsky deduced that a disruption in the smooth flow of activity is "an important stimulus for egocentric speech", and that it illustrated the general awareness of the child, and the fact that speech is an expression of that process of becoming aware, and becomes an instrument of thought itself in seeking and planning solutions to any problems.

"The inner speech of the adult represents his 'thinking for himself' rather than social adaptation; i.e. it has the same function that egocentric speech has in the child. It also has the same structural characteristics"[12].

Vygotsky's conclusion was that the primary function of both the child's and adult's speech is communication and social contact. This means that the earliest speech of the child is essentially social; at first, multifunctional, but later on differentiated. Piaget was unacquainted with these criticisms made by Vygotsky until 1962, when, characteristically, he wrote a pamphlet relating his development since the early 1930's to the work of Vygotsky[13].

II. The Schemata, or Mental Patterns, in Children's Thinking

Piaget used two main methods in his researches; one was the recording of everything said by children in their activity at the J. J. Rousseau Institute over a period of time, and the other was to set a number of standard questions or tasks to the children, in situations which were obviously contrived or "clinical", and to record their answers. The latter were classified according to three stages:

> *Stage I:* Answers which characterize those children who cannot answer the question because they do not understand the nature of the task itself, or the principles involved in the task, or those who try to answer the questions but show, by their conclusions, that they are not thinking along the same lines as adults; i.e., their thinking is pre-operational.
>
> *Stage II:* Answers which represent a traditional phase and which are groping towards the right solution, sometimes correct and sometimes incorrect.
>
> *Stage III:* Answers which show a correct response and are justified by an explanation. These answers demonstrate that the child has attained a steady understanding of the concepts involved; i.e., their thinking is operational.

Since his first work in 1923 Piaget has developed considerably his ideas about the *syncretic* character of children's thinking. Syncretic thinking is "wide and comprehensive, but obscure and inaccurate"[14]; it is a type of thinking in which analysis based upon objective relations, as conceived by most adults, plays little or no part. In the child's mind everything is connected with everything else, but not in terms of the adult's conception of causation, or of time and space. In order to investigate further this type of thinking, and in order to elucidate further the growth of mental structures in the child mind, Piaget devised a number of experiments which children could perform for themselves and which could be studied by the psychologists in a rather less "clinical" manner. These experiments will not be described here, but the reader is strongly urged to look at what must be one of the best outlines to date of the experimental work of Piaget, namely

A Teacher's Guide to Reading Piaget, by two very clear inter-preters of his theory and practice[15].

According to Piaget, each experience which a child has, and absorbs, will help to establish what he calls *schemata* (or "schemas") which, when firmly fixed, will enable the child to extend his knowledge. A *schema* is an elementary structure, particularly in the beginning of psychological life. The average child passes through a number of distinguishable, but not separate or discrete, phases. These phases, although not completely divorced from one another, represent very clearly defined stages of the development of the child from a primitive form of reasoning to an adult, logical form. In this very brief and inadequate state-ment of Piaget's idea of the development of the schemata, two criticisms are already anticipated and partially answered. One is that Piaget is concerned only with the internal mental develop-ment of the child, unaffected by anything outside himself: and the other is that Piaget's stages of development are too hard-and-fast, and do not fit the facts of the development of many children. We shall enter more fully into a discussion of such criticisms later.

(a) *The Sensori-Motor Phase* (From 0 to 2 years): In this phase the child is able to perform only motor actions, and he has very little language or thought at his command. At first, an object will exist for the infant only when it is in sight; but gradually, as his spatial field expands, he is able to construct the permanent object through organizing the field by co-ordinating actions and to some extent reversing them. As the child develops he is, in fact, building up a series of *invariants*, upon which he draws for any further development in his thinking.

During this first phase the child co-ordinates the perceptive and motor functions, and begins to elaborate an elementary behaviour pattern for dealing with things outside himself. This, in turn, involves the process of *differentiation* of one object from another, and the discovery of the very fact that they *are* outside himself.

Towards the end of this stage language begins to develop, and so the mind is provided with verbal symbols by means of which it can register and store a sequence of experiences, past and present.

There are two functions in this phase which the child in parti-cular employs: there is the function of *assimilation*, which is the means whereby the child absorbs and incorporates new experiences into what he has already established; and there is the function of *accommodation*, which is the means whereby what has been established is modified further in the light of fresh experiences. There are three possible relationships between assimilation and accommodation:

1. Equilibrium, in which case there is adaptation. The higher forms of this adaptation result in intelligent activity.
2. Primacy of assimilation over accommodation: This may reveal itself in an insufficient "decentration" of the child's actions with regard to external consequences; or it may reveal itself in the inadequacy felt between the schema of assimilation and the external movements and objects. Every degree of this primacy is found, and in its extreme form it is characteristic of play, and all the intermediary stages linking play with adaptation.
3. Primacy of accommodation over assimilation: This is characteristic of imitation, even as early as the level at which the child merely reproduces known gestures and sounds.

The Schemata of Assimilation are further illustrated and developed in detail in Piaget's *La Formation du Symbole*, which was published in English in 1951 under the title *Play, Dreams and Imitation in Childhood*. Attention is particularly drawn to the diagram opposite the first page of the Introduction to this book, which is in itself an admirable summary of the theme[16]. The development of the idea of these functions of the mind, working at the sensori-motor phase, emphasizes (as M. Brearley and E. Hitchfield have pointed out) that the stages outlined by Piaget are not maturational levels, nor yet educational ones, but that, as a result of accommodation and assimilation, they are dependent upon the interaction between maturation and experience[17].

(b) *The Pre-Conceptual or Pre-Operational Phase* (From 2 to 4/5 years): This is the first development in overt relation-finding. The child begins to organize his world and the inner model of it that he is gradually constructing. Actions are internalized into thoughts largely through imaginative play, and through experiment. He still finds time relations difficult, and there is a great instability in his mental images. Up to the age of four or five the child fails to distinguish adequately between generic concepts, in which words are used as common names, and specific concepts, in which words are used to relate to individual objects.

(c) *Growth into the Concrete Operational Phase* (From 4/5 to 7 years): Gradually, after about four or five years, the child advances to the stage of concrete operations. There is a slow sorting out of the state of mental fluxion in relation to notions of time, speed, movement, space, shape, number, measure, size, mass, weight, distance, length and so on. Development is gradual, and until about six or seven children tend to be guided by perceptual intuitions. This is sometimes referred to as the Intuitive Phase. A single relationship at a time only can be grasped, and other relationships will be ignored or distorted. There is a certain inability to reverse thinking at this stage, and when it is tried it usually ends in confusion.

There is the same interdependence here between the various forms of representation (play, imitation, and conceptual representation) as was evident in the sensori-motor phase. *Egocentrism* is characterized by its centrations, that is, the child tends to assimilate reality to his activity, rather than accommodate his activity to reality. His inability to view things from another angle tends to distort relationships, and a true equilibrium between assimilation and accommodation can be achieved only through *decentration*, that is, by moving away from the egocentric view. Thus "egocentrism" is one of the chief limiting factors in these earlier stages. There may be certain objections to the term "egocentrism" on semantic grounds insofar as it has other connotations; B. Inhelder seems to prefer to use the term "unidirectional thinking"[18].

(d) *The Concrete Operational Phase* (From 7 to 11 years): The average child of about seven or eight is now able to perform mental operations with regard to concrete situations, actions, and visual and sensory data; he can classify, serialize and correlate objects. In such operations *reversibility* is now clearly evident. At first the child will concentrate upon relating things which are visible and tangible, but gradually, as he approaches the upper limit of this stage, he is able to attempt abstract and propositional thinking. There may still be little generalization from one field of reference to another, but he will be able to some extent to go back over his ideas and arguments in some logical detail.

The child has now reached the level of *conservation* as well as reversibility. Speed, distance, length, number and so on, now stand for *constant* values, or invariants, and Piaget terms this type of thinking "operational". It is reasoning based upon concepts accepted as constant, and the child using this form of reasoning allows the possibility of applying the principles which are characteristic of logical and mathematical "operations".

(e) *The Formal Operational Phase* (From 11 to 16 years): The final phase of reasoning begins at about eleven or twelve years of age and develops up to about sixteen. The data of thinking begin to change, and situations are seen in terms of propositions which may be logically true or false, and which can be tested in the crucible of thought. Facts given in experience are recognized as the expression of necessary laws (like the laws of science); and, further, the developing child now recognizes the possibility of examining such laws in a hypothetical sense in order to discover whether they are in accord with the totality of facts. Logical thinking now becomes fully possible in abstract or symbolic terms; reasoning is reversible in terms of propositions, as well as in relation to objects and actions. Both deduction and induction are now being used.

Piaget is quite prepared to admit that all of us, both children and adults, are capable of regressing to earlier and simpler phases of thought on occasion, particularly when the individual is tired, or weakly motivated, or when the problem presents too many difficulties.

D. SOME CRITICISMS OF PIAGET

Many of the criticisms of Piaget's work stem from the fact that his books are not particularly easy to read since he presents his theories in a technical, abstract, even Piagetian vocabulary. M. Brearley and E. Hitchfield remark, in their Preface to *A Teacher's Guide to Reading Piaget*:

"It is not only the fact that Piaget's books have to be read in translation by most people that makes them difficult but the ideas themselves are revolutionary in that they seek to explain the child's intellectual life in terms of his own action and its internalization rather than as the emergence and training of an inherited ability"[19].

The actual experiments devised by Piaget are concrete situations in which children like to participate and which they find intriguing. Many of the earlier criticisms by Susan Isaacs and L. S. Vygotsky are either no longer valid, or less valid than they were, because of Piaget's own development of his ideas and the refinement of his terminology, experiments and controls, and also because many of his findings have been confirmed by researchers in other countries during more recent years.

In her *Intellectual Growth in Young Children*, Susan Isaacs attacked the view of Piaget that young children are involved in the Egocentric Stage in a sort of "collective monologuism". She maintained very strongly, and with specific evidence, that her children at Malting House School, Cambridge, talked *to* one another, and quite rarely to themselves in the presence of others. She further insisted that there were no successive "structures" in the child's intellectual development such as Piaget had outlined; there was, in fact, a continuous progression in both the scope and clarity of their thought, their "noetic synthesis", and in their ability to handle experience in more and more complexity. There are two points here—collective monologuism and mental structures, and we will look at each in turn[20].

As already mentioned, Vygotsky did some experimentation along similar lines to those of Piaget, and he did, in fact, confirm Piaget's results. Even up to their seventh year he found that his children, on whom he experimented, were largely egocentric in their talk, and that nearly fifty per cent of their recorded "pseudo-conversation" was of this order. But, as we noted, Vygotsky came to very different conclusions with regard to this monologuism, which he considered to be a stage of internalization of problems which adults think about, without talking. And yet it is interesting to note that many adults revert to this form of monologuism when faced with problems—and not all of them are senile. At any rate, Vygotsky concluded that all the "inner speech" of the adult had

"the same function that egocentric speech has in the child. It also has the same structural characteristics"[21].

It has been argued that the sampling at Malting House was not a representative one, since most of them were children with above average I.Q's.

The clinical method which Piaget used, so highly praised by Professor Claparède (*vide supra*), has been strongly criticized on the grounds that it tends to bring the deeper phantasies of children to the surface rather than to provide a picture of the ordinary intellectual tools of children which they are using in their day-to-day life. In this connexion it is worth quoting two passages from L. S. Vygotsky's writings. In his essay entitled "Learning and Mental Development at School Age", he argues that researches into the development of thinking in the school child take as their starting point the tenet that the process of development is independent of the process of learning; and that the child's understanding and reasoning, his ideas about the world, explanations of physical causes, mastery of abstract logic and logical forms of thought, are all considered as if they were processes which took place of themselves without at all being influenced by the child's learning in school. He goes on:

"For Piaget this is a question of principle, not of technique; his method, when investigating the child's mental development, is to set tasks which are not only foreign to school work but also exclude any sort of readiness on the child's part to give the necessary answer. A typical example, illustrating clearly the strong and weak aspects of this method, is Piaget's questions in his clinical dialogues with children. When a child of five is asked why the sun does not fall, the idea in mind is not merely that the child has no prepared answer but that he is in no position—even were he a genius—to give anything approaching a satisfactory answer. The object of posing such entirely inaccessible questions is completely to exclude the influence of previous experience, previous knowledge; to force the child's thought to work on what are known to be new and inaccessible problems so that tendencies in his thinking can be studied in a pure form, in absolute independence from his knowledge, experience and learning"[22].

He can still say, however, in *Thought and Language*,

"His clinical method proves a truly invaluable tool for studying the complex structural wholes of child thought in its evolutional transformations. It unifies his diverse investigations and gives us coherent, detailed, real-life pictures of child thinking"[23].

These two evaluations of Piaget's clinical method, made by Vygotsky at about the same time, are not necessarily opposed. But they tend to give a view of Piaget which is surely unrealistic; a Piaget rummaging around in a world of his own, totally and hermetically sealed off from the external world of experience and of education, classifying children rather in the manner of a brilliant zoologist, which he certainly was, classifying the molluscs of the Neuchâtel Jura—with no purpose other than to produce hypotheses or schemata which all could applaud. As I hope we shall see in the next section this is certainly not the case. But as far as his "clinical" technique is concerned Piaget has certainly modified his methods; he eradicated a great deal of the verbal questionings which many critics have objected to, and replaced them with concrete experimental situations and games in which the children were given the opportunity to participate. Much of the sheer verbalism was taken out of Piaget's investigations and replaced by activity.

We now return to Susan Isaacs' criticism of Piaget's "mental structures". Both she and Nathan Isaacs have attacked Piaget's use of the term "animistic" in relation to the young child's view of life. According to Piaget the child in the egocentric stage is a "realist"—he does not distinguish between the thing signified and the sign, between external and internal, between physical and psychical. He has spontaneous ideas of almost a "magical" nature, he experiences what L. Lévy-Bruhl referred to as *participations mystiques*[24]. In this "pre-logical" type of thinking life, the world, everything is impregnated with the self. The child, like the primitive, *is* the Universe, and the mystic properties with which things and people are imbued form a part of a synthetic whole. The child is "egocentric", everything is in communion with him and obedient to him; he invents his own truth and reality; and everything that moves in any way is conscious. The term "animism" is for some people a very emotive word, and we must be careful that we do not object to the term on the grounds of association with primitive devil worship and magic, or because we consider that it has some pejorative connotation. Nathan Isaacs' comment seems to be a justifiable one, namely, that the child's *belief* and his *ignorance* should not be confused: it is not that the child believes that everything is alive; he just does not know that everything is not alive.

Susan Isaacs has argued[25] that Piaget's "phases" of development cannot be taken as the way in which the child's mind invariably works at any particular stage. At all ages we get monologues, communicative speech, phantasy, magic, realism, and so on, all intermingled in such a way that it requires close observation and analysis to detect any transition from one to another—transitions which are rapid, frequent, and reversible. In his lecture, "Children's 'Scientific' Interests"[26], Nathan Isaacs points out that the chronological age-ranges that Piaget gives for the various phases represent a *majority* of the children tested (typically 75 per cent).

"As Piaget himself has declared, he is concerned not with age-levels as such, but merely with the *order of unfolding* of human mental growth. Average chronological age-ranges serve simply as the most convenient frame of comparison and reference"[27].

The ages must not, therefore, be regarded as setting any hard and fast bounds. Nathan Isaacs goes on to point out that advance to the "concrete operational" level of thought takes place between about five and seven or eight years of age. How many, he asks, take three years, two years, one year or six months? In this connexion M. Brearley and E. Hitchfield say:

"It will be readily seen that these stages merge gradually into each other through many sub-stages and that in fact the earlier stages are absorbed into later thinking"[28].

And the authors have kept to this line of argument from the very beginning of the book, where they speak in terms of "growth into the concrete operational stage", "growth within the concrete operational stage", and "growth into the formal operational stage"[29].

The last point from Nathan Isaacs that I want to quote links up with what was said previously concerning Vygotsky's idea of Piaget's work: the complete independence of the processes of development from the process of learning. Isaacs maintains that not only do Piaget's findings *not* rule out the idea that children's intellectual growth *could* be influenced from without; "his basic

G

analysis implies that this *must* happen". Piaget is not in any way precluded from acknowledging the great importance of external factors, "they are merely not his chosen field". And Piaget is not committed to anything more maturational than the truism "that the *fundamental direction* of human mental growth is determined from within"[30].

How does Piaget regard the development of the *social* factor within the human psyche? Although he tells us that the social stage begins to appear at about the age of seven or eight years, (*Vide* Section I on "The Language and Thought of the Child"), he does not seem to offer any ideas as to its psychological genesis. Are we left to assume, as some have suggested, that these social impulses are the result simply of some biological process in which there is some modification of the nervous system? Or is Susan Isaacs correct in her view that the process of socialization is a gradual and continuous one, beginning before the fourth year, or even the third, and marked by certain phases of development?[31] In *The Normal Child*, C. W. Valentine has attempted to show some evolution of the social impulses from the age of about two years and throughout the child's school career. He says of the three-year-old:

"The child now tends to play with another child, or at times in a group of three or four. There are often brief conflicts, even with special friends, the conflicts often being about the possession of some toy. Yet most children will sometimes sympathize with and help others"[32].

And Dr W. McDougall has maintained that the basis of all social feeling and development is tender emotion, which is the affective side of the parental instinct[33]. In his examination of the various mental structures and concepts of time, space, velocity, duration, succession, number and even moral judgement, the social impulse seems to have eluded Piaget. Perhaps it belongs to that realm of "genetic epistemology"[34] whereby we may arrive at the solution to "scientific" problems by the study of the child's mental structures. In other words, perhaps the genesis of what we are pleased to term the "social impulse" is itself no more than the child's capacity successfully to reach a reciprocal standpoint in relation to other children and to adults, just as it does in relation to objects. And although he seems to have regarded the Social

Stage as beginning at about the age of seven, no doubt, again, this is rather the onset of a more settled mental structure than a description of sociality *ab initio*. This development of a reciprocal standpoint in relation to people, and behaviour with others, is not unlike G. H. Mead's concept of the internalization of "the Generalized Other"[35].

Despite all the criticisms, however, it is generally agreed today that Piaget has considerably advanced our knowledge of the child mentality. He has sought to demonstrate in practice what Jean-Jacques Rousseau asserted in theory—that the child was not just a little man, thinking in the same way, if at a less mature and knowledgeable level. He has drawn our attention to some general lines, or "phases", of development at certain chronological, or mental ages. Piaget has also provided us with material for comparative psychology by indicating some of the general features of the primitive mind within the egocentric stage, and by demonstrating the fact that the autistic stage resembles very closely that of certain types of mental derangement in the forms of autism, phantasy and regression.

In Great Britain, in recent years, many of the results of Piaget have been verified by E. A. Lunzer[36] who has used more stringent experiment, sampling, analysis, and statistical techniques. Most of the recent studies tend to support Piaget's general phases of operational thinking. Other researches have taken place in mathematical thinking (E. M. Churchill, 1958), in logical thinking in relation to historical prose (A. R. Lodwick, 1958), in children's perception and thinking (E. A. Peel, 1959), in children's understanding of terms used in history (J. B. Coltham, 1960), in the growth of pupils' judgements (E. A. Peel, 1961), and in the growth of scientific and mathematical processes (K. Lovell, 1961)[37]. In general, critics seem to be agreed that cultural *milieux* are significant, whilst mental age is more important than chronological age.

E. THE SIGNIFICANCE OF PIAGET'S WORK FOR EDUCATION

In *Training for Teaching*, A. N. Gillett and J. E. Sadler make the following comment on the work of Jean Piaget:

"Jean Piaget has done great service to teachers by showing how various concepts do develop naturally and therefore by implication how teachers can build on nature in their methods of teaching. It may not be clear how the various factors in the development of abstract thinking are related—natural maturation, concrete experience and language experience—but this does seem to be an area where teachers can expect positive guidance from Child Study"[38].

And already such guidance is forthcoming by such researchers as E. A. Peel, K. Lovell, E. A. Lunzer and R. Goldman. Throughout, the work of Piaget has led to a stress on the role of maturation in the learning process—the word "readiness" is one which is today constantly being used in connexion with the child and his work, his curriculum, his syllabuses, various processes and techniques that he is being taught, and so on. Is he "ready" for these things? Not so very long ago such questions would hardly have been considered. There was a certain amount of ground to be covered in a certain time, and you obviously took the "easiest" material first, and then went on to something "harder". But Piaget has shown that a great deal of this sort of thinking was meaningless without some consideration of how, for example, children formed mathematical concepts and discovered spatial relationships.

Whilst scientific geometry began with the Euclidean system, and then developed projective geometry (concerned with problems of perspective), and finally came to topology (the description of spatial relationships in a general qualitative way), the child begins with topology, and

"Not until a considerable time after he has mastered topological relationships does he begin to develop his notions of Euclidean and projective geometry. Then he builds those simultaneously"[39].

Thus it is becoming increasingly clear that the time of introduction of any material, and the methods employed in teaching it, are very closely interrelated. As a result of his extensive researches, Dr R. Goldman produced his *Religious Thinking from Childhood to Adolescence*, in which he analyses and describes the capacities of pupils of a variety of background, or cultural *milieux*, and of varying ages and abilities, to understand religious ideas and teaching. This was one of the first real attempts, and based upon Piagetian psychology, to consider at what point in their development children were really *ready* for certain types of Biblical story, whether Old Testament history and prophecy, or New Testament parable. It had almost always been tacitly assumed that the child was capable of receiving anything provided it was watered down a little, the difficult passages expurgated, and when necessary the whole put into some sort of baby-language; the parables had always seemed sound material for even the youngest—they were already couched in picture language. But

"In the light of Piaget's work, the young child's understanding of the parables is questionable. Since the significance of the parable is abstract rather than concrete, is it possible that the child will understand this before he has reached the formal stage in his development?"[40]

And the answer given by D. Ainsworth is that only the beginnings of understanding the simplest parables appeared by the age of ten. Dr R. Goldman has since produced other books as a basis for developmental Religious Education, in particular *Readiness for Religion*[41], which considers the natural limitations of children as well as their basic needs, and shows how matter and method may be adjusted to meet both.

Piaget was the first psychologist to consider in detail the development of what he calls "schemata", or mental structures, and their relevance to the problem of how children learn. To advance learning itself we must bring the child face to face, by means of practical situations, with the inadequacy of existing schemata. He should not, of course, be left there. A child requires all the help and guidance he can get in order to make new accommodations to his environment and experience. With the help of such guidance the individual will be encouraged, and will learn how, to integrate his new experiences or "accommodations", with the existing schemata. Piaget has thus devised a method of approach which has both diagnostic and educational value.

The days when "getting the right answer" was of paramount importance may not be completely over in practice, judging from the examinations and type of questions still set in those examinations. But in theory, at any rate, it has been long accepted that an understanding of the *method* in order to obtain the correct solution is much more important. We now add, in Piagetian fashion, that it is more important to develop the right mental structure, so that complete understanding and confidence may help to mediate both method and solution; since, of course, it is quite possible to know the right method, and even be able successfully to manipulate it, without fully understanding it or knowing why it works. Piaget insists that *rules* for getting things right are not what is needed, but rather *concepts* of number, measurement, length, breadth, height, quantity, and so on, so that each child will know what the problem is. And it would seem likely that the same is true in the realm of religious and moral education—that concepts, rather than rules, are what we have to mediate.

In *Some Aspects of Piaget's Work*[42], Nathan Isaacs in his concluding section remarks that "true education is what the child's own work achieves in himself". In this section he further intimates that it is integrated growth at which educators should aim from the very start, and that their chief task should be to co-operate to the utmost with all those forces and interests in the child that may "help towards the organic growth" of such central organizing ideas as a structured sense of time, space, reality, causality, chance, probability, measure, number and order. Growth will ensue only if the child really wants to do the work which is set before him; the teacher can guide, help, even at times lead, but in the long run, says N. Isaacs, "what the child makes of all this depends entirely upon himself". Once more, responsibility is thrown heavily upon the educand; he must be made to feel and know this responsibility for his own development as *per se* one of the structures of the mind. Whether Piaget has actually said this I am not sure, but it seems to be one of the inevitable concomitants of everything else he has written. In the words of Nathan Isaacs:

"The *inward world he eventually inhabits*, its breadth, its depth, its organization and integration, can only be the world which *by his own cumulative thought-work on his own experience* he himself has built up"[43].

The ways and means of developing such organization and experience in terms of the classroom may be seen in such books as *Communication and Learning* by L. G. W. Sealey and V. Gibbon,

and *A Teacher's Guide to Reading Piaget* by M. Brearley and
E. Hitchfield[44].

There are two final points the writer would like to mention;
one is on the question of morality and the other on the question of
"syncretic" thought. For Piaget morality was a question of
gradual development from the stage where rules were being imposed from outside to the stage of autonomy, or near-autonomy.
Children pass through various phases in their attitude towards
rules; they accept their validity even though they are external to
themselves, and even though they sometimes quite deliberately
break them. But eventually they will internalize them, or at least
some of them. Some they will reject. In this way they will reach a
stage of relative autonomy in which they feel they are doing things
because they want to do them, even though, as Professor R. S.
Peters points out, "in all of us, in varying degrees, our father's
voice lives on"[45]. Maturity is the acceptance of our morality as
our own, and as our personal responsibility. As Piaget himself has
indicated in *The Moral Judgment of the Child*:

"It is at the end of knowledge and not in its beginnings that the
mind becomes conscious of the laws immanent to it. . . . For conduct to be characterized as moral there must be something more
than an outward agreement between its content and that of the
commonly accepted rules: it is also requisite that the mind should
tend towards morality as to an autonomous good and should
itself be capable of appreciating the value of the rules that are
proposed to it. . . . Co-operation alone leads to autonomy"[46].

Here again, a sound education will seek to elicit this "structure"
in the child mind.

The second point is one which is becoming agonizingly clear
to many educationists or educators. Piaget categorized "syncretic"
thinking as belonging to the earlier stages of the child's development; and the mental growth of the child gradually replaces this
type of thinking with one which is analytic and exact. In our
modern society we have become masters of differentiation, of
classification, of analysis; we can count the hairs on a flea, measure
the perspiration of an Olympic athlete, codify the S-R co-efficient
of a food-deprived rat, and reduce almost everything—from love
and sex to crime and delinquency—to a statistical skew. But when
we have helped to develop the structures in the child mind

capable of performing all this analysis, may we not have neglected to provide the means for the development of a structure of some higher level of "syncretism" and reintegration? The fully evolved, matured and structured mind, unless motivated by social and community spirit, can be a very dangerous and destructive one. This has been stated far more cogently by Professor G. H. Bantock in an essay, "What is Wrong with English Education?":

"It may very well be that in our education we should do more to nurture neglected aspects of that syncretism which Piaget describes as constituting an essential stage in child development; that the process of 'objectification' from egocentrism in which he sees the ideal course of development to logico-empirical modes of thought needs refining by concentration on other, more affectively based modes of apprehension; so that the particular progress towards which Piaget calls 'objectification'—which is, roughly, science—is seen as only one possible mode of development implicit in childish egocentrism—there are other modes of objectification"[47].

When we have finished with all our analysis and differentiation, like the Zen Buddhist, perhaps, we must seek once more to integrate, to see life whole. Before a student begins the study of Zen, mountains are mountains, trees are trees, and rivers are rivers to him. Gradually, as he glimpses into the truth through the help (but not the forcing) of a good master, mountains are no longer mountains, trees are no longer trees, and rivers are no longer rivers. They are scientifically and minutely analysed, classified, stratified and structured. Later, however, when the student has really reached the place of Rest, and has attained to a perfect understanding of life's meaning and purpose, mountains are again mountains, trees are again trees, and rivers are once more rivers.

REFERENCES

1. Brearley, M.: *First Years in School*. (Studies in Education). Univ. of Lond. Inst. of Ed., published by Evans Bros., 1963. In his contribution, "The Young Child's Thought", pp. 36–

48, Piaget says (on p. 38): "It was when I had children myself that I understood better, through studying them, the importance of action, and in particular I understood that actions are the point of departure for the future *operations* of intelligence, the operation being an internalized action which becomes reversible and is co-ordinated with others into an operational whole."

2. *Ibid.* pp. 44–8.
3. *Vide* Simon, B. & J. (ed.): *Educational Psychology in the U.S.S.R.* Routledge, 1963, p. 22. (N.B. Vygotski = Vygotsky).
4. Piaget, J.: *The Language and Thought of the Child.* Routledge, 1926; 3rd Edition, 1959 (Reprinted 1965); Preface, p. xiv.
5. Brearley, M. (ed.): *Op. cit.*, p. 37.
6. Hadfield, J. A.: *Childhood and Adolescence.* Penguin Books (Pelican), 1962.
7. *Vide* Valentine, C. W.: *The Normal Child.* Penguin Books (Pelican), 1956 (Reprinted 1962).
8. Isaacs, S.: *Intellectual Growth in Young Children.* Routledge, 1930, (8th Impression, 1963), *passim.*
9. Vygotsky, L. S.: *Thought and Language.* (First published in Moscow, 1934); The M.I.T. Press, 1962, p. 11.
10. Bantock, G. H.: *Education and Values.* Faber, 1965, p. 21.
11. Vygotsky, L. S.: *Op. cit.*, pp. 15ff.
12. *Ibid.* p.18.
13. Piaget, J.: *Comments on Vygotsky's Critical Remarks.* The M.I.T. Press, 1962.
14. Thouless, R. H.: *General and Social Psychology.* U.T.P., 4th Edition, 1958 (Reprinted 1963).
15. Brearley, M. & Hitchfield, E.: *A Teacher's Guide to Reading Piaget.* Routledge, 1966.
16. Piaget, J.: *Play, Dreams and Imitation in Childhood.* Heinemann, 1951.
17. Brearley, M. & Hitchfield, E.: *Op. cit.*, p. 169.
18. *Vide* Goldman, R.: *Religious Thinking from Childhood to Adolescence.* Routledge, 1964, p. 21.
19. *Op. cit.*, pp. x–xi.
20. Isaacs, S.: *Op. cit.*, Chapter III.
21. Vygotsky, L. S.: *Op. cit.*, p. 18.
22. Simon B. & J.: *Op. cit.*, p. 22.
23. Vygotsky, L. S.: *Op. cit.*, p. 11.
24. *Vide* Lévy-Bruhl, L.: *Primitive Mentality.* Macmillan, 1923.
25. *Op. cit.*, Chapter III.
26. *Vide* Brearley, M. (ed.): *First Years in School*, pp. 49–92; particularly pp. 59–62.

27. *Ibid.* p. 59.
28. *Op. cit.*, p. 168.
29. *Ibid.* p. 3.
30. Brearley, M. (ed.): *First Years in School*, pp. 60–1. Quotations in this paragraph are from Nathan Isaacs' Lecture.
31. Isaacs, S.: *Social Development in Young Children*. Routledge, 1933 (9th Impression 1964).
32. Valentine, C. W.: *Op. cit.*, Chapter 11: "Social Development at School", p. 169 *et passim.*
33. McDougall, W.: *An Introduction to Social Psychology.* First published, London, 1908; Methuen Univ. Paperback.
34. Brearley, M. (ed.): *Op cit.*, pp. 36 and 44–8.
35. *Vide infra* Chapter 12.
36. Lunzer, E. A.: *Recent Studies in Britain based on the Work of Jean Piaget.* (Occasional Publication No. 4), National Foundation for Educational Research, 1961. I am greatly indebted to this work for the whole of this section on Piaget.
37. The Researches referred to are as follows:
Churchill, E. M.: "The Number Concepts of Young Children" Research and Studies, Univ. of Leeds Inst. of Ed., 17/18; 1958.
Lodwick, A. R.: "Inferences drawn in History compared with Piaget's stages of mental development", unpublished Dip.Ed. dissertation, Univ. of Birmingham; 1958.
Peel, E. A.: "Experimental Examination of Piaget's Schemata concerning Children's Perception and Thinking, and a Discussion of their Educational Significance", *Brit. J. Ed.* Psych. xxix, Part 2, 89–103; 1959.
Coltham, J. B.: "Junior School Children's Understanding of Some Terms commonly used in the Teaching of History", unpublished Ph.D. thesis, Univ. of Manchester; 1960.
Peel, E. A.: "The Growth of Pupils' Judgments—Thinking Comprehension", unpublished account of research at Princeton, New Jersey; 1961.
Lovell, K.: *The Growth of Basic Mathematical and Scientific Concepts in Children.* U.L.P., 1961.
38. Gillett, A. N. & Sadler, J. E.: *Training for Teaching.* Allen & Unwin, 1962, p. 265.
39. Piaget, J.: "How Children Form Mathematical Concepts". Scientific American Offprint, No. 420 (November 1953), W. H. Freeman & Co.
40. Goldman, R.: *Op. cit.*, p. 6. Quoted from D. Ainsworth's "A Study of Some Aspects of the Growth of Religious Understanding of Children aged between 5 and 11 years",

unpublished Dip.Ed. Dissertation, University of Manchester; 1961.
41. Goldman, R.: *Readiness for Religion*. Routledge, 1965.
42. Lawrence, E., Theakston, T. R. & Isaacs, N.: *Some Aspects of Piaget's Work*. National Froebel Foundation, 5th Edition, 1963, pp. 44–6.
43. *Ibid*. p. 46.
44. Sealey, L. G. W. & Gibbon, V.: *Communication and Learning in the Primary School*. Blackwell, 1963 (Revised; Reprinted 1964). Brearley, M. & Hitchfield, E.: *Op. cit*., particularly pp. 23–4; 36–9; 56–7; 70–2; 103–6.
45. Peters, R. S.: *Authority, Responsibility and Education*. Allen & Unwin, 1959, p. 31. See also p. 130 for further comments on Piaget.
46. Piaget, J.: *The Moral Judgment of the Child*. Glencoe, Ill., The Free Press, 1948, pp. 404–11 in particular.
47. Bantock, G. H.: *Op. cit*., p. 23.

BIBLIOGRAPHY

A. BOOKS BY PIAGET

The Language and Thought of the Child. Routledge, 1926; 3rd Edition (Revised), 1959; (2nd Impression, 1962).
Judgment and Reasoning in the Child. Routledge, 1928 (3rd Impression, 1961).
The Child's Conception of the World. Routledge, 1929 (4th Impression, 1965).
The Moral Judgment of the Child. Routledge, 1932 (4th Impression, 1965).
The Psychology of Intelligence. Routledge, 1950 (4th Impression, 1964).
Play, Dreams and Imitation in Childhood. Heinemann, 1951; also Routledge, 1951 (Reissued 1962).
The Child's Conception of Number. Routledge, 1952 (3rd Impression, 1964).
The Origin of Intelligence in the Child. Routledge, 1953.
Logic and Psychology. University of Manchester Press, 1953.
The Child's Construction of Reality. Routledge, 1955.
Comments on Vygotsky's Critical Remarks. The M.I.T. Press, 1962.
Piaget, J. & Inhelder, B.: *The Child's Conception of Physical Causality*. Routledge, 1930.

Piaget, J. & Inhelder, B.: *The Child's Conception of Space.*
    Routledge, 1956 (2nd Impression, 1964).
—: *The Growth of Logical Thinking.* Routledge, 1958.
—: *The Early Growth of Logic in the Child: Classification &
    Seriation.* Routledge, 1964.
Piaget, J., Inhelder, B. & Szeminska, A.: *The Child's Conception of
    Geometry.* Routledge, 1960.
Piaget, J.: "How Children Form Mathematical Concepts". No.
    420 (November 1953), Scientific American Offprint. W. H.
    Freeman & Co.

B. OTHER BOOKS OF REFERENCE

Brearley, M. (ed.): *First Years in School* (Studies in Education).
    Univ. of Lond. Inst. of Ed. Published by Evans Bros.,
    1963.
Brearley, M. & Hitchfield, E.: *A Teacher's Guide to Reading Piaget.*
    Routledge, 1966.
Flavell, J. H.: *The Developmental Psychology of Jean Piaget.* Van
    Nostrand, 1963.
Gesell, A. & Ilg, F. L.: *The Child from Five to Ten.* Hamish Hamil-
    ton, 1946.
Goldman, R.: *Religious Thinking from Childhood to Adolescence.*
    Routledge, 1964.
—: *Readiness for Religion.* Routledge, 1965.
Isaacs, N.: *The Growth of Understanding in the Young Child—A
    Brief Introduction to Piaget's Work.* Ed. Supply Assoc.,
    1961.
—: *New Light on Children's Ideas of Number.* E.S.A.,
    1960.
Isaacs, S.: *Intellectual Growth in Young Children.* Routledge, 1930,
    (8th Impression, 1963). (Particularly Chapter III and
    Appendix).
—: *Social Development in Young Children.* Routledge, 1933,
    (9th Impression, 1964).
Lawrence, E., Theakston, T. R. & Isaacs, N.: *Some Aspects of
    Piaget's Work.* National Froebel Foundation, 1955 (5th Edition,
    1963).
Lovell, K.: *The Growth of Basic Mathematical and Scientific Con-
    cepts in Young Children.* U.L.P., 1961.
Lunzer, E. A.: *Recent Studies in Britain Based on the Work of Jean
    Piaget.* (Occasional Publication No. 4), National Foundation
    for Educational Research, 1961.
Peel, E. A.: *The Pupil's Thinking.* Oldbourne Press, 1960.

Sealey, L. G. W. & Gibbon, V.: *Communication and Learning in the Primary School*. Blackwell, 1963 (Revised Edition; Reprinted 1964).
Vygotsky, L. S.: *Thought and Language*. The M.I.T. Press, 1962.

CHAPTER 9

B. F. SKINNER (b. 1904)

A. THE BACKGROUND OF BEHAVIOURISM

Professor B. F. Skinner is a behaviourist, and it is therefore important to know something of the general background and development of Behaviourism, which begins with cats in puzzle boxes and
ends with men operating teaching machines. Since Behaviourist
Psychology derives from physiology, and is a development of
reflexological theory, it will be useful to start with the doyen of
the physiologists in this field, Ivan P. Pavlov (1849–1936).

Pavlov had been experimenting with the salivary secretion of
dogs during the process of digestion, and he sought to measure
the amount of secretion produced when they were presented with
differing types of food, such as milk, meat and bread. In the
course of his experiments, Pavlov met with a practical difficulty in
that the dogs began to salivate in response to almost anything
associated with their food—not merely its smell, but also food
dishes and even the sounds of preparation of the food. Pavlov
referred to the natural stimulus as the "unconditioned" one
(UnCS), and the associated stimulus as the "conditioned" one
(CS).

Pavlov now developed a skilled laboratory technique whereby
reflex responses could be aroused not merely by the natural and
unconditioned stimulus, but also by any other stimulus which had
been presented in association with the natural one. An unconditioned stimulus produced an unconditioned reflex; similarly a
conditioned stimulus produced a conditioned reflex. More recently the producing of the conditioned reflex has been termed
the formation of an "association", and the Principle of Association states that when there are two experiences occurring together
they tend to be held in association, and the occurrence of one will
tend to revive the other.

Pavlov experimented mainly with dogs, and in particular with the salivary glands and the salivary reflex in them, the natural and unconditioned stimulus being food. He found that when some other stimulus, such as a bell, light flash, or musical note, was repeatedly presented just before or at the same time as the food the dogs would begin to salivate as soon as the signal was given, with or without food.

It was thought at one time that Pavlov's experiments confirmed the view that the formation of conditioned responses, or associations, depended upon the processes in the cortex, and that a decorticated dog lost all the conditioned reflexes which had been formed before the operation; and that, furthermore, it was incapable of forming new ones[1]. Recently, however,

"experimenters have succeeded, with great difficulty, in establishing conditioned responses in decorticate dogs and cats, thus showing that, in these animals at all events, certain rudimentary forms of conditioning can take place at a sub-cortical level. There can be no doubt, however, that in the intact animal the cortex plays a dominant part in the conditioning process"[2].

Many other experimenters have worked along lines similar to those of Pavlov with both animal and human subjects. In America, J. B. Watson (b. 1878) performed a series of experiments upon children, in particular in relation to their fear responses. He discovered that there were three types of experience only which elicited instinctive reactions of fear in very small children, namely a sudden loud noise, any sort of pain, and the sensation of being dropped. The end-product of his experiments was a demonstration that anything frequently associated with these experiences would become a conditioned stimulus to the fear-response. In a very interesting chapter, entitled "Little Hans or Little Albert", Professor H. J. Eysenck has given an account of Watson's experiment, and has shown the contrasting ways in which psycho-analysis and behaviourism attempt to understand the same, or similar, data in human behaviour[3].

J. B. Watson took up an extreme view as a behaviourist and asserted that the science of psychology was a purely objective and experimental branch of natural science, and that it required "introspection" just about as much as the sciences of physics and chemistry. He believed that the behaviour of animals could, and must, be considered on the same plane[4]. Certainly extreme behaviourists accept this view and consider that all our activity can ultimately be reduced to the S-R, or stimulus-response, formula; it is all a question of reflexes. Psychology thus becomes a branch of physiology. Some suggest that there are no *mental* processes as such: they are in reality identical with brain processes— whether we call them sensations, ideas, thoughts, concepts, emotions, and so on. The less extreme behaviourists withhold judgement about brain-mind relationships, and, while accepting the existence of mental processes, suggest that the only useful approach to psychology is a physiological one, and not an introspective one. On this matter, B. F. Skinner says:

"The objection to inner states is not that they do not exist, but that they are not relevant in functional analysis. We cannot account for the behaviour of any system while staying wholly inside it; eventually we must turn to forces operating upon the organism from without"[5].

B. FURTHER EXPERIMENTS WITH ANIMALS

It is not the author's purpose here to give a detailed description of the experiments which have been carried on with animals, from hens and pigeons to mice, rats, cats, apes and monkeys; but merely to point out that since E. L. Thorndike (1874–1949) began some experiments with cats in cages in 1897 there has been a steady increase in the examination of animals under all sorts of conditions—natural, artificial and problematic—down to the present time. Man's curiosity is insatiable, and it is not beyond the realms of possibility that before the century is out we shall have experimented with even lower forms of life, and have discovered under what conditions it is possible to produce neurosis in a flea. Have all these experiments really any relation to man's behaviour, and in particular to his learning processes and activity? Without attempting in any way to prejudge such an issue it is important to note what some of the experimenters have thought and said about their own experiments. In his *Authority, Responsibility and Education*, Professor R. S. Peters refers to the visit of the Soviet psychologist, Professor A. R. Luria, to this country. Professor Luria "stated categorically that Pavlov, in his later years, proclaimed explicitly that his laws were relevant only to animal learning. Human learning, he maintained, needs a quite different set of laws. Luria then went through the Pavlovian laws and demonstrated how all of them were false at the human level"[6].

Professor Peters also quotes from an article by E. C. Tolman in which he concludes with "a final confession of faith":

"I believe that everything important in psychology (except perhaps such matters as the building up of a super-ego, that is *everything save such matters as involve society and words*) can be investigated in essence through the continued experimental and theoretical analysis of the determiners of rat behaviour at a choice point in a maze"[7].

If this "confession of faith" has any sort of meaning at all it would appear to be that, whilst the building up of the super-ego, of verbal and social communication and organization, is important, the study of the behaviour of rats and its determiners cannot help us very much in this particular field. To some educators this will be a very consoling confession, even though within the realm of the super-ego and social confrontation much of our behaviour may, anecdotally and analogically speaking, appear somewhat "rat-like".

From his experiments with animals, E. L. Thorndike established that trial-and-error learning takes place in accordance with three laws:

1. *The Law of Frequency*—This law indicates that movements which are most frequently performed tend to be repeated.
2. *The Law of Recency*—Those movements which are most recently performed tend to be repeated.
3. *The Law of Effect*—This states that correct movements tend to be stamped in by the satisfaction of success, and incorrect ones tend to be stamped out by the dissatisfaction of failure.

Thorndike considered that his results were valid only for animals which were at or below the evolutionary level of cats; and his experiments with monkeys seemed to indicate that they learned by another method. R. H. Thouless maintains that experimental evidence is "strongly against the legitimacy of any such extension of the blind and mechanical operation of the law of effect . . . to learning at the human level, and gives grave reason for doubting whether such blind learning is characteristic of any animal, even of Thorndike's own cats"[8].

The *gestalt* psychologists, M. Wertheimer, W. Köhler and K. Koffka, were all very interested in animal experiments[9]. One experiment, attributed to Köhler[10], involved the training of hens to respond to certain stimuli, in particular to the darker of two greys, by rewarding them with food when they responded to the darker, and by not rewarding them when they responded to the lighter. When this discrimination had been reliably established, a new task was presented to the hens in which they had to choose between the original grey, which had been *reinforced*, and a grey which was still darker. In this experiment the hens responded to the darker grey. On the basis of this sort of experiment, Köhler argued that the animals had, in fact, learned to respond to the *relationship* between the stimuli (i.e. the "darker than" relationship) rather than to the absolute properties of the stimuli, since, if the latter were the case, they should have responded to the grey which was originally reinforced. H. Ellis[11] refers to this phenomenon of responding to a new task on the basis of the discrimination of relationships as *transposition*; and the Gestalt psychologists have argued that their transposition is an element in the "insight" learning of both animals and men. This does not mean that they necessarily reject a physiological explanation; it simply means that they reject the S-R conceptions of discrimination learning. R. and M. Knight point out that the Gestalt school have, in fact, proffered "a tentative explanation of insight in terms of brain physiology"[12], namely that the relational properties of the "wholes", "patterns", "structures" (*gestalten*) that we perceive have their counterparts in similar relational properties in the brain nerve-cells.

Since the late thirties some of the more important experiments carried out on animals have been performed by Professor B. F. Skinner and his associates. Skinner, who was born in 1904, graduated first in English and then in psychology, and in 1936 he was appointed to the Psychology Department of the University of Minnesota. In 1945 he became Chairman of the Department of

Psychology at Indiana University, and in 1948 he went to Harvard where he became Professor of Psychology. Skinner has devised many different types of experimental environments for his animals under test—perhaps none more famous than the "Skinner box", in which, for example, a rat may learn how to press a lever in order to obtain a food pellet which drops into a pan. Of this latter invention H. F. Harlow said, in his Presidential Address of the Division of Experimental Psychology of the American Psychological Association:

"The Skinner box is a splendid apparatus for demonstrating that the rate of performance of a learned response is positively related to the period of food deprivation . . . the results from the investigation of simple behaviour may be very informative about even simpler behaviour but very seldom are they informative about behaviour of greater complexity. I do not want to discourage anyone from the pursuit of the psychological Holy Grail by the use of the Skinner box, but as far as I am concerned, there will be no moaning of farewell when we have passed the pressing of the bar"[13].

Another contemporary experimenter, using techniques similar to those of Professor Skinner, is Dr D. S. Blough at Brown University, U.S.A. His "Experiments in Animal Psychophysics"[14] discusses new techniques for controlling the behaviour of animals which make it possible to measure their response to varying stimuli. In these experiments pigeons are trained "to tell" what they see.

Professor Skinner maintains that the techniques which he and others such as Dr Blough are using are much more effective than the rule-of-thumb methods of the past, and that they are calculated to give far more accurate results. When they have been tested on animals these new techniques have proved far superior to traditional methods of the professional animal trainers[15]. A typical animal experiment might be reduced to the following chief factors:

1. *Subject:* Rat.
2. *Reinforcement for required behaviour:* Food—cheese.
3. *Particular Condition of Experiment:* Hunger in the rat.
4. *Control:* Reinforcement as a means of control over the rat.

5. *Principle Involved:* Whenever any particular form of activity in an organism is reinforced, there is an increase in the probability that the organism will repeat that activity.

6. *Efficiency:* To be really efficient and effective a reinforcement must be given without delay, i.e. almost simultaneously with the desired activity.

7. *Conditioned Reinforcer:* This is a signal of some sort (e.g. a light flash or a sharp noise) which the rat is conditioned to associate with the cheese. The stronger this association between the signal and the food the better the result; and the signal itself becomes the reinforcer.

Skinner has extensively experimented, in the Skinner box, with pigeons; one assignment was to teach a pigeon to identify the visual patterns on cards, and to discriminate among them. For example, he would reinforce on diamonds, not on clubs. The pigeon's progress could be speeded up to complete rejection of clubs by discontinuing the experiment, even for a moment, as a mild form of punishment, whenever it pecked a club. An effective conditioned punishment is simply to turn off the light, or cover or remove the card; after about half a minute the light should be turned on again, or the card replaced, and the experiment continued[16].

According to Skinner the chief reinforcements in learning are attention, approval and affection, followed by other such generalized reinforcers as the submissiveness of others, and tokens (such as money). Money, of course, is not the only token; in education, the student behaves in part because of the grades and diplomas he receives, and ultimately because of the esteem and prestige which these provide[17]. Skinner agrees, however, that the science of behaviour is not yet as successful in controlling *emotion* as it is in shaping practical behaviour. This is largely where the hiatus between animal and human behaviour occurs. A mother may give her child attention, affection and approval, and they will act as very powerful reinforcers. And, as Skinner points out, any behaviour on the part of the child that produces these consequences is likely to be further strengthened. But the mother may, through reinforcement, promote the very behaviour she is seeking to prevent.

"One might even say that 'annoying' behaviour is just that behaviour which is especially effective in arousing another person to action. The mother behaves, in fact, as if she had been given the assignment to teach the child to be annoying!"[18]

When she is busy she will probably respond to the child only when it shouts; this encourages the child to shout; the mother gets accustomed to this level and ignores it; this reinforces the child's behaviour and it shouts louder—and so on. Skinner's solution is a simple one—the mother must make sure that she responds with attention and affection to most, if not all, of the responses of the child, which are at a level of intensity that is acceptable; and that she never reinforces annoying forms of behaviour.

C. SKINNER'S THEORY OF HUMAN BEHAVIOUR

I. The Possibility of a Science of Human Behaviour

In his book *Science and Human Behaviour*, Skinner discusses the possibility of a science of human behaviour. Whilst it is obviously better to be exact than inexact, we may nevertheless be scientific, in an elementary way, without the mathematical tools required to translate our reports into more general statements. Science, he insists, must not be *identified* with precise measurements—we may measure or be mathematical without being, necessarily, scientific. But if science is not precise measurement, it is not just a set of attitudes. It is a search for uniformities, for order, for relations in natural events.

Behaviour is, of course, difficult subject matter to examine; this is not because it is inaccessible, but rather because it is complex in the extreme. Unlike a piece of rock, or a fossil, it is not a thing that can be held still for observation—it is changing, in a constant state of flux, and so demands ever new and more inclusive techniques for adequately assessing it. Skinner sees nothing "essentially insoluble", however, about the problems which arise from this fact[19].

Skinner accepts that there *is* a science of behaviour and that it is amenable to the same sort of disciplines as any other science. He believes also that the Principle of Indeterminacy, particularly applicable to physics at the sub-atomic level, applies also to human behaviour. At our present stage of know-ledge in the physical realm it would appear that certain events are unpredictable—but this does not thereby make the whole of the Universe a disordered and capricious arrangement. Similarly,

"since human behaviour is enormously complex and the human organism is of limited dimensions, many acts may involve pro-cesses to which the Principle of Indeterminacy applies. It does not follow that human behaviour is free, but only that it may be beyond the range of predictive or controlling science"[20].

Despite this limitation, Skinner believes that the science of be-haviour is capable of a degree of prediction and control quite similar to that achieved by the physical sciences. He maintains, further, that the arguments sometimes proposed against the science of behaviour apply no more to behaviour than to the realms of chemistry or physics or medicine. Every action of the individual is unique as well as every event in physics; but scien-tific laws are now accepted as statements of statistical averages, and the laws of behaviour are also of this order. We cannot expect *absolute* uniformity, but we can expect *some* sort of uniformity. For example, a general consistency of character may be expected. It is also argued that study distorts the thing studied; but this again is not something peculiar to human behaviour. In the act of observing any scientific phenomenon, it is necessary, in how-ever small degree, to interfere with it; in a sense, to participate in it. And in sound scientific method it is equally necessary to make some allowance for it. In the same way, in the process of observing human behaviour and analysing it, the scientist may have an effect upon it; but it is something that he will take into account, and he will further seek to control it.

Skinner attacks the attempt to look for "inner causes" in human behaviour, which are "mental" or "psychic". Such causes are fictions and their fictional nature is demonstrated by the ease with which the mental process is discovered, in a Freudian manner, to have just the properties needed to account for the behaviour. This practice of "looking inside" the organism for an explanation of behaviour

"has tended to obscure the variables which are immediately available for scientific analysis. These variables lie outside the organism, in its immediate environment and in its environmental history"[21].

His main objection to such inner states is that they are not relevant in a functional analysis. If we stay wholly inside a system we cannot account for its behaviour; we must eventually turn to forces that are operating upon the organism from outside.

The material for analysis in a science of behaviour derives from many sources:

    (a) Our casual observations.
    (b) Controlled field observation.
    (c) Clinical observation.
    (d) Industrial, military and other institutional research.
    (e) Laboratory studies of human behaviour, using careful controls.
    (f) Laboratory studies of the behaviour of animals below the human level.

II. The Analysis of Behaviour

To a large extent Skinner follows the Pavlovian line on reflexes and conditioned reflexes. But reflexes, whether conditioned or not, are mainly concerned with the organism's internal physiology; on the other hand, we are most frequently interested in the behaviour of humans which has some effect upon the external world. It is such behaviour which, on analysis, raises most of our practical problems, and whose consequences begin to "feed back" into the organism. In this process of "feed back" the probability of a repetition of the behaviour is relatively increased. Pavlov himself referred to all events which strengthened behaviour as *reinforcement* and all the resulting changes as *conditioning*, and Skinner uses these terms.

A *response* is the movement of an organism; and a response which has already occurred cannot, of course, be predicted or controlled: we can predict only that similar responses will occur again. Skinner concludes that the unit of a predictive science is "not a response but a class of responses"[22], and the word *operant* is used to describe this class. This term simply means that the behaviour operates upon the environment to generate consequences, and these consequences define the properties concerning which responses are termed "similar". Thus, in an experiment, in which for example a pigeon is induced to raise its head, a single instance of the raising of its head is called a response; it is a "bit of history which may be reported in any frame of reference we wish to use"[23]. The behaviour called "raising the head" is an operant. If food is presented to the pigeon as an inducement to raise its head, the food acts as a *reinforcer*, and presenting food when a response is emitted is the *reinforcement*. Finally, the operant is defined by the property upon which reinforcement is contingent—in the experiment referred to, the height to which the head of the pigeon must be raised; and the alteration in the frequency with which the head is lifted to this height is the process of *operant conditioning*.

Reinforcements may be positive or negative. Some consist in presenting stimuli, such as giving food or water or affection; some consist in removing stimuli, such as a loud noise, a bright light or heat. In either case the effect of reinforcement is the same, namely, the probability of response is increased.

"A survey of the events which reinforce a given individual is often required in the practical application of operant conditioning. In every field in which human behaviour figures prominently—education, government, the family, the clinic, industry, art, literature, and so on—we are constantly changing probabilities of response by arranging reinforcing circumstances"[24].

There is reinforcement in industry by means of acceptable wages and suitable working conditions; there is reinforcement in education by the sense of achievement which is rewarded in various ways, and so on. Generalized reinforcers have already been mentioned under Section B.

III. The Control of Human Behaviour

Skinner holds that the notion of control is implicit in a functional analysis, and he goes on to discuss some of the problems in "self-determination" of conduct, and some of the techniques of control[25]. Skinner has throughout insisted that the application of scientific method to the study of human behaviour depends upon the hypothesis that man is not free; and, even in what we are pleased to term "self-control", Skinner sees only behaviour for which we must account in terms of other variables in the history and environment of the individual[26]. Practically no ultimate control remains with the individual. In a rather inconclusive discussion of the concept of "the self", Skinner, whilst rejecting "any analysis which appeals to a self or personality as an inner determiner of action", yet finds that the three selves of the Freudian scheme—the ego, the super-ego, and the Id—"represent important characteristics of behaviour in a social milieu"; but he finds that "a concept of self is not essential in an analysis of behaviour"[27].

Skinner then goes on to discuss some of the controlling agencies which affect the behaviour of individuals and groups in any society, such as government and law, religion, psychotherapy, economics and education. In his chapter on "Education", Skinner begins:

"In an American school if you ask for the salt in good French, you get an A. In France you get the salt. The difference reveals the nature of educational control. Education is the establishing of behaviour which will be of advantage to the individual and to others at some future time. The behaviour will eventually be reinforced in many of the ways we have already considered; meanwhile reinforcements are arranged by the educational agency for the purposes of conditioning. The reinforcers it uses are artificial, as such expressions as 'drill', 'exercise' and 'practice' suggest"[28].

As far as Skinner is concerned education emphasizes the acquisition of behaviour rather than its maintenance; and he suggests that it is non-educational consequences that eventually determine whether any individual will continue to behave in the same fashion. And then, in a rather revealing statement on his view of education in general, Skinner adds that:

"Education would be pointless if other consequences were not eventually forthcoming, since the behaviour of the controllee at the moment when he is being educated is of no particular importance to any one"[29].

Can Skinner really mean this? If he does, then even his own extensive efforts in the field of programmed learning and teaching machines seem rather pointless. His acute and intensive examination of pupil and student responses as they work his sample programmes surely indicates that they are of some importance to the programmer, if only in order that he may improve his programme; but the object of improving the programme is to affect the behaviour of the controllee whilst he is working the improved programme.

Skinner goes on to consider some of the reinforcements of education, both positive (rewards) and negative (punishments). To him the term "progressive education" describes roughly a concerted effort to discover substitutes for "the spurious reinforcements of educational control". Such substitutes are "natural" and "functional" reinforcements, such as the pleasure derived from reading books written in French, and from effective communication with people in France, not an A for producing a correct exercise in written French. In a similar way, a science student is reinforced as quickly as possible by his ever-increasing ability to deal with nature[30].

Skinner finally discusses the designing of a culture and the deliberate construction of a social environment for the reinforcement of certain forms of behaviour. He suggests that experimental curricula in schools and colleges, and books on child care which recommend substantial changes in family practices, are attempts to manipulate important parts of a culture. The religious books exemplify a deliberate construction of a social environment —whether it be in the Ten Commandments, which codified both existing and proposed practices, or in the teaching of Jesus, which represented a new design. In both instances, behaviour was to be reinforced by the group, or by the religious agency, or by the application of sanctions, earthly or heavenly. In government control the passing of a law usually establishes new cultural phases and practices, and on a broader scale a constitution is a similar undertaking. An experimental environment is created by social legislation; through these means behaviour is more often reinforced with housing, food, clothing, medical attention, and so on, and deprivation is less likely to occur. The deliberate manipulation of culture is itself very often a characteristic of cultures, and this is another fact to be noted in any scientific analysis of human behaviour. Skinner considers that the greatest contribution which can be made by any science of behaviour to the evaluation of cultural practices is "an insistence upon experimentation"[31].

D. PROGRAMMED LEARNING AND TEACHING MACHINES

Skinner believes very firmly that the conditions for learning which he set up in his laboratory, and used in experiments with animals, can also be applied to human beings in their verbal learning. In order to demonstrate this he had to be able to apply the same sort of control over human behaviour as he had achieved over animal, and as a result he began to construct teaching machines and programmed texts which would have control over the teaching situation. In the construction of a programme the teacher must decide on the precise response that he wants from the student, and he must give it immediate reinforcement. Provided he does this accurately and expertly he can shape the student's behaviour just as surely as the behaviour of the hen, the pigeon, the dog or the monkey was shaped in the laboratory. But just as the animal experiments proceeded gradually, step by step, so too must the teaching programme, each step containing one single piece of information, linking closely with the previous step and with the following one.

Skinner's linear programmes have followed these general lines, and the steps are so gradual and so small in each successive frame that one is hardly aware of a progression. *The Analysis of Behaviour*, which Skinner produced with his collaborator, J. G. Holland, in 1961, is in itself a programme for self-instruction[32]. As each frame, or piece of information, is presented to the student, so the latter must make his own free and *constructed response*, by filling in blank spaces. The missing words are invariably obvious and requiring but brief thought, and the response made by the student is immediately reinforced by the programme itself, which provides the answer by directing the student to the page and frame where the answer will be found. It is one of Skinner's principles that the student should be right as often as possible, thus giving further reinforcement to his behaviour. In his machine programmes and texts the same material is presented to all students who can work at their own pace without leaving out any of the steps or frames.

Skinner has argued that telling the student he is correct will reinforce the response; and he has provided sufficient evidence to establish that the time interval between the response and its reinforcement is a crucial variable. But Professor H. Kay, of Sheffield

University, has argued that Skinner has not shown that the same time intervals are significant with a human being as with an animal, and that there is some reason for doubting whether this is so. The human subject *knows* what his response was, and may even know *why* he gave it: what he really wants to know is whether it is correct. Professor Kay further asks whether knowledge of results acts as a reinforcement.

"The consensus of opinion is that when knowledge of results confirms that a response is correct it does act as a reinforcer, but where the response is wrong it does not"[33].

And so in linear programming the accent is upon *being correct*. Professor Kay objects further that confirming a response to be correct may have quite varying effects since not all humans are "hungry" for knowledge; it is not nearly so easy to set up a deprivation schedule with human beings as with animals: not all students are motivated to learn. Moreover the effect of reinforcement on animal behaviour depends upon the size of the reward, and we know little about the effect of continuously giving small rewards to human subjects. Nothing, says Professor Kay,

"is more stable than the operant behaviour of a well-trained rat in a Skinner box, but it has yet to be demonstrated that this procedure of small but continuous rewards will hold for the behaviour of children and adults"[34].

Other procedures have been developed in Programmed Learning, such as the Multiple-Choice programmes and the Ruleg system. In the Multiple-Choice programme the student is presented with a number of alternative answers to any particular question, these answers being placed at the end of each frame. The student is required to choose the answer which he believes to be the right one. The programme is generally arranged in a number of branches, and the branch which a student takes will be determined by his answer to any particular question. The difference between the *constructed response* type of programme already mentioned and this one is that the emphasis in the Multiple-Choice programme is upon *recognition*, whilst in the former it is upon *recall*. The Skinnerian type of programme offers the subject the opportunity of making a constructed answer in a free choice situation, whereas the Multiple-Choice type of programme pre-

sents the subject with an opportunity of recognizing the answer
in a multiple-choice situation. This latter type of programming is
also referred to as *intrinsic*, since the student's own responses will
determine the route to be followed. S. L. Pressey has emphasized
the value of immediate knowledge of results (I.K.R.) in a branching programme, so that the progress of the student may be constantly guided by knowledge of his performance.

The Ruleg System is based on the same premises as the programming of Skinner and Holland, but all verbal subject matter
is divided into two classes of statements:

(a) Rules to be learned—RU's.
(b) Examples or illustrations—EG's.

The System, Ruleg, derives its name from the linking of these
two abbreviations. It is impossible here to go into all the detail
involved in the construction of such a programme, and you are
recommended to read the relevant section in E. B. Fry's *Teaching
Machines and Programmed Instruction*[35]. There are, however,
four main stages: firstly, a rule is given; secondly, a particular
example is given by way of illustration; thirdly, the student is
prompted to provide his own illustration; and, fourthly, he is left
to supply others.

With regard to Teaching Machines, Skinner has said that

"Some see the machines as a threat to the teacher, which they are
not. Some fancy that they will make education a cold, mechanical
process. Others fear that they will turn students into regimented
and mindless robots. Such fears are groundless. The purpose of a
teaching machine can be simply stated: to teach rapidly,
thoroughly and expeditiously a large part of what we now teach
slowly, incompletely and with wasted effort on the part of both
student and teacher"[36].

Skinner further holds out the hope that such teaching machines
may one day be capable of teaching behaviour of a kind and
subtlety that until now has seemed beyond the reach of explicit
teaching methods. He sees the machine as a means of developing
a *technology* of education, which will follow the practice of the
experimental laboratory, and which will use instrumentation
to equip our students "with large repertoires of verbal and
non-verbal behaviour"[37]. This instrumentation will, in turn,

be able to "nurture enthusiasm" for further and continued study.

Skinner quite readily agrees that no machine is better than the material fed into it, and therefore programmes have to be designed with great care, accuracy and thoroughness. An adequate teaching machine provides the reinforcement, or reward, which Skinner feels that the traditional classroom lacks; and it permits the pupil to learn the validity of his answer as soon as he has made it. The machine is not an elaborate or ingenious toy to keep recalcitrant pupils amused or at bay; it is a part of the very theory of teaching, based upon a scientific diagnosis and prognosis of human verbal behaviour and response; it is part of the science of Cybernetics, or the theory of communication and control mechanisms. On the other hand, the authors of the B.B.C. publication, *What is Programmed Learning?*, state that they believe, on the basis of research evidence, that teaching machines

"are not essential, except where, for example, the subject is a non-reader and a tape-recorder is needed. There are probably other situations in which a machine has advantages. In the majority of cases, however, equally good results will be obtained from the use of programmes in book form. The great cost of a machine to present a branching programme seems excessive, merely to spare the pupil the inconvenience of turning the pages in a 'scrambled' text book, and even the more modest cost of linear machines is probably an unjustified extravagance"[38].

This is the considered judgement of responsible people, but this is the Age of Automation, the Computer Age, and it would be conservative indeed to imagine that although, in a century (if Skinner is to be believed) the typical classroom and the techniques of teaching have hardly changed[39], the classroom can remain for long unaffected by machines which are becoming a vital part of scientific equipment, as well as of industry, commerce and military enterprise. The classroom is specifically concerned with communication and communication problems[40]; and it would be surprising if such machines did not in some way and in some areas of education affect our teaching methods and their very *milieu*. Moreover, in an age in which vast sums of money are spent on abortive experiments and destructive instruments, one wonders whether, even at the experimental stage, the expense of teaching machines is really such an "unjustified extravagance".

E. BEHAVIOURISM, PROGRAMMING AND EDUCATION

Every new development in learning, whether it be in philosophy, psychology, technology or whatever, tends to present an exaggerated perspective of one view of "reality". The old dualisms perpetually reappear in our doctrines: heredity—environment, determinism—freewill, freedom—authority, and so on. It is the wisdom of the East, the Taoist philosophy, which accepts the "opposites" for what they are. In the symbol of Yang-Yin, at the centre and circumference all things are one—the positive and negative, male and female, light and dark, active and passive— they all complement and counterbalance each other; they are not really opposed, merely in a state of tension; each invades the other's hemisphere, each establishes itself in the other's territory.

It seems to the writer just as inconceivable, and undemonstrable, that man is absolutely determined as that he is absolutely free. In his criticism of the "Hobbes-Hull-Skinner approach", Professor R. S. Peters makes the point that, unlike animals or machines, man does not act merely "*in accordance with* rules; he acts because of his *knowledge* of them"[41]. Man has a store of knowledge, he has a history, he has institutions, he has conventions, and he has concepts of past and future, of progress, development, improvement, health, happiness and values such as animals never elicit. Of course he is determined by his genetic heredity and environment. Yet if there is any truth in Skinner's theories at all, man also determines, and calculatingly constructs his own environment—if only, in turn, to determine himself. Thus, Skinner has remarked:

"When we say that an organism has failed to solve a certain problem, it may very well be that we ourselves have failed to construct the necessary teaching programme. In particular, no one knows what the human organism is capable of because no one has yet constructed the environment that will push human achievement to its limits"[42].

Skinner, in his behaviouristic theory, seems to forget at times that the box in which he has placed his experimental man, in order to determine his activity and response, was freely constructed by man himself; and that it is further being adapted by him in order to condition his prisoner in the way he conceives best. But man is himself the *conditioner*; he is perpetually changing and adapting his environment in an active, purposive way in order to recreate himself in his "ideal" image. Skinner may argue that it is the stimulus of man's desire to create a better world that calls forth the response whereby he changes his environment; but he doesn't *have* to change it in the one particular way that he chooses; in fact, his multiple-choice programme, which he works out for himself, has no *one* correct solution capable of immediate reinforcement. And the choice, which he freely makes, may in fact prove, in the long run, not to be the best.

Operant conditioning has been validated within certain limits of animal behaviour and learning, and even human learning. But, as every teacher knows, there are all sorts of factors, known and unknown, that enter into children's learning—and adults' learning as well—besides operant conditioning in behaviouristic terms. Some children learn better within a group atmosphere than by working on their own; questions of temperament, aptitude, ability, and maturation are all part of the process of learning. To some extent Skinner recognizes this, although it will make little difference to the programme—it is the same programme for everybody, but, like a personal tutor, the "machine presents just that material for which the student is ready"[43]. So the "readiness" of the pupil is implicit in the stages or frames of the programme; he goes at his own rate, and according as he has success in his answers.

Skinner's position, however, is no better revealed or criticized than in his own comments on the question of the difference between just learning subject matter and causing the pupil to "think":

"If we want to teach students to think, a more sensible procedure would be to analyse the behaviour called 'thinking' and produce it according to specification. A programme specifically concerned with such behaviour could be composed of material already available in logic, mathematics, scientific method and psychology"[44].

It is difficult to know whether Skinner means that no "thinking" is done in (say) history, geography, and English literature, or simply that in his programmed learning in such subjects no "thinking" is necessary—one is just making a physiological response, or making an effort of recall. One can almost visualize a curriculum comprising programmed history, geography, mathematics, physics, "naming of parts", and "thinking". It is pretty certain that, since in all his programmes there can be only one correct solution to each frame, unless man is to become simply a recording machine capable only of recall and recognition, he would assuredly need some teaching in the process of "thinking". If nothing in his learning is "open-ended", he would never be able to make a decision on a question where there can be no certainty as to the correct conclusion, simply because there *is* no right answer to some questions—at least, not in the sense that their correctness is predictable. It is interesting to note that Skinner maintains that the *behaviour* of making decisions is usually deficient:

"It is not present in any degree in the behaviour of lower organisms or of many people. When present, it is usually the result of special reinforcements applied by the community"[45].

If this really *is* true, then without some very special programming in social decision making, and in personal trouble-shooting, Skinner's programmes would seem to make it even more difficult for people to make decisions (even wrong ones) on any questions which involved vigorous analysis and thought. But Skinner is confident that "there is no reason why we cannot teach a man how to think"[46]. Perhaps it would not be too much to say that some educators have believed this for a very long time, and that they have even been sufficiently conceited as to think that they have helped to achieve it—without the process of programmed learning, and within the framework of their "subject"—be it geography, history, social studies, English literature, chemistry, physics or mathematics. But the idea of extrapolating "thinking" as a special process of behaviour for programming purposes reminds one very forcibly of the objection made by the psychologist, philosopher and educationist, Professor Peters, to much of the argument based upon Freudian and Pavlovian theory—however misconceived such argument may be:

"What I object to is when the unconscious wish or conditioned response is taken not as a brilliant hypothesis to explain certain

H

limited phenomena but as an all-inclusive postulate to explain things as various as salivation, pressing a lever, cutting potatoes with a knife, talking, being honest and decent, being taken in by a business man, and making a clever finesse at Bridge"[47].

When all this has been said, it still remains a fact that, within the limits of the subject matter which is being taught, individual instruction can, by means of programmed books and teaching machines, be adapted at each step to the progress of the individual pupil; and, further, that the teaching skill and ability of a competent tutor are on tap all the time for that one pupil. Such individual tuition could easily be made available on a mass scale.

K. Austwick has pointed out that programming has inevitably led to a much more detailed study of subject matter; to a more precise consideration of the type of student for whom the programme is intended (e.g. primary, grammar, technical, university, etc.); to an examination of the order of topics within subjects, based upon the work of experimental psychology (e.g. the work of Piaget); and to the ascertainment that the selected order is appropriate to the development of mental structures and abilities in the children for whom the programme is being prepared[48].

Programmers argue that machines and programming generally will not displace teachers; that many different types of machine and programme will be needed—but so also will the teacher. Programmed learning will be particularly useful in teaching basic material, which is repeated in the classroom year after year without change, and in a somewhat mechanical and repetitive way. The programmed course is also of value in "levelling". Before beginning a new course it is sometimes important to make sure that all pupils have the same basic background and foundation. Such courses are also of value to new pupils who may well be starting a subject which has been followed by the rest of the class for some time. Programmed courses also have their uses for enriching the knowledge of brighter pupils who are sufficiently advanced in the general work of the class to be able to study on their own. Equally they may be used in a remedial way for backward pupils for whom no personal tutor is available.

It is envisaged that in this new situation the teacher will also have a new role or function; or rather, perhaps for the first time he will be enabled to become less of the drillmaster, often (if we are honest) bored with the annual repetition of the same mechanical processes, and more of the educator at last freed for the really creative activities of the classroom; and

"in assigning mechanizable functions to machines, the teacher will emerge in his proper role as an indispensable human being"[49].

REFERENCES

1. *Vide* Knight, R. & M.: *A Modern Introduction to Psychology*. U.T.P., 2nd Edition 1951, p. 51.
2. *Ibid* 6th Edition, 1959 (Reprinted 1964), p. 52.
3. Eysenck, H. J.: *Fact and Fiction in Psychology*. Penguin Books (Pelican), 1965, Chapter 3, pp. 95–131.
4. *Vide* Watson, J. B.: *Psychology from the Standpoint of a Behaviourist*. Lippincott, 1919; and *Behaviourism*. Kegan Paul, 1925.
5. Skinner, B. F.: *Science and Human Behaviour*. Collier-Macmillan, 1953; Free Press paperback, 1965, p. 35.
6. Peters, R. S.: *Authority, Responsibility and Education*. Allen & Unwin, 1959, p. 128.
7. *Vide* Peters, R. S.: *The Concept of Motivation*. Routledge, 1958 (Reprinted 1960), p. 96. Professor Peters is quoting from E. C. Tolman's article, "The Determiners of Behaviour at a Choice Point", *Psychological Review*, 45; pp. 1–41, 1938. The italics are Professor Peters'.
8. Thouless, R. H.: *General and Social Psychology*. U.T.P., 4th Edition, 1958 (Reprinted 1963), p. 100.
9. *Vide* in particular Köhler, W.: *The Mentality of Apes*. Kegan Paul, 1925; Penguin Books (Pelican), 1957.
10. Ellis, H.: *The Transfer of Training*. Collier-Macmillan, 1965, p. 76. Cf. also Grey Walter, W.: *The Living Brain*. Penguin Books (Pelican), 1961 (Reprinted 1963), p. 120, where a similar experiment is attributed to M. Wertheimer.
11. *Op. cit.*, p. 76.
12. Knight, R. & M.: *Op. cit.*, 6th Edition, pp. 148–9.
13. Harlow, H. F.: "Mice, Monkeys, Men and Motives", Sept. 3, 1951. Printed in *Psychological Review*, 60; pp. 22–32, 1953; and reprinted in Fowler, H.: *Curiosity and Exploratory Behaviour*. Collier-Macmillan, 1965, p. 98.

14. Blough, D. S.: "Experiments in Animal Psychophysics". Scientific American Offprint, No. 458 (July 1961), W. H. Freeman & Co.
15. *Vide* Skinner, B. F.: "How to Teach Animals". Scientific American Offprint, No. 423 (December 1951), W. H. Freeman & Co.
16. *Ibid.* p. 3.
17. *Science and Human Behaviour*, pp. 77–81.
18. "How to Teach Animals", p. 5.
19. *Op. cit.*, p. 15.
20. *Ibid.* p. 17.
21. *Ibid.* p. 31.
22. *Ibid.* p. 65.
23. *Ibid.* p. 65.
24. *Ibid.* p. 73.
25. *Ibid.* pp. 227ff.
26. *Ibid.* pp. 240–1.
27. *Ibid.* pp. 284–5.
28. *Ibid.* pp. 402–12. Chapter XXVI on "Education".
29. *Ibid.* pp. 402–3.
30. *Ibid.* pp. 406–7.
31. *Ibid.* pp. 426–36. Chapter XXVII on "Designing a Culture".
32. Holland, J. G. & Skinner, B. F.: *The Analysis of Behaviour*. McGraw-Hill, 1961.
33. *Vide* Austwick, K. (ed.): *Teaching Machines and Programming*. Pergamon Press, 1964, pp. 25–33. Quotation from p. 29.
34. *Ibid.* p. 31.
35. Fry, E. B.: *Teaching Machines and Programmed Instruction*. McGraw-Hill, 1963, pp. 53–8.
36. Skinner, B. F.: "Teaching Machines". Scientific American Offprint, No. 461 (November 1961), W. H. Freeman & Co., p. 4.
37. *Ibid.* pp. 3–4.
38. Montagnon, P. & Bennett, R.: *What is Programmed Learning?* B.B.C. Publication, 1965, p. 97.
39. "Teaching Machines", p. 3.
40. *Vide* Sealey, L. G. W. & Gibbon, V.: *Communication and Learning in the Primary School*. Blackwell, 1963 (Revised; Reprinted 1964), pp. 162–3 *et passim*.
41. Peters, R. S.: *Authority, Responsibility and Education*, p. 121; *Vide* also p. 124.
42. "Teaching Machines", pp. 6–7.
43. *Ibid.* p. 9.
44. *Ibid.* p. 13.
45. *Science and Human Behaviour*, p. 244.

46. *Ibid.* p. 256.
47. *Authority, Responsibility and Education*, p. 134.
48. *Vide* Austwick, K. (ed.): *Teaching Machines and Programming*, pp. 174–201, "Automation in Schools".
49. "Teaching Machines", p. 13.

BIBLIOGRAPHY

A. BOOKS BY SKINNER

The Behaviour of Organisms. Appleton-Century, 1938.
Science and Human Behaviour. Collier-Macmillan, 1953; Paperback 1965.
Verbal Behaviour. Appleton-Century, 1957.
Cumulative Record. Appleton-Century, 1961.
Ferster, C. B. & Skinner, B. F.: *Schedules of Reinforcement.* Appleton-Century, 1957.
Holland, J. G. & Skinner, B. F.: *The Analysis of Behaviour.* McGraw-Hill, 1961.
Skinner, B. F.: "How to Teach Animals". Scientific American Offprint, No. 423 (December 1951), W. H. Freeman & Co.
—: "Teaching Machines". Scientific American Offprint, No. 461 (November 1961), W. H. Freeman & Co.

B. OTHER BOOKS OF REFERENCE

Blough, D. S.: "Experiments in Animal Psychophysics". Scientific American Offprint, No. 458 (July 1961), W. H. Freeman & Co.
Frolov, I. P.: *Pavlov and his School.* Kegan Paul, 1937.
Hebb, D. O.: *The Organization of Behaviour.* J. Wiley, 1949.
Hull, C. L.: *Principles of Behaviour.* Appleton-Century, 1943.
—: *A Behaviour System.* Yale Univ. Press, 1952.
Koffka, K.: *Principles of Gestalt Psychology.* Kegan Paul, 1935.
Köhler, W.: *The Mentality of Apes.* Kegan Paul, 1925; Penguin Books (Pelican), 1957.
—: *Gestalt Psychology.* Liveright, 1930.
Loeb, J.: *The Mechanistic Conception of Life.* Chicago, 1912.
Pask, G.: *An Approach to Cybernetics.* Hutchinson, 1961.
Pavlov, I. P.: *Conditioned Reflexes.* O.U.P. 1927 (and various Reprints).
Peters, R. S.: *The Concept of Motivation.* Routledge, 1958 (Reprinted 1960).

Tolman, E. C.: *Purposive Behaviour in Animals and Men.* Appleton-Century, 1932.
Watson, J. B.: *Psychology from the Standpoint of a Behaviourist.* Lippincott, 1919.
—: *Behaviourism.* Kegan Paul, 1925.
Wiener, N.: *Cybernetics.* J. Wiley, 1948.
Woodworth, R. S.: *Contemporary Schools of Psychology.* Methuen, 1931,

C. BOOKS ABOUT PROGRAMMED LEARNING

Adam, J. B. & Shawcross, A. J.: *The Language Laboratory.* Pitman, 1963.
Austwick, K. (ed.): *Teaching Machines & Programming.* Pergamon Press, 1964.
Carr, R.: *Training for Skill.* H.M.S.O., 1957.
Coulson, J. (ed.): *Programmed Learning and Computer Based Instruction.* Prentice-Hall, 1962.
Cram, D.: *Explaining Teaching Machines & Programming.* Fearon, 1961.
de Cecco, J. P. (ed.): *Educational Technology.* Holt, Rinehart, 1964.
Deterline, W. A.: *An Introduction to Programmed Instruction.* Prentice-Hall, 1962.
Fry, E. B.: *Teaching Machines & Programmed Instruction.* McGraw-Hill, 1963.
Galanter, E. (ed.): *Automatic Teaching: The State of the Art.* J. Wiley, 1959.
Goldsmith, M. (ed.): *Mechanisation in the Classroom.* Souvenir Press, 1963.
Green, E. J.: *The Learning Process & Programmed Instruction.* Holt, Rinehart, 1962.
Kay, H. *et al.*: *Teaching Machines & their Use in Industry.* H.M.S.O., 1963.
Leedham, J. & Unwin, D.: *Programmed Learning in the Schools.* Longmans, 1965.
Leith, G. O. M.: *A Handbook of Programmed Learning.* Univ. of Birmingham Ed. Dept., 1964.
Lysaught, J. P. et al.: *Handbook on Programmed Instruction.* J. Wiley, 1962.
Margulies, S. et al.: *Applied Programmed Instruction.* J. Wiley, 1962.
Markle, S. J.: *Good Frames & Bad: A Grammar of Frame Writing.* J. Wiley, 1964.

Montagnon, P. & Bennett, R. (ed.): *What is Programmed Learning?* B.B.C. Publication, 1965.
Richmond, W. K.: *Teachers and Machines*. Collins, 1965.
Smith, W. I. & Moore, W.: *Programmed Learning*. Van Nostrand, 1962.

D. SOME PROGRAMMED TEXTS

Austwick, K.: *Simultaneous Equations*. Methuen, 1963.
—: *Brackets*. Methuen, 1964.
Carman, R.: *Programmed Instruction to Vectors*. J. Wiley, 1963.
Clarke, J.: *A First Book of Sets*. Longmans, 1965.
—: *A Second Book of Sets*. Longmans, 1965.
Harries, C.: *Geometry of the Point & Line*. Longmans, 1965.
Harris, R.: *Angles*. Methuen, 1964.
—: *Triangles*. Methuen, 1964.
—: *Rectangles*. Methuen, 1964.
Hartley, J.: *Logarithms*. Methuen, 1964.
Leedham, J.: *Area and Volume*. Longmans, 1965.
McCollough *et al*: *Statistical Concepts*. McGraw-Hill, 1963.
Unwin, D.: *Kinematics*. Methuen, 1964.

PART THREE

Sociological

CHAPTER 10

SOCIOLOGY AND EDUCATION

A. THE NATURE AND SCOPE OF SOCIOLOGY

In his *Sociology: The Study of Social Systems*, G. D. Mitchell defines sociology as a

"descriptive and analytical discipline concerned with the structural aspects of human society"[1].

Human society is a network of relationships and structures, and these relationships and structures may be viewed in many different ways. Thus, for example, when man (particularly primitive man) is studied in terms of the whole scheme of his activities, his productions, his techniques and his artefacts, his myths and superstitions, the resultant body of knowledge is usually referred to as "cultural anthropology"; the study of the record of man and his activity in chronological sequence is "history"; "economics" examines man and his activity as a producer, consumer and dispenser of wealth, and studies the relationship between the supply and demand of goods, and between wealth and welfare. Sociology examines social relationships as objective facts. They are *social*, but they may also, of course, be cultural, economic, historical, political, religious or psychological; sociology, however, is interested in them primarily because they are social.

Durkheim certainly accepted that sociology was concerned with a wide range of institutions and social processes. He said that

"There are, in reality, as many branches of sociology, as many particular social sciences, as there are varieties of social facts"[2].

Thus there have developed general sociology, the sociology of religion, the sociology of law, the sociology of crime, the sociology of ethics or morals, and so on. Society, then, is the intricate, complex, and ever-changing pattern of the totality of all types of human relationships, in all aspects in which man relates himself to man, and it is these patterns with which sociology concerns itself. As a science, sociology deals with facts, data, and factual-judgements; social philosophy deals with judgements upon these facts and data, that is, with value-judgements.

But how far can it really be said that sociology is a science? According to W. F. Ogburn and M. F. Nimkoff[3] a science is to be judged by three main criteria: the reliability of its information or body of knowledge, its organization, and its method. With regard to the reliability of its knowledge, as these two writers point out, there are many more variables in the data of sociology —variables concerned with time and place. In physics and chemistry there are many generalizations which can be made with a great deal of certitude, and with a minimum of exceptions. In sociology, however, one is involved in the development and change of individual groups, cultures and societies over a wide area and over a long period of time. The very example which Ogburn and Nimkoff give of the success which sociologists have had in their generalizations illustrates the limitations of both data and method. They say:

"Still, sociologists seek generalizations that are universal, and they have had some success, as, for instance, in finding that societies always regulate marriage in such a manner as to prevent incest, *though incest may be variously defined*"[4].

If, however, "incest" may be variously defined, and there is no general agreement upon its limits, any generalization made about the information acquired is hardly "scientific" in the strict sense of the term. If what constitutes "incest" for one society, or one group in that society, is not incest for another society, or for another group in that society, it is not very helpful to speak of sociologists "finding that societies always regulate marriage in such a manner as to prevent incest"—particularly when even marriage itself may also be variously defined according to the society. The authors maintain that a "very good test of the reliability of knowledge is the test of prediction"[5] and that while prediction in the field of sociology is "liable to error", that error is small, as in the prediction of the social effects of trade and business cycles, and of inventions.

With regard to the organization of its knowledge, Ogburn and

Nimkoff point out that a miscellaneous and unrelated body of facts, such as may be found in an encyclopaedia, is not a science. The facts must be related, classified and systematized, as for example in the natural sciences of physics and chemistry. The value of such organization of relationships is that through a closer examination of the pattern of things there is always the possibility of further discovery. Sociology provides many interrelationships, and some of these lead to further discovery. Sociology provides possibilities of relationships, but the organization is not yet sufficiently strong "to yield a very adequate synthesis for the whole field"[6]. It becomes increasingly important that sociologists should not merely amass more data and information on every conceivable social topic, though this of course is vital, but that they should also develop some general organization and synthesis of the material, in order to make sociology a more reliable field of scientific study.

The third criterion provided by Ogburn and Nimkoff was that of method, and here they suggest that the statistical methods, as well as controlled and regulated social experiments, of sociology are "quite adequate", but that the cost of obtaining the data is almost prohibitive. One census alone in the United States, that of 1950, cost 90 million dollars[7]. In general, however, sociology has steadily developed its techniques and methodology over the years, and it has increasingly become a science in which statistical analysis has been used to establish the facts of society and social structure. One of the difficulties, however, about establishing a "science" of society is that we often reach the point where the collection of mere data becomes almost an end in itself, and the reliable knowledge acquired is carefully filed away and never used to increase man's happiness and awareness of social life. Professor P. L. Berger has pointed out, in this connexion, that

"it is quite true that some sociologists, especially in America, have become so preoccupied with methodological questions, that they have ceased to be interested in society at all. As a result, they have found out nothing of significance about any aspect of social life, since in science as in love a concentration on technique is quite likely to lead to impotence"[8].

Nevertheless, without techniques and methodology, sociology would remain very much at the level of anecdote and travellers' tales. Emile Durkheim set a standard for sociological method in his *Rules of Sociological Method*, first published in 1895[9], as we shall see in Chapter 11. In this book Durkheim emphasized that the methods used by the natural sciences were valid also in the field of social science. In addition, he sought to establish sociology as a science in its own right, at a time when the data of social science were being absorbed into psychology. Unfortunately, Durkheim went to extremes in his sociological approach by denying, or simply leaving out of account, all personal motives; for example, in his study of *Suicide*[10], the individual and personal motives of those who commit suicide, or attempt to do so, are almost completely ignored. To him, suicide was a *social fact* and, therefore, there must be some social explanation of that fact. As Professor P. L. Berger remarks,

"In the Durkheimian perspective, to live in society means to exist under the domination of society's logic. Very often men act by this logic without knowing it"[11].

It is, of course, true that we all do act by a "latent" logic, a social logic of which we are unaware; but it is also true that much of our individual activity, particularly that of a pathological nature, cannot be explained simply in social or sociological terms, except without a great deal of forcing of the facts into some preconceived social hypothesis or sociological pattern.

In general terms, then, sociology is the scientific study of social life, and social organization; and whilst of course it cannot avoid description, sociology is much more concerned with the causes of what it sees and discovers than with mere description.

Sociology is concerned to examine the physical and psychological bases of social life. These factors vary from one society to another, so that this discipline becomes involved in questions of biological heredity and natural environment, and the influence which both of these factors may exert on any group of people. The variability of culture-patterns is now a commonplace in sociological study[12]; and it is as important for the sociology of education as it is for the study of comparative sociology, as we shall presently see. The very concepts of "culture" and "civilization" require closer definition and analysis, before we can even begin to talk about the role of either. And in a consideration of cultures, whether ancient or modern, simple or complex, primitive or developed, we are involved in the folkways, the customs, the *mores* of these varied societies; problems of how, and why, these customs, taboos, and forms of "morality" developed are important in any sort of appreciation of the growth and structure of societies.

As a study of social relations, sociology is primarily concerned with groups and group behaviour. The extent to which groups are integrated will certainly affect their behaviour, and much of Durkheim's study on suicide was concerned with this very problem. In a consideration of group integration, sociology is concerned to discover why it is that human groups are formed at all, what it is that produces group cohesiveness and provides the components of integration. In his *Human Groups*, Professor W. J. H. Sprott points out that in all groups there is a "moral" element, that "there are standards or 'norms' of conduct incumbent upon its members to obey", and that groups "have purposes which are collectively pursued"[13]. It is part of the function of sociology to examine these norms of behaviour and to discover the collective purposes of any group. Ogburn and Nimkoff state that "consensus on 'Rules of the Game' is a unifying force"[14]. There are rules of behaviour in any society or group, regulating such things as division of labour (even, for example, in home life), sex roles and sexual behaviour.

"When there is agreement on opinions or values, we say there is *consensus*. Consensus is then a measure of integration; since consensus is a matter of degree, scales can be devised to measure the extent to which a given opinion is held by the members of a group"[15].

The integration of any group or groups is effected by assimilation, co-operation, and accommodation. *Assimilation* occurs when a person or a group acquires the values, standards or tastes of another person or group. But assimilation does not, by itself, effect integration; it frequently happens that a coloured individual, and sometimes a whole group, becomes assimilated to the *mores* of a white society, but will yet lack anything like complete integration within the larger white society. Despite their assimilation, and their complete equality and identity in habits, customs and interests, the coloured group may still be regarded as inferior, and integration may be refused. Within any group *co-operation* will always represent an integrating factor. Ogburn and Nimkoff cite an experiment which took place in America in which two class-room groups were created.

"One was told that all the members would get the same grade depending upon the quality of the collective product. The other was told that they would be rewarded differentially, each in terms of his achievement. Tests showed that the co-operative groups were more highly integrated, more friendly, liked one another better"[16].

Accommodation relates to the adjustment of hostile groups and individuals. Sometimes the accommodation is merely temporary, and the latent hostility breaks out at a later stage; it is a matter of degree, just as any social process is. In fact, as R. M. MacIver and C. H. Page have pointed out, civilized man is rarely in perfect harmony with all the other members of his group and his environ-ment. His wants and environing conditions are so complex "that a perfect sense of equilibrium is hard or impossible to attain"; and it is this element of eternal discontent which spurs man ever on towards new achievement[17]. When group solidarity is at any time weakened by conflict or competition, the techniques of accommodation, such as arbitration, conciliation or compromise, are used in order to effect some form of temporary integration.

Sociology is very much concerned with the problems of social differentiation, of role and status, and social class and stratifica-tion. It is interested in the establishment and ascription of *élites* in societies, and the extent to which there may exist social mobility, or movement from one class or caste to another. Both the effi-ciency of social life and its continuity depend to a large extent upon the individuals within their society knowing their role, or function, and upon the stability of social differentiation. Patterns of behaviour, life-styles, sub-cultures, all depend very much upon social position, and even class-consciousness or class-awareness. A society in which there is a maximum of social mobility is referred to as an "open-class" society; whilst one in which social mobility is at a minimum is a "caste" society. Mobility is effected by means of education, inherited special abilities and intelligence, marriage, or the acquirement of wealth; it is furthered by culture-contact, migration, the development of technology, invention, and urban life.

The existence of "norms" of behaviour simply implies that those who deviate from these standards are, through various forms of pressure and control, made to conform. Through these "norms" of behaviour the group provides an influence for conserving what it regards as best in social relationships, and the sanctions it brings to bear upon those guilty of deviant behaviour will vary according to the society and the seriousness with which it regards the offence as a possible means of social disruption. In a modern, complex society deviant behaviour demands a disproportionate share of both the attention and the economic resources of that society. The simpler the society, the more expeditious the punishment: the more humane the society, the less efficient the sanctions seem to be.

One of the most important topics, both for general sociology as well as for education, is the process whereby the child grows and develops into a socialized being. This process of socialization and internalization of the culture of the child's society is well described in Professor P. L. Berger's *Invitation to Sociology*:

"What happens in socialization is that the social world is internalized within the child. The same process, though perhaps weaker in quality, occurs every time the adult is initiated into a new social context or a new social group. Society, then, is not only something 'out there', in the Durkheimian sense, but it is also 'in here', part of our innermost being. Only an understanding of internalization makes sense of the incredible fact that most external controls work most of the time for most of the people in a society. Society not only controls our movements, but shapes our identity, our thought and our emotions. The structures of society become the structures of our own consciousness. Society does not stop at the surface of our skins. Society penetrates us as much as it envelops us"[18].

There are, of course, many theories concerning the process of internalization and the manner or mechanics of its operation. According to Freud it was through the operation of the Super-Ego that the Ego became socialized, and there was a steady adjustment between the various elements of the personality—the Id, the Ego, and the Super-Ego. According to George H. Mead, the self developed through the gradual internalization of the "generalized other", through taking on the roles of others in society. The whole question of socialization, internalization and role-taking is of prime importance for the educationist.

One of the most important branches of sociological study is that concerned with the origin, growth, change and function of social institutions, such as the family, kinship, marriage, religion, and government. It is not our purpose to deal with these institutions in any detail, but it is important to note here that different countries, societies, and even social groups within the same macro-society, have very different views about both the nature and the function of these institutions. The function also changes from one age to another within the same society. In modern times, for example, functions which formerly appertained to the family or the church have now been adopted by the State. In consequence, government has extended both its social functions and its social control, even within the "open society"; whilst many of the functions of the school, such as moral and religious education, the provision of meals, etc., were originally the concern of the family. The patterns of culture and institutions are changing rapidly even although the average person is almost unaware of the transformations taking place around him. And it is the concern of sociology to investigate the principles of change, diffusion and contact, as well as of continuity. This is particularly important at the present time in face of considerable social disorganization. Ogburn and Nimkoff have summed this situation up in the following words:

"When culture begins to change, the modifications do not occur evenly in all parts of the social heritage. Some parts change faster than others. When the different parts are interrelated, the varying rates of change produce a strain between the unequally moving parts. The part that is moving at the slowest rate of speed constitutes the cultural lag. Since the other part of culture has already changed, as a rule the most practicable method of effecting a better integration between the two parts is to make some adjustment in the part that is lagging. Modern technology is changing at a rapid rate and creating important social changes, with which our social institutions have not yet caught up. Analysis of important modern social problems, such as unemployment, poverty, and family disorganization, shows that much of our contemporary social disorganization issues from the irregular changes of our culture"[19].

The scope of sociology is as wide as social life itself; its implications in an age, in which men are journeying into Space and even talking in terms of colonizing other planets, defy our imagination; but one thing is clear and that is that its ramifications are by no means exhausted. It has explored the inner sanctum of the bedchamber, often in a rather unimaginative way; and it must face the possibility of an evaluation of human relations at a cosmic level. In its exploration of all our interrelations it will do well to take note of Professor Berger's warning not to

"fixate itself in an attitude of humourless scientism that is blind and deaf to the buffoonery of the social spectacle"[20].

We tend in all our disciplines, but perhaps particularly in relatively new ones, to develop a grammar and terminology that begins with clarifying by definition, and ends by stupefying through esoteric mystification. It becomes almost a point of honour to develop a language which no one else can understand. It would be a sad thing if the very discipline which seeks to explore and explain man's social behaviour were to make itself quite unintelligible except to an *élite*.

B. THE SOCIOLOGY OF EDUCATION

If the central concern of sociology is the social relationships of mankind, that of the sociology of education is the study of relations between education and society as a whole. It is virtually impossible today to think about educational problems, with any sense of reality and purpose, without also thinking about the social context of the problem. As P. W. Musgrave points out, in *The Sociology of Education*, a science should contain no prejudice, and so "a sociology of education must give a neutral analysis"[21]. At the same time, such an analysis must have a purpose, for education, other than just a delineation of things as they are, and A. K. C. Ottaway, for example, makes it quite clear that we must eventually go beyond sociology to the sphere of social philosophy, because

"we cannot avoid some responsibility for deciding in which direction we think our society ought to develop"[22].

Margaret Mead, who has made a study of education in the context of both simple and complex societies, has repeatedly emphasized that educators cannot succeed unless they are able to adjust, adapt and rethink their methods in order to meet the changing demands of a changing world[23]. The sociology of education is concerned with the aims of education, its methods, its institutions, its administration and curricula all viewed in relation to the various social forces in which they function—forces such as the religious, the cultural, the economic and the political. A society grows and changes, it is never static; it comprises a collection of people who are interested in the present, the past, and the future; and it is surely one of the tasks of education to prepare these people to become full members of their society.

It is, therefore, not surprising that the Newsom Report, which was published in August 1963, lays great emphasis upon the relationship between the educand and his society. In Chapter 9 the Report deals with the question of "Going out into the World", and states that some form of social studies should feature in the school programme[24]. Equally significantly, in its discussion of "Teachers Needed", in Chapter 12, it says that

"all teachers in training should have some introduction to sociological study, such as many colleges now offer, in order that they may put their own job into social perspective and be better prepared to understand the difficulties of pupils in certain types of area. They need, we suggest, some straightforward courses in recent social history; a study of the family and its changing function and structure in present day society; and guidance in understanding the current literature of sociology and psychology and the implications of research results"[25].

Obviously, the discipline of the sociology of education is particularly concerned with the influence which society has upon its children through its various structures and institutions; and whilst any environment or experience *may* be educative, not all experiences are of equal value, whilst some may be positively deleterious. Only teachers who know their society, its values, its dangers and its depths, are able to see their work properly orientated in its social context.

It was suggested earlier that no society is ever completely static; even the most simple or primitive society must adapt its customs, its mores and institutions according to the various new culture-contacts it makes, and even according to the vagaries of geographical environment. Sometimes, for example, the marriage taboos of aboriginal tribes have to be broken through lack of suitable and permissible mates; whilst dress, feeding and other habits have radically changed among many Pacific groups through the increasingly intensive contact of Western culture and civilization. Many of the old gods have disappeared, and new gods (such as those associated with the "cargo cult") have usurped their thrones. The primitive *rites de passage*, or initiation ceremonies from one peer group to another, are the educational means for mediating to the novitiate the accepted relationships, taboos, and culture of his society. And as his society changes, and is inevitably modified by these culture-contacts, and also by new internal stratifications, so the very nature and content of the *rites de passage* are changed.

More complex societies, like our own, are really in a very similar position. We live in social environments which are in a state of perpetual flux, whether we think in terms of roads, buildings, art, literature, morals, technology or traffic. And as the structure of our society changes, and the nature of its complexity alters, so also do our attitudes and relationships. It is the duty of every member of society, and particularly of the more intelligent, to understand something of the nature of his society, how it has developed, how it works, and where it is going. In the past it has almost always been assumed, in a rather facile manner, that our first educators, our parents, would pass on to their children the essential knowledge concerning their society, their social responsibilities and obligations. When the family was a close-knit organization, and when society was less complex than it is now, this was frequently done in an adequate manner. But, in contemporary society, family ties have been considerably weakened by technical change, the restlessness of youth, and their economic and general independence. In the words of P. W. Musgrave:

"the roles that an adult in contemporary Britain needs to learn cannot all be taught within the nuclear family. A very simple example will show this to be true. A nuclear family is of one social class and mainly meets members of the same or almost the same social class. In industry, however, a manager or a workman must meet all social classes and know how he is expected to behave in each different social situation. The school can provide experience of a wider range of adult roles in a less emotional frame of reference than the family. This opening of the world to the child is one important function of the school that is often forgotten by teachers in their stress on sheer knowledge and on the inculcation of moral virtues"[26].

The school must, more and more, concern itself with the mediation not merely of knowledge and morals, but also of acceptable, valuable and right social relationships, and also with the explication of social values, social institutions and social behaviour. It is the concern of education to inculcate in all pupils the full nature and function of the society and the culture in which they are being nurtured. Professor M. V. C. Jeffreys has expressed it in the following way:

"Education, properly understood, is an activity of the whole community. At the same time, the greatest contribution that the school can make towards the realization of this ideal of the educative society is the education of its members in the meaning of community"[27].

Thus, in the process of education the child and his social environment must always be considered together as two interacting elements; and the nature of his society must be transmitted to him.

Durkheim considered that there were as many different kinds of education as there were social *milieux* in any given society[28]. Now each child has certain social positions by ascription: it is born into a family as a male or female, and in a relative position with regard to brothers and sisters—the child may be the eldest or youngest or at some point in between, but each different position in the family organization provides, in fact, a slightly different *milieu*. But his position even within the family is not a static one; older children may leave home in order to get married, younger children may be born. The child is also born into a family which will belong to a particular part of the structure of society—it may be a working-class family; it may be a middle-class one, and so on. Here, again, the family fortunes may change, and so the social *milieu* may be a moving one. The family will live in a certain area which may be rural, urban, agricultural, industrial small town, large city, etc. Inequalities in opportunity for educational development may arise out of any of the factors—familial, economic, or regional. Studies such as those by Dr J. W. B. Douglas[29], J. E. Floud, A. H. Halsey and F. M. Martin[30], A. Davis [31], and J. B. Mays [32], are all concerned to show the effects of environmental factors upon the child. Thus there are many social determinants affecting education, and education is clearly a dependent variable; a comprehensive system of secondary education may be wholly successful in one area because of certain favourable regional factors, whilst in another area it may be a comparative failure. Discipline, and consequently learning, may be a problem in a slum area within a large city situated in an industrial region; in a rural area the children may be equally poverty-stricken and yet present few disciplinary problems.

Education cannot afford to ignore such facts as these, and it must adapt itself to the particular needs of particular social *milieux* as well as to particular children. But finally, as A. K. C. Ottaway has amply demonstrated[33], it must also consider the needs of our future society. We are fast moving through the Nucleotechnic and Biotechnic phases of the new Industrial Revolution, and we are now entering the third, or Cybernetic, phase. Automation, calculating machines, electronic brains, self-guiding missiles, and programmed-learning machines are all just ahead of us. These automatic machines will all help to reduce the number of brains as well as hands required for any particular operation; and they will reduce man's drudgery and increase the leisure time at his disposal. It is obvious that the education of the future, and the teacher-training of the present, cannot afford to ignore these facts. In particular, those who do not possess sufficient intelligence or capacity to have a real, active and useful part in this Cybernetic Revolution must, nevertheless, be educated for the emergent society and for living in it. This means we must not be surprised if our youth try out a great variety of jobs before they finally settle; indeed, this may prove to be a good thing. But whilst educating for adaptability we must also educate for *leisure*. This may not be the best way to express the educational need of our future society, or at least one of its needs; but it is a way of expressing the problem in such a way that it is immediately understood. Ultimately we are educating people *to be*, that is, to live the fullest and most integrated life possible within their society. To do this they must first understand both society and themselves.

REFERENCES

1. Mitchell, G. D. *Sociology: The Study of Social Systems.* U.T.P., 1959 (Reprinted 1963), p. v.
2. Durkheim. E.: *De la Méthode dans les Sciences.* Paris, Alcan, 1902, p. 242. Quoted by Inkeles, A.: *What is Sociology?* Prentice-Hall, 1966, pp. 5–6.
3. Ogburn, W. F. & Nimkoff, M. F.: *A Handbook of Sociology.* Routledge, 1960 (4th Edition, Revised), pp. 10–15.
4. *Ibid.* p. 11; my italics.
5. *Ibid.* p. 11.
6. *Ibid.* p. 11.
7. *Ibid.* p. 12.
8. Berger, P. L.: *Invitation to Sociology.* Penguin Books (Pelican), 1966, p. 24.
9. *Vide* Durkheim, E.: *The Rules of Sociological Method.* Collier-Macmillan, Free Press, 1964.
10. *Vide* Durkheim, E.: *Suicide: A Study in Sociology.* Routledge, 1952.
11. *Op. cit.*, p. 53.
12. *Vide* Benedict, R.: *Patterns of Culture.* Routledge, 1935 (7th Impression, 1961).
13. *Vide* Sprott, W. J. H.: *Human Groups.* Penguin Books (Pelican), 1958 (Reprinted 1964), pp. 11–12.
14. *Op. cit.*, p. 87.
15. *Ibid.* p. 88.
16. *Ibid.* p. 108.
17. MacIver, R. M. & Page, C. H.: *Society: An Introductory Analysis.* Macmillan, 1957, p. 123.
18. *Op. cit.*, pp. 140–1.
19. *Op. cit.*, p. 547.
20. *Op. cit.*, p. 187. The whole chapter, "Sociology is a Humanistic Discipline", is a most timely one.
21. Musgrave, P. W.: *The Sociology of Education.* Methuen, 1965, p. 11.
22. Ottaway, A. K. C.: *Education and Society: An Introduction to*

the Sociology of Education. Routledge, 1960 (4th Impression), p. 161.

23. Mead, M.: *Coming of Age in Samoa.* Penguin Books (Pelican), 1943 (Reprinted 1963), Chapters 13 and 14, pp. 157–97; and *Growing Up in New Guinea.* Penguin Books (Pelican), 1942 (Reprinted 1963), Chapters 13–16, pp. 161–208.
24. Newsom Report: *Half Our Future.* H.M.S.O., August 1963, p. 73.
25. *Ibid.* p. 103.
26. *Op. cit.*, p. 33.
27. Jeffreys, M. V. C.: *Glaucon.* Pitman, 1950, p. 71.
28. Durkheim, E.: *Education and Sociology.* Glencoe, Free Press, 1956, p. 67.
29. Douglas, J. W. B.: *The Home and the School.* MacGibbon and Kee, 1964.
30. Floud, J. E., Halsey, A. H. & Martin, F. M.: *Social Class and Educational Opportunity.* Heinemann, 1957.
31. Davis, A.: *Social Class Influences on Learning.* Harvard Univ. Press, 1948.
32. Mays, J. B.: *Education and the Urban Child.* Liverpool Univ. Press, 1962.
33. *Vide Op. cit.*, Chapter V, pp. 76–100.

BIBLIOGRAPHY

A. GENERAL BOOKS ON SOCIOLOGY

Berger, P. L.: *Invitation to Sociology.* Penguin Books (Pelican), 1966.
Bottomore, T. B.: *Elites and Society.* Watts, 1964.
Brown, R.: *Explanation in Social Science.* Routledge, 1964.
Davis, K.: *Human Society.* Macmillan, N.Y., 1948.
Erikson, E. H.: *Childhood and Society.* Penguin Books (Pelican), 1957 (Reprinted 1965).
Fletcher, R.: *The Family.* Penguin Books (Pelican), 1962.
Fyvel, T. R.: *The Frontiers of Sociology.* Cohen & West, 1964.
—: *The Insecure Offenders.* Penguin Books (Pelican), 1963.
Ginsberg, M.: *The Psychology of Society.* Methuen, Univ. Paperbacks, 1964.
—: *On Justice in Society.* Penguin Books (Pelican), 1965.
Glass, D. V. (ed.): *Social Mobility in Britain.* Routledge, 1954 (2nd Impression 1963).

Homans, G. C.: *The Human Group*. Routledge, 1951 (5th Impression 1965).

Inkeles, A.: *What is Sociology?* Prentice-Hall, 1964 (5th Printing 1966).

Johnson, H. M.: *Sociology: A Systematic Introduction*. Routledge, 1961.

Jones, H.: *Crime in a Changing Society*. Penguin Books (Pelican), 1965.

Klein, J.: *The Study of Groups*. Routledge, 1956.

Lewin, K.: *Field Theory in Social Science*. Tavistock Pub., 1952.

MacIver, R. M. & Page, C. H.: *Society*. Macmillan, 1950 (Reprinted 1957).

Maus, H.: *A Short History of Sociology*. Routledge, 1962.

Mead, G. H.: *On Social Psychology*. Univ. of Chicago Press, 1964 (Revised Edition).

Mead, M.: *Coming of Age in Samoa*. Penguin Books (Pelican), 1943 (Reprinted 1963).

—: *Growing Up in New Guinea*. Penguin Books (Pelican), 1942 (Reprinted 1963).

Merton, R. K.: *Social Theory and Social Structure*. Glencoe, Free Press, 1951.

Mitchell, G. D.: *Sociology: The Study of Social Systems*. U.T.P., 1959 (Reprinted 1963).

Myrdal, G.: *Value in Social Theory*. Routledge, 1958.

Ogburn, W. F. & Nimkoff, M. F.: *A Handbook of Sociology*. Routledge, 1947; 5th Edition (Revised) 1964.

Parsons, T. *et al.: Theories of Society*. Collier-Macmillan, Free Press, 1965.

Sprott, W. J. H.: *Human Groups*. Penguin Books (Pelican), 1958 (Reprinted 1964).

Sumner, W. G.: *Folkways*. Mentor, New English Library, 1960.

Tiryakian, E. A.: *Sociologism and Existentialism*. Prentice-Hall, 1962.

Weber, M.: *Basic Concepts in Sociology*. Citadel Press, N.Y., 1962.

Wootton, B.: *Social Science and Social Pathology*. Allen & Unwin, 1959.

B. SOCIOLOGY OF EDUCATION

Banks, O.: *Parity and Prestige in English Secondary Education*. Routledge, 1955 (2nd Impression, 1963).

Bantock, G. H.: *Education and Values*. Faber, 1965.

—: *Education in an Industrial Society*. Faber, 1963.

Bear, R. M.: *The Social Functions of Education*. Macmillan, 1937.

Blyth, W. A. L.: *Primary Education. A Sociological Description.* Routledge, 1965.

Brown, F. J.: *Educational Sociology.* Technical Press, 1947.

Clarke, F.: *Freedom in the Educative Society.* U.L.P., 1948.

—: *Education and Social Change.* Sheldon Press, 1940.

Collier, K. G.: *The Social Purposes of Education.* Routledge, 1959 (2nd Impression, 1962).

Douglas, J. W. B.: *The Home and the School.* McGibbon & Kee, 1964.

Durkheim, E.: *Education and Sociology.* Collier-Macmillan, Free Press, 1956.

Elvin, H. L.: *Education and Contemporary Society.* Watts, 1965.

Evans, K. M.: *Sociometry and Education.* Routledge, 1961.

Fleming, C. M.: *The Social Psychology of Education.* Kegan Paul, 1944.

Floud, J. E., Halsey, A. H. & Martin, F. M.: *Social Class and Educational Opportunity.* Heinemann, 1957.

Folsom, J. K.: *Youth, Family and Education.* Washington, 1941.

Halsey, A. H. *et al.*: *Education, Economy and Society.* Collier-Macmillan, Free Press, 1963.

Halsey, A. H. (ed.): *Ability and Educational Opportunity.* O.E.C.D., Paris, 1961.

Jackson, B. & Marsden, D.: *Education & the Working Class.* Routledge, 1962.

Lester Smith, W. O.: *The Impact of Education on Society.* Blackwell, 1949.

Mannheim, K. & Stewart, W. A. C.: *An Introduction to the Sociology of Education.* Routledge, 1962.

Mays, J. B.: *Education and the Urban Child.* Liverpool Univ. P., 1962.

—: *Growing Up in a City.* Liverpool Univ. Press, 1951.

Mercer, B. E.: *Education and the Social Order.* Holt, 1957.

Musgrave, P. W.: *The Sociology of Education.* Methuen, 1965.

Musgrove, F.: *Youth and the Social Order.* Routledge, 1964.

Newsom Report: *Half Our Future.* H.M.S.O., 1963.

Ottaway, A. K. C.: *Education and Society.* Routledge, 1953 (4th Impression, 1960).

Reeves, M.: *Growing Up in a Modern Society.* U.L.P., 1946.

Stanley, W. O.: *Social Foundations of Education.* Holt, 1946.

Wiseman, S.: *Education and Environment.* Manchester Univ. Press, 1964.

CHAPTER 11

EMILE DURKHEIM (1858–1917)

A. DURKHEIM AND THE DEVELOPMENT OF SOCIOLOGISM

Auguste Comte (1798–1857) died in the year before Emile Durkheim was born, and he has been called the father of modern sociology. Comte was trained in engineering, mathematics and the natural sciences, and he looked at society with a scientific eye; in consequence, he saw the science of society as a positive one, concerned with the delineation of the structures of society, *as it is*. The word "sociology" first appeared in one of Comte's volumes entitled, *Cours de Philosophie Positive*, in which Comte considered that one could discern the natural development of society in accordance with some law within the history of mankind. Comte believed that there was some form of progress attending this natural development of society, and that the main task of sociology was concerned with the reconstruction and progress of social forms and structures. According to him there were three definite stages in the law which governed such progress:

(a) the theological or fictive;
(b) the metaphysical or abstract; and
(c) the scientific or positive.

This third stage, the phase of science, included sociology which was, to Comte, the very crown of science and of intellectual achievement.

Comte saw sociology as a humanizing science. It would react upon the other sciences and show their true function in the fabric of man's intellectual achievement. Sociology was, therefore, of pre-eminent importance. Moreover, it was a *positive* science; it was a science in its own right and not simply as a specialized application of one or more of the other sciences. Comte looked for the laws that governed the actual observed phenomena, and not for any ultimate or absolute inner essences of a metaphysical order. These latter were neither knowable nor useful; but the laws behind and in observable phenomena were facts both discoverable and socially helpful. Thus Comte sought to separate philosophy and sociology, and, in the judgement of Professor E. A. Tiryakian of Princeton University, U.S.A., the consequences of this separation have been twofold:

"On the positive side, one may mention that it has enabled sociology to become an academic discipline in its own right, free from the shackles of subordination. In divorcing itself from metaphysics and social philosophy, sociology became an empirical science"[1].

On the negative side, however, he feels that sociology has tended to concentrate on "problems at the microscopic level"[2], and that, in consequence, research projects tend to accumulate rather than to be cumulative.

The Sociologistic School of sociologists is, in general, characterized by the belief that society, or sociality, is something *sui generis*; it exists apart from, and is different from, the individuals of which it is composed. Its source and its essence are to be found in the phenomena of social interaction; and sociology becomes irreducible to psychology—it is in itself both necessary and sufficient for the complete explanation of social reality.

Emile Durkheim was a Jew, and the son of rabbinical parents, and his general ethos of ideas was formed by two traditions—the secular-rationalist and the Christian-conservative[3]. He was an agnostic in religious matters, but an agnostic who was deeply interested in religion and in its function and causative influences in society, as his *Elementary Forms of Religious Life* bears witness. In the realm of the sociology of religion he provided not only a method of functional analysis, but also, according to Professor R. A. Nisbet, perhaps

"the most convincing proof ever written of the functional indispensability of religion in one form or other and of the historical primacy of religion among all symbols and modes of thought"[4].

In 1887 Durkheim was given an appointment at the University of Bordeaux and put in charge of the teaching of the social sciences and pedagogy. Nineteen years later, in 1906, he was granted the Chair at the Sorbonne, Paris, in the Science of Education, which became in 1913 the Chair of the Science of Education and Sociology.

At first, Durkheim accepted the positivist position of Comte and Herbert Spencer (1820–1903). When, however, he wrote *The Rules of Sociological Method* in 1895 he was highly critical of Spencer's view of the social order[5]; Durkheim broke from the positivist and utilitarian tradition in which sociology was developing. He maintained that the method of sociology must be absolutely objective, and must be dominated by the view that "social facts are things" and that they must be treated as such (*comme les choses*). Any preconceptions which the sociologist might have about the facts he must forthwith disregard, and he must face the facts themselves[6]. The sociologist *qua* sociologist was not immediately concerned with the psychological or biological processes: he was concerned specifically with the facts of social life, and such facts should be those which are general throughout the extent of any given society, and at any given stage in the evolution of that society.

B. THE RULES OF SOCIOLOGICAL METHOD

Durkheim's book, *The Rules of Sociological Method*, was written in 1895 and is one of his shortest works; yet it raises "most of those theoretical problems which are fundamental" to a study of human society. It is, in fact, a classic in the methodology of political science[7]. In it Durkheim considers the possibility of a social science, or sociology, and the existence of measurable facts in the realm of social phenomena. He argues that there is a distinction between the social and natural sciences in their universe of operation, but that the methods employed by the natural sciences are valid for sociology. Social phenomena, however, are not the product of the individual will, or idea; on the contrary, they exercise constraint upon the members of a society; they are "exterior" and "resistant"; they are objective and influence the behaviour of both the individual and the aggregate of individuals, to the extent that, for example, crime leads to measures to deal with it.

Durkheim defines a "social fact" as

"every way of acting, fixed or not, capable of exercising on the individual an external constraint . . . every way of acting which is general throughout a given society, while at the same time existing in its own right independent of its individual manifestations"[8].

It is the collective aspects of the practices, beliefs and tendencies of any particular social group that characterize truly social phenomena. Currents of opinion are social facts; such currents of opinion vary according to time and place, and impel or constrain certain groups to more suicides, or fewer marriages, or a higher birth-rate, for example[9]. Such social facts may be recognized by their power of external coercion, which they are able to exercise over individuals—a power which is recognizable by the existence of some sanction or by the resistance which it offers to every individual effort that attempts to violate it[10].

Durkheim, in the second chapter, provides certain "Rules for the Observation of Social Facts". These may be summarized as follows:

(a) We must consider social facts as *things*; "and, in truth, up to the present, sociology has dealt more or less exclusively with concepts and not with things"[11]. And Durkheim accuses both Comte and Spencer of taking ideas for the subject matter of study. The point of departure of science is the consideration of phenomena as things, and thereby to treat them as data.

(b) We must consider social phenomena in themselves, as distinct from any consciously formed representation of them which we may possess in the mind; they must be studied objectively as external things. We should never assume beforehand, for example, the voluntary character of an institution or practice.

(c) We must eradicate all preconceptions; the basis of all scientific method is logical doubt. Our sentiments, our religious beliefs, our political prejudices, our moral standards—all carry an emotional tone which is deleterious to the delineation and explanation of such phenomena.

(d) The subject matter of every sociological study should comprise a group of phenomena which has been defined in advance by certain, specific, external characteristics; and all phenomena so defined should be included within such a group. Durkheim gives the example of certain acts which evoke from society the particular reaction which we term "punishment". Thus punishable acts come under the general heading "crime", and become the province of a special science termed "criminology".

(e) When sociology undertakes to investigate some order of social facts, it must try and consider them from an aspect that is independent of their individual manifestations. For example, different family types should be studied via the legal structure of the family, or the right of succession, not on the basis of literary descriptions provided by travellers and historians[12].

In the third chapter, Durkheim considers the "Rules for Distinguishing between the Normal and the Pathological". In general comment he remarks:

"Briefly, for societies as for individuals, health is good and desirable; disease, on the contrary, is bad and to be avoided. If, then, we can find an objective criterion, inherent in the facts themselves, which enables us to distinguish scientifically between health and morbidity in the various orders of social phenomena, science will be in a position to throw light on practical problems and still remain faithful to its own method"[13].

He then proceeds to develop certain objective criteria which he feels will fulfil these requirements. They are as follows:

(a) A social fact is *normal*, in relation to a given social type and at a given stage in its development, when present in the average society of that species at the corresponding stage of its evolution.

(b) The results of this method may be verified by demonstrating that the generality of the phenomenon is bound up with the general conditions of the collective life of the social type which is being considered.

(c) Such verification is necessary when the fact in question occurs in a special species in society which has not yet attained full evolution[14].

In this section, Durkheim underlines the "normalcy of crime". The existence of criminality in a society is normal, provided that it does not exceed a certain level for each social type in society, which Durkheim felt might well be fixed in conformity with the rules he had laid down. Durkheim hastened to add, in a foot-note[15], that, whilst crime may be regarded as a phenomenon of normal sociology, it does not follow that the criminal may be regarded from a biological and/or psychological point of view, as an individual normally constituted. Crime is necessary, and bound up with the fundamental conditions of our social life, and

"by that very fact it is useful, because these conditions of which it is a part are themselves indispensable to the normal evolution of morality and law"[16].

In chapters four and five, Durkheim goes on to consider the "Rules for the Classification of Social Types", or Social Morphology, and "Rules for the Explanation of Social Facts". In his discussion of the latter he suggests that when the explanation of a social phenomenon is sought, the investigator must seek separately the efficient cause which produces it and the function it fulfils[17]. Moreover, he maintains, we must not seek to explain social facts in a psychological way; if we do, our explanation will be false, since collective representations (*représentations collectives*), tendencies and emotions are not caused by certain states of individual consciousness, "but by the conditions in which the social group in its totality is placed"[18]. Rather, the determining *cause* of any social fact should be sought among the preceding social facts; and the *function* of any social fact should be sought in its relation to some social end. Durkheim makes it clear that he does not deny that psychology and psychological explanation may have some value for the sociologist; the latter should utilize every aid available. But there can be no reduction of sociological study to psychological analysis; it is in social facts that the sociologist must establish himself, and in the internal constitution of the social group; i.e., in things, persons, law, established customs, literary and artistic works, etc. The human *milieu* remains as an active factor, and so it is the principal task of the sociologist to discover the many and various aspects of this *milieu* which can exert some influence upon the course and direction of social phenomena[19].

In chapter six, Durkheim concludes with two "Rules Relative to Establishing Sociological Proofs". They are:

(a) A given effect has always a single corresponding cause.
(b) A social fact of any complexity cannot be explained except by means of following its complete development through all social species[20].

Durkheim regards sociological method as entirely independent of philosophy: sociology does not need to choose between great hypotheses; all that it requires is that the principle of causality should be applied rigorously to all social phenomena. Sociology *per se* is not positivistic, evolutionary, idealistic, individualistic, naturalistic, communistic or socialistic; sociology, with its method, is *objective*. Social facts are social things and the method of sociology is exclusively "sociological": a social fact can be explained only by another social fact[21].

C. THE SOCIAL MIND, GROUP MIND, OR COLLECTIVE CONSCIOUSNESS

Durkheim's theory of society has sometimes been referred to as a psycho-mysticism. In *The Rules of Sociological Method*, Durkheim says that

"Individual minds, forming groups by mingling and fusing, give birth to a being, psychological if you will, but constituting a psychic individual of a new sort. It is, then, in the nature of this collective individuality, not in that of the associated units, that we must seek the immediate and determining causes of the facts appearing therein"[22].

Of the concept of the "group mind", or "collective consciousness", George E. G. Catlin, in his Introduction to the English translation of this work, has said that it results in a "deplorable effort to interpret social phenomena in terms of this alleged consciousness"[23]. Professor Morris Ginsberg has attacked the whole of the doctrine of the Group Mind in *The Psychology of Society*, and he is very critical of Durkheim's theory of the social mind[24]. There is no doubt that a great deal of the language of Durkheim suggests the creation of a monster, monolithic, psychic entity which might be called the Collective Consciousness; and yet other statements he makes seem to indicate, not only that he was aware of the danger of the language he was using, but that he did not, in fact, mean quite the sort of thing that many of his interpreters have suggested. Although some writers have referred to his theory as an "organismic" interpretation of society[25], the idea of organic development does not necessarily imply that society possesses a separate organ, called the "Group Mind" or "Collective Consciousness". Indeed, Durkheim seems explicitly to deny this in one passage:

"The totality of beliefs and sentiments common to average citizens of the same society forms a determinate system which has its own life; one may call it the *collective* or *common conscience*. No doubt, it has not a specific organ as a substratum; it is, by definition, diffuse in every reach of society"[26].

Yet he still goes on to add that it has "specific characteristics which make it a distinct reality"[27]. It is a distinct reality, and yet not a separate personal, or supra-personal, existence. It is clearly something special, and it requires a special term to designate it, "simply because the states which constitute it differ specifically from those which constitute the individual consciousness"[28].

Morris Ginsberg, however, makes three particular points in relation to Durkheim's theory, which seem to be a fair summary of what Durkheim has said—individual passages apart. Firstly, Durkheim seems to maintain that the "collective representations" are exterior to the individual consciousness. The individual is able to possess only a *parcelle* of the social mind, and the collective consciousness comes to his mind as something exterior (in the form, for example, of moral, religious, juridical and logical rules). Secondly, the "collective representations" differ in kind from "individual representations". The new production, through the aggregation of these "collective representations" has all the appearance, from Durkheim's statements, of a "psychical individuality *sui generis*". And the "representation" content of this new production is different from that of the individual[29]. Certainly Durkheim has said this in his *Sociology and Philosophy*:

"Society transcends the individual's consciousness. It surpasses him materially because it is a result of the coalition of all the individual forces. ... Society is something more than material power; it is a moral power. It surpasses us physically, materially and morally"[30].

And this leads to Professor Ginsberg's third point, namely, that Durkheim claims for the social mind a superiority over the individual mind[31]. Durkheim considers that the collective consciousness is the highest form of psychic life because it is "a consciousness of consciousness"; it is superior to the individual in every way—a "hyperspirituality". Society is God; or God is but a "mythicization of society"[32]. Professor Ginsberg suggests that, if such a "social mind" exists, we have no direct way of discovering what it thinks; indeed, the lack of a sense of purpose, or clear perception of ends, observable in society would seem to indicate that it is a "conglomeration of elements" far inferior to the greatest individual minds that we have known[33].

There is, however, another point of view presented by several Durkheimian defenders. Professor J. G. Peristiany has commented:

"Durkheim, of course, is fully aware that it is individuals who think and not a monstrous Group Mind. What he wishes to suggest is that the pattern, the grammar of thought, of a certain society is connected with its historical development and with the structure of society and of its system of values, which is something other than the structure and development of individual minds"[34].

This seems to suggest something symbolic, or in the nature of a personification, rather than organic; that the Collective Consciousness, or Group Mind, is a sort of mythicization of society, in much the same way as Durkheim seems to suggest that God himself is. But this does not seem to do justice quite to what Durkheim in fact said; it seems rather to be an attempt to defend him against those who would accuse him of an organismic view of society. If society is, in Durkheim's view, a "coalition of all the individual forces", an aggregation of individual consciousnesses, a synthesis, *sui generis*, arising out of the fusion or compounding of individual representations, then it must surely be a form of consciousness, of mind. The sum total of all the individual consciousnesses in our society can give us only Consciousness; it may or may not be

I

different in quality (Durkheim thinks that it is); it may or may not be separate (Durkheim has certainly maintained that it is); but it must surely be of the same nature and order. Professor R. A. Nisbet argues that, for Durkheim, society is

"neither an inert monolith nor a brooding, ghostly presence epiphenomenal to the individual and discoverable only by the kind of mystic intuition that had produced Rousseau's vision of the general will . . . society is indistinguishable from the observable data of human conduct. What one actually sees are not 'individuals', not 'instincts', but rather human beings inextricably involved in institutionalized and associative patterns of behaviour"[35].

Thus, in Professor Nisbet's view, for Durkheim man and society were fused, and society was not in reality external to man, but inseparable from man and his mind. Indeed, Durkheim had explicitly said that man is not truly himself nor fully realized "except on the condition that he is involved in society"[36].

Professor Tiryakian argues in a chapter entitled, "Durkheim's Conception of Society", that, instead of collective life arising from the individual, in Durkheim's view "*the individual personality is a product of society*"[37]. Tiryakian goes on to suggest that for Durkheim collective beliefs are manifestations of a reality "which transcends and yet is immanent in the individual"[38]. Society does not depend upon any single individual for its reality, and therefore it must transcend the individual. Moreover, when the individual dies, society still persists. On the other hand, it is the individual who is "the ultimate vehicle of social life", and so society is immanent[39].

The concept of the Group Mind has found support from a number of thinkers, including Professor W. McDougall, who defined "mind" in behavioural terms, but not to imply a "super-individual group consciousness"[40]. Professor C. G. Jung wrote of the Collective Unconscious as if it were a reality, a self-existent, an extra-personal psychic force acting upon the individual[41]. And in his essay on "The Formation of the Noösphere", Pierre Teilhard de Chardin has stated that

"We feel that the relation between Society and Social Organism is no longer a matter of symbolism but must be treated in realistic terms"[42].

These may not be either popular or generally accepted views—that man shares a realm of Collective Unconsciousness, or that there is a Social Organism of a psycho-biological nature developing into a Supra-Organism, the Noösphere—but, at the same time, it is not denied by the critics of Durkheim, McDougall, Jung or de Chardin that there is *some* sort of group consciousness, or group awareness, however difficult it may be to define. The individual both acts and thinks differently within the group from the way in which he does when he is alone; but to make this group or collective consciousness something *distinct from* the individual consciousness is to make the group in some way an organism. This few critics are able to accept, whilst yet agreeing that social interaction *is* a factor in the explanation of social and psychical phenomena.

D. SUICIDE: A STUDY IN SOCIOLOGY

Since 1897, when Durkheim first produced his monumental work on *Suicide*, our statistical methods have improved infinitely, largely through the development of the whole field of biometrics under the influence of Professor Karl Pearson, and through his refinement of the correlation factor. Durkheim set out to apply his sociological method to particular aspects and problems of society, such as religion, morality, education and so on. Historically, his work on the problem of suicide is of importance because it was the first thorough-going study in social causation, and the first piece of investigation to demonstrate a rigorous sociological method. The subtitle for this book is not "A Sociological Study", which of course it is, but "A Study in Sociology"—it is not simply a cogent sociological study into the problem of suicide; it is a model of method and approach for the investigation of any sociological problem; it is a study in sociology itself, as a science objectively at work, amassing social facts or data, and arranging them in some order of significance. As K. D. Naegele points out in an article entitled, "Some Observations on the Scope of Sociological Analysis",

"The logic that arranged and interpreted the facts of suicide will serve equally well with the puzzles of alcoholism or cross-cousin marriage. In all these cases we must distinguish between rates and

individual histories; we need to search for types among a determinate, and hence apparently uniform, category of events"[43].

This remark indicates how thorough-going was this particular
piece of analysis by Durkheim, setting a pattern for future studies.

Any particular suicide might be explained in terms of the
psychological effects of mental sickness, financial or domestic
problems, general failure and disappointment, and so on. In such
examples as these there is some attempt to explain matters in
terms of motivation—it is an attempt at a psychological analysis.
It is Durkheim's aim, however, to demonstrate that there is a
sociological explanation for all types of suicide; that when all the
suicides occurring in any society, and in any one period, are
analysed and classified, and are then compared with the numbers
which have occurred at any other period, the *proportions* falling
into each class tend to remain constant, although the general rate
of suicide may vary. The rates may, in fact, indicate wide variations: this phenomenon Durkheim designates as a "social fact" or
datum requiring investigation. Moreover, it is a fact which must
be studied at the *sociological* level, and not at the psychological
one. More recently Maurice Halbwachs, a former student of
Durkheim's, has developed his research further, and he has indicated that there is no real antithesis between the sociological and
the psychological explanations of suicide, but that they complement each other[44]. And Erwin Stengel, who has made several
studies of this problem, remarks that

"Durkheim and Freud seem to be worlds apart. No two theories
of human behaviour could be more different than the conception
of the collective mind coercing the individual to kill himself and
pyschoanalytical notions of the origin of suicidal tendencies. Yet
the two theories have one important aspect in common; both see
the individual's actions as the result of powerful forces over which
he has only limited control. Durkheim located those forces in
society, Freud in the unconscious. Durkheim's "collective mind"
supposed to be extra-personal has, in the psycho-analytical theory,
its counterpart in the innate drives and the super-ego, i.e. the
mental representation of the moral demands. The drives are
modified and the super-ego is shaped by society"[45].

Thus Freud and Durkheim are perhaps not really so incompatible
in their approach as might at first sight appear.

Durkheim, then, relates suicide to social concomitants and he distinguishes three types according to the sort of disturbance in the social-individual relationship—Egoistic, Altruistic and Anomic:

(a) *Egoistic:* This is found mostly among people who have no strong group attachments, and who, therefore, lack integration with their society. For example, the suicide rate is lower among married people than among single, widowed or divorced. Again, among those who are married the rate is lower among those who have children than among those who have none. According to Durkheim, the rate is lowest among Catholics, i.e. followers of a branch of a religion which integrates the individual very closely into the collective life. It is higher among Protestants, where a high state of individualism exists.

(b) *Altruistic:* The integration of the individual is comparatively great where his life is rigorously governed by custom and habit. This is particularly so amongst the lower societies. The individual's own existence has become of little account compared with what he believes are his social obligations. Examples of suicide that fall within this category are *suttee* among Indian widows, and *hara-kiri* among the *bushido* observing knights of Japan.

(c) *Anomic:* Lack of regulation of the individual by society may result in what Durkheim terms "anomic" suicide. The French word *anomie* is derived from the Greek ἀνομία (anomia), meaning "lawlessness" or "normlessness". The English equivalent "anomy" is also used, with the adjective "anomic", meaning "lawless" or "normless". Durkheim maintained that anomy resulted from a breakdown in the regulation of goals such that, as a result, men's ambitions and aspirations create a constant pressure for deviant behaviour. In such conditions social norms of behaviour no longer control men's actions, and society has failed to regulate the behaviour of individuals.

"Anomy indeed springs from the lack of collective forces at certain points in society; that is, of groups established for the regulation of social life. Anomy therefore partially results from the same state of disaggregation from which the egoistic current also springs"[46].

When the regulation of the individual is upset so that his scope is broadened beyond the powers of endurance, or when it is unduly narrowed so that he feels frustrated, then conditions for anomic suicide tend to be maximized. Durkheim discovered correlations between suicide and periods of marked economic prosperity (high rate), and periods of marked economic depression (high rate). These are both periods during which the normal expectations of people are disturbed, and there is a resultant confusion, disorientation, and increased strain and stress.

In his Introduction to Durkheim's *Suicide* the editor, George Simpson states that

"the individual inclination to suicide is explicable scientifically only by relation to the collective inclination, and this collective inclination is itself a determined reflection of the structure of the society in which the individual lives"[47].

This is the view of Durkheim. Further, suicide, like crime, is "normal" in any society, but when the rate of suicides rapidly increases it is a symptom of some breakdown in the social consciousness. This cannot be remedied by education, which is but "the image and reflection of society"[48]. Altruistic suicide, found principally in lower societies, was losing ground—at least, so Durkheim thought. The Second World War and events since, particularly in Eastern countries, do not seem to bear this out. The only remedy for egoistic suicide was to restore enough consistency to social groups in order that they might obtain a firmer hold upon the individual, and so that he might feel more closely bound to them. Anomic suicide would be alleviated by similar attempts to control and organize social behaviour. Durkheim considered that religion modified the inclination to suicide only to the extent that it prevented men from thinking freely.

E. SOCIOLOGY AND EDUCATION

Although Durkheim has explicitly stated that sociology *per se* affirms neither free-will nor determinism, and that all it asks is "that the principle of causality be applied to social phenomena"[49], yet it seems clear from all Durkheim's writings that he has more than just a *causal* view of education; he has a *deterministic* one. In *The Rules of Sociological Method*, for example, he states that

"all education is a continuous effort to impose on the child ways of seeing, feeling, and acting which he could not have arrived at spontaneously ... the aim of education is, precisely, the socialization of the human being; the process of education, therefore, gives us in a nutshell the historical fashion in which the social being is constituted.... This unremitting pressure to which the child is subjected is the very pressure of the social *milieu* which tends to fashion him in his own image, and of which parents and teachers are merely the representatives and intermediaries"[50].

Durkheim seems thoroughly preoccupied with fitting the child into his environment, that is, his present and immediate future society. But, again, we must remember that to Durkheim education was a "social thing", and it was concerned with mediating to the child a particular and given society, not society in general. He recognized, as a student of comparative education as well as of comparative sociology, that education varies from one society to another, and even within each society. To Durkheim the psychological analysis of the child, however useful, was not enough; it was inadequate to analyse for the child the nature of the civilization in which he was living, and which education was seeking to transmit.

In critically examining the various definitions of education and its nature, Durkheim argues that it is not the aim of education to present some picture of an ideal society to the child; nor is it the object of the educationist to consider some ideal form of education for such a society. To inquire what such an ideal form of education must be, when abstracted from conditions of both time and place, is "to admit implicitly that a system of education has no reality in itself"[51]. There is not just one form of education, ideal or actual, but many forms: there are, in fact, as many different forms of education "as there are different *milieux* in a given society"[52]. And so, society as a whole, and each particular *milieu*, will determine the type of education that is realized. Whilst, however, it is vital through education to preserve a degree of "homogeneity", and that by establishing in the child from the very beginning the "essential similarities" of collective life, it is also very important to ensure that there is a certain amount of "diversity" in society, without which all forms of co-operation would be impossible. Durkheim suggests that this diversity is assured by the very diversification and specialization of education itself[53].

Durkheim presents us with his own definition of education in terms which underline the demands and essential conditions of society, which are necessary for its very existence:

"Education is the influence exercised by adult generations on those that are not yet ready for social life. Its object is to arouse and to develop in the child a certain number of physical, intellectual and moral states which are demanded of him by both the political society as a whole and the special *milieu* for which he is specifically destined"[54].

Durkheim's view of education is that of a methodical socialization of the younger generation by the older; the teacher's natural ascendancy over his pupils, because of his superior culture and experience, will donate the required force to his influence. The individual, according to Durkheim, is a *homo duplex*: he is an individual being, made up of all the mental states that apply only to him and to the events of his personal life; and he is a social being, with a system of sentiments, ideas and practices which express in him, not his own discrete personality, but the group or groups of which he is a part. This social being (the *We* as opposed to the *I*) is composed of religious beliefs, moral beliefs, moral practices, collective opinions, and national or professional traditions. And it is the end of education to constitute this social being in each of us[55].

It would, perhaps, be too facile and dangerous, to make comparisons between Durkheim's "individual being" and "social being", and Freud's Ego and Super-Ego, to say nothing of George H. Mead's "Self" and the "Generalized Other". The detailed examination of these concepts would require far more space than we have here at our disposal; but it is interesting, to say the least, that in general terms the great psychologist and psycho-analyst, Freud, the greatly neglected social psychologist and philosopher, George H. Mead, and the sociologistic sociologist, Durkheim, all found a duality in man, a bipolarity of the "self" and "the other", the "I" and the "We", the individualized person and the socialized self. And, moreover, that there seems to be general agreement among them that self-fulfilment is achieved only when there is a correct balance between these two forces. It is, according to Durkheim, the great function of education to internalize the standards and beliefs of society and to socialize the individual. Durkheim did not dismiss entirely the influence of heredity and the *given* element in the child, but it is quite clear from one passage in *Education and Sociology* that he minimized it. One of his earliest comments on heredity, made in 1893 in *The Division of Labour*, was that there was room for believing that

"the hereditary contribution diminishes, not only in relative value, but in absolute value. Heredity becomes a lesser factor of human development, not only because there is an ever greater multitude of new acquisitions it cannot transmit, but also because those it transmits disturb individual variations less"[56].

In *Education and Sociology*, published posthumously in 1922, his view remains unchanged. He regards the tendencies which can be attributed to heredity as "vague and indefinite"; and the child, on entering life, effectively brings to it only his "nature as an individual". It is not quite clear what Durkheim means by this, although his next words seem to imply that the phrase connotes the fact of his individuality, and not any specific inherited factors. He continues:

"Society finds itself, with each new generation, faced with a *tabula rasa*, very nearly, on which it must build anew. To the egoistic and asocial being that has just been born it must, as rapidly as possible, add another, capable of leading a moral and social life. Such is the work of education, and you can readily see its great importance. It is not limited to developing the individual organism in the direction indicated by its nature, to elicit the hidden potentialities that need only be manifested. It creates in man a new being"[57].

But Durkheim still maintains that, contrary to the belief of Locke, education does not "make a man out of nothing", but that he has certain very general and vague predispositions which are also very malleable and flexible[58].

Durkheim discusses the role of the State in the process of education. It is obvious, he says, that society must be very interested in a procedure which is seeking to adapt the individual to itself, i.e. to his social *milieu* in which he is destined to live. And so society, or the State, must inform and constantly remind the teacher of those sentiments and ideas which it requires to be mediated to the child in order to adjust him to this *milieu*. Everything that in any way pertains to education must, therefore, to some extent, be submitted to the influence of the State. Durkheim discusses what some of these ideas and sentiments must be, in much the same way as some educationists today might discuss the "Core Values" which, they believe, should form a basis of their philosophy of education. He is willing to admit the great divergence of opinion here, but despite all this he considers that there exist, implicitly or explicitly, certain principles common to all, such as respect for reason, for science, for ideas and sentiments, which are at the base of democratic morality[59]. These principles the State should outline and ensure that they are taught in schools.

There are, however, apparent contradictions in Durkheim's writings. It would seem, according to some passages, that the educational system can change neither society nor itself. He states that:

"To the extent that real life increasingly takes possession of him [the child], it will come to destroy the work of the teacher. Education, therefore, can be reformed only if society itself is reformed"[60].

But how can society reform itself, except through some means or agent such as education? If each society seeks to train the type of human being it *needs* for its particular stage of civilization, and if it wants to change that stage, it would seem a reasonable assumption that society must train for this more desirable stage (and, therefore, more desirable type of human being), through its educational system. Again, in the same section of *Suicide*, Durkheim remarks that education is only "the image and reflection of society"; it imitates and reproduces the latter in an abbreviated form, but it does not *create* it[61]. This, once more, reflects a very deterministic view; and according to it all educators and teachers are simply the passive servants of the State, carrying out its decrees. As J. Barron Mays comments:

"To ignore the creative and moral significance of the individual altogether is, in the last analysis, untenable. Not only is it true that the net result of innovations within the educational field, by virtue of the fact that they work towards greater equality of opportunity, assists large numbers of people to rise in the socio-economic scale with important (sometimes perhaps unforeseen) consequences for social structure, but it is further clear that individuals within the system may elect to facilitate or obstruct the attainment of ultimate objectives"[62].

There is, and must be, an interaction between education and society. It is not merely a one-way process, as Durkheim seems to suggest, in which education is wholly determined by the State or the demands of society; but the structure of education can, in turn, change the social structure. Society at large may dictate the change, through the free election of political parties to power; and in turn the programme of education, its forms and structure will be to a large extent directed and controlled by the political and social aims of society at any particular time. The study of comparative education adequately reveals the fact that the ideologies, the political ideals, and the social aims of such a variety of countries as China, U.S.A., France, Germany, Malaysia, U.S.S.R. and England, are reflected in the educational systems of those countries. Education, however, does not merely reflect society; it co-operates with society to change it.

Despite his avowedly "sociological" approach to his problems, Durkheim does at times, as G. H. Bantock has noted[63], appear to move from the realm of fact to that of value, and makes what at first sight appears to be a value-judgement. In chapter three of *Education and Sociology*, Durkheim discusses "Pedagogy and Sociology". During the course of the discussion he maintains that "our pedagogic ideal is explained by our social structure", and suggests that society builds the model of the human type that it requires. He goes on to say that

"The man whom education should realize in us is not the man such as nature has made him, but as the society wishes him to be; and it wishes him such as its internal economy calls for. . . . Every change of any importance in the organization of a society results in a change of the same importance in the idea that man makes of himself. . . . Thus, in the present as in the past, our pedagogical ideal is in every detail the work of society. It is society that draws for us the portrait of the kind of man we should be, and in this portrait all the peculiarities of its organization come to be reflected"[64].

Professor G. H. Bantock has criticized Durkheim's position here by suggesting that even if education does often reflect the nature of the social system, it does not necessarily follow that it *ought* to, as Durkheim's use of "should" twice in the above passage seems to imply. Bantock maintains that there is actually "no necessary correlation between change in social structure and change in social doctrine"[65]. No doubt Bantock is justified in his criticism and in his conclusion; but there are one or two points to note in relation to Durkheim's use and concept of judgements. In his *Sociology and Philosophy* he draws the distinction between a judgement of reality, which is simply a judgement of existence, and a judgement of value, which expresses a relation between a socially held ideal and an object. The value-judgement is neither a statement about the nature of things nor yet a subjective appreciation: it is *a social, an objective evaluation*. He goes on to say that

"The principal social phenomena, religion, morality, law, economics and aesthetics, are nothing more than systems of values and hence ideals. Sociology moves from the beginning in the field of ideals—that is its starting-point and not the gradually attained end of its researches. The ideal is in fact its peculiar field of study. . . . It does not set out to construct ideals, but on the contrary accepts them as given facts, as objects of study, and it tries to analyse and explain them. . . . The aim is to bring the ideal, in its various forms, into the sphere of nature, with its distinctive attributes unimpaired"[66].

No doubt Durkheim would argue that his "should" or "ought" in the previously quoted passage connotes "in order to be socially successful" or "socially adapted", rather than the fulfilment of any particular preconceived ideal, whether related or unrelated to the present society. He would, perhaps, further argue that we tend to become like the portrait drawn for us by society because, basically, we want to conform to the level of success and adjustment or adaptation that we see around us. Durkheim is thinking of the actualization of the social ideal in terms of social realism or social pragmatism. It would have made no difference to Durkheim's argument or meaning if, instead of "should", he had used the word "must". Durkheim, as Bantock has pointed out, is an environmentalist; to him nurture, from the time of birth to the completion of school education, is paramount. He was convinced that if pupils were to be prepared for life and society, it was first of all necessary to have an objective, methodical, and thorough-going "break-down" of the society for which they were being prepared. This meant an investigation both of the macro-society and also of the more immediate micro-society in which the pupils lived. Uppermost in his mind was the aim of mediating to the pupils the nature of the larger society into which they were born, and of the local community and *milieu* in which they were nurtured. In this way, the individual would learn the sort of man he *must* be in his society and how he might live maximally in his world. Education was the *agency* whereby society perpetually recreated itself; an agency both uniform and diverse. But Durkheim's complete neglect of the factor of heredity in this educative process is just as unjustifiable as any complete rejection of environmental factors; in the words of G. H. Bantock:

"Hereditary factors place considerable limitations on human adaptability. More important, the very power assigned to the environment should inhibit us from thinking that school education can bring about rapid reorientation"[67].

Perhaps the foregoing might appear to give a picture of personality which is completely formed by society and determined by its cultural *milieu*, its beliefs, its ideas and its practices, without any freedom to disagree or be different. Yet, to Durkheim, freedom ultimately derived from the acceptance of the rationality of the internalization of social demands. "To be free is not to do what one pleases"[68], it is to know how to act with reason, how to perform one's duty, how to take on self-responsibility. The ultimate autonomy of the individual does not imply anarchy of thought and behaviour; it is for this very reason that the authority of the teacher is employed, in order gradually to endow the individual with self-mastery. The authority of the teacher is, for the child, an aspect of the authority of reason and of duty; it is an element which the child internalizes and to which he later returns and finds, when necessary, within his own conscience[69]. The element of discipline is strong in Durkheim's pedagogy because, he feels, it is only through the initial external discipline which the individual experiences that he learns to become self-disciplined and autonomous. If the first element of morality is the external imposition of it, and the second element is the gradual internalization of it, then the third element is the understanding and rational acceptance of it—which is the greatest freedom we can enjoy. Discipline is indispensable to the child's equilibrium: without it, both within and outside the child, there would exist a state of anomy. Thus education becomes a means of organizing the individual self and the social self, or the *homo duplex*, into a disciplined, stable, meaningful unity.

The "interiorization" or "internalization" of values and discipline, then, represented for Durkheim the child's initiation into his society; and perhaps all that one can really say about this view is that if the values are "good" (i.e. have survival value), then the child will be "good" according to the standards of his society, and he will survive. But if the society's values are "bad" (i.e. self-destructive), then they will be reflected in the sort of citizens that the society produces—anomic, destructive and deviant. It was in the realm of moral education that Durkheim did some of his most critical, as well as constructive, work. He recognized that it was ultimately the *moral values*, and not discipline, which were of paramount importance. Discipline, he accepted, was "only a means of specifying and imposing the required behaviour"[70]; although it was an indispensable means. But to act morally, to respect discipline, to be committed to a group, were not enough. We must know *why* we behave in a particular way, we must know the reasons for our conduct[71]. But if we attain to this, then the ancient, God-sanctioned *ipse dixit* will no longer suffice. Indeed, Durkheim in a very real way saw our modern dilemma in relation to religious and moral education; and in his *Moral Education* he sees the new approach to morality as both scientific and rationalistic; moral re-education will be lay education, it will set forth new ideals and provide a new set of moral beliefs, informing individuals with a sense of purpose.

"We can no longer make use of the traditional system, which, moreover, has for long only kept itself going by a miracle of balance, by the force of habit. For a long time now it has not rested on a solid enough basis; for a long time it has not rested on beliefs strong enough to enable it effectively to discharge its functions. But to replace it usefully it is not enough to tear off the labels. It will not do to take away a few tags, at the risk moreover of taking away at the same time substantial realities. We have to go forward to a recasting of our educational techniques"[72].

REFERENCES

1. Tiryakian, E. A.: *Sociologism and Existentialism*. Prentice-Hall, 1962, p. 4.
2. *Ibid.* p. 4.
3. *Vide* Nisbet, R. A.: *Emile Durkheim*. Prentice-Hall, 1965, p. 28.
4. *Ibid.* p. 28.
5. Durkheim, E.: *The Rules of Sociological Method*. Collier-Macmillan, Free Press, Glencoe, 1938 (Paperback Edition, 1964). *Vide* especially pp. 20–1, 29, 81–2, 99–100. Note his comment on p. 21: "So here again a certain conception of social reality is substituted for reality itself. What is thus defined is clearly not society but Spencer's idea of it."
6. *Ibid.* pp. 143–4.
7. *Vide The Rules of Sociological Method*, Introduction by George E. G. Catlin, p. xi *et passim*.
8. *Ibid.* p. 13.
9. *Ibid.* p. 8.
10. *Ibid.* p. 10.
11. *Ibid.* p. 18.
12. *Vide ibid.* pp. 27–46.
13. *Ibid.* p. 49.
14. *Vide ibid.* pp. 50–64.
15. *Ibid.* p. 66, n. 10.
16. *Ibid.* p. 70.
17. *Ibid.* p. 95.
18. *Ibid.* p. 106.
19. *Ibid.* p. 113.
20. *Vide ibid.* pp. 125–40.
21. *Vide ibid.* pp. 141–6.
22. *Ibid.* p. 103.
23. *Ibid.* p. xiv.
24. Ginsberg, M.: *The Psychology of Society*. Methuen, 1964 (9th Edition), University Paperback, pp. 46–51.
25. *Vide* Nisbet, R. A., *Op. cit.*, p. 26.

26. Durkheim, E.: *The Division of Labour in Society*. Free Press, Glencoe, Collier-Macmillan, 1964, p. 79.
27. *Ibid*. pp. 79–80.
28. *The Rules of Sociological Method*, p. 103n.
29. Ginsberg, M.: *Op. cit.*, pp. 47–8.
30. Durkheim, E.: *Sociology and Philosophy*. Cohen & West, 1965 (Revised Edition), p. 54.
31. Ginsberg, M.: *Op. cit.*, p. 48.
32. *Vide* Nisbet, R. A.: *Op. cit.*, p. 41.
33. Ginsberg, M.: *Op. cit.*, p. 51.
34. Durkheim, E.: *Sociology and Philosophy*, Introduction, p. xxiii.
35. Nisbet, R. A.: *Op. cit.*, p. 48.
36. Durkheim, E.: *Moral Education: A Study in the Theory and Application of the Sociology of Education*. Glencoe, Free Press, 1961; *Vide* pp. 67–8.
37. *Vide* Tiryakian, E. A.: *Op. cit.*, Chapter III, pp. 22–46 *passim*. Quotation from p. 22.
38. *Ibid*. p. 22.
39. *Ibid*. p. 23.
40. *Vide* Thouless, R. H.: *General and Social Psychology*. U.T.P., 1958 (4th Edition, Reprinted 1963), p. 269.
41. *Vide* Jung, C. G.: *The Archetypes and the Collective Unconscious*. Routledge, 1959.
42. *Vide* de Chardin, P. T.: *The Future of Man*. Collins, 1965.
43. Parsons, T. *et al.* (ed.): *Theories of Society*. Free Press, Collier-Macmillan, 1965, p. 15.
44. Halbwachs, M.: *Les Causes du Suicide*. Paris, 1930. *Vide* Durkheim, E.: *Suicide*, Editor's Introduction, p. 17.
45. Stengel, E.: *Suicide and Attempted Suicide*. Penguin Books (Pelican), 1964, p. 47.
46. Durkheim, E.: *Suicide*. Routledge, 1952 (Reprinted 1963), p. 382.
47. *Ibid*. p. 16.
48. *Ibid*. p. 372.
49. *The Rules of Sociological Method*, p. 141.
50. *Ibid*. p. 6.
51. Durkheim, E.: *Education and Sociology*. Free Press, Glencoe, 1956, pp. 64–5.
52. *Ibid*. p. 67.
53. *Ibid*. p. 70.
54. *Ibid*. p. 71.
55. *Ibid*. p. 72.
56. *The Division of Labour in Society*, p. 321.
57. *Education and Sociology*, p. 72.

58. *Ibid.* pp. 82–3.
59. *Ibid.* p. 81.
60. *Suicide*, p. 373.
61. *Ibid.* p. 372.
62. Mays, J. B.: *Education and the Urban Child.* Liverpool Univ. Press, 1962, p. 9.
63. Bantock, G. H.: *Education and Values.* Faber, 1965. *Vide* his essay, "Education and Society", pp. 118–37.
64. *Education and Sociology*, pp. 122–3.
65. Bantock, G. H.: *Op. cit.*, pp. 119–20.
66. *Sociology and Philosophy*, p. 96.
67. *Op. cit.*, p. 133.
68. *Education and Sociology*, p. 89.
69. *Ibid.* p. 90.
70. *Vide Moral Education*, pp. 31–2.
71. *Ibid.* p. 120.
72. *Ibid.* This passage is quoted by H. L. Elvin in his *Education and Contemporary Society*, Watts, 1965, p. 206, at the conclusion of a valuable discussion on "Moral Values in Education", pp. 193–206.

BIBLIOGRAPHY

A. BOOKS BY DURKHEIM

The Division of Labour in Society. (1893) Macmillan, 1933; Collier-Macmillan, 1964.

The Rules of Sociological Method. (1895) Univ. of Chicago Press, 1938; Collier-Macmillan, 1964.

Suicide: A Study in Sociology. (1897) Glencoe, Free Press, 1951; Routledge, 1952.

The Elementary Forms of Religious Life. (1912) Allen & Unwin, 1915; Glencoe, Free Press, 1954.

Education and Sociology. (1922) Glencoe, Free Press, 1956.

Sociology and Philosophy. (1924) Glencoe, Free Press, 1953; Cohen & West, 1965 (Revised Edition).

Moral Education: A Study in the Theory and Application of the Sociology of Education. (1925) Glencoe, Free Press, 1961.

Socialism and Saint-Simon. (1928) Routledge, 1959.

Professional Ethics and Civic Morals. (1950) Routledge, 1957.

Montesquieu and Rousseau. (1953) Univ. of Michigan Press, 1960.

Durkheim, E. & Mauss, M.: *Primitive Classification.* Cohen & West, 1963.

B. OTHER BOOKS OF REFERENCE

Alpert, H.: *Emile Durkheim and his Sociology*. Columbia Univ. Press, 1939; Russell, Inc., N.Y., 1961.

Bantock, G. H.: *Education and Values*. Faber, 1965.

Ginsberg, M.: *On the Diversity of Morals*. Heinemann, 1956. (Section on "Durkheim's Ethical Theory").

—: *The Psychology of Society*. Methuen, University Paperbacks, 1964 (9th Edition), pp. 46–51.

Nisbet, R. A.: *Emile Durkheim*. Prentice-Hall, 1965.

Parsons, T. *et al.* (ed.): *Theories of Society*. Free Press, Collier-Macmillan, 1965.

Parsons, T.: *The Structure of Social Action*. Glencoe, Free Press, 1949 (2nd Edition) (especially chapters VIII–XII).

Tiryakian, E. A.: *Sociologism and Existentialism*. Prentice-Hall, 1962.

Wolff, K. H.: *Emile Durkheim, 1858–1917*. Ohio State Univ. Press, 1960.

CHAPTER 12

GEORGE H. MEAD (1863–1931)

George H. Mead was born at South Hadley, Massachusetts, U.S.A., on February 27th, 1863. His father was the pastor of the local congregation at South Hadley and was eventually appointed to the Chair in Homiletics at the Theological Seminary, Oberlin, in Ohio. It is clear that social relationships and their problems interested George H. Mead from quite an early age, and in 1879 he entered Oberlin College to study for the A.B. degree. This degree involved a large range of subjects including classics, rhetoric, literature, moral philosophy, mathematics and a certain amount of elementary science. The range of thought observable in Mead's work—most of which has been collated from his students' notes—may be attributed to this broad, non-specialist study for his first degree.

He graduated in 1883 and began teaching in what was regarded at the time as a very tough school, and one in which many of the pupils learned virtually nothing. Apparently Mead was determined that some of them at least should learn something, so he began to weed out the roughest characters and sent them home. He then got down to the serious work of teaching those who were really interested. The authorities, however, frowned on this attempt to educate an élite, so Mead left the school to do some private tutoring and land surveying.

In 1887, after several years of intensive reading in all branches of learning, he entered Harvard University and graduated in 1888. He then went abroad, travelling in Europe and studying in particular philosophy and psychology. He married an old friend, Helen Castle, in 1891 and settled down at Ann Arbor, Michigan, where he became an instructor in the Department of Philosophy and Psychology. This work suited him admirably and in 1893, at the age of thirty, he went to the University of Chicago where John Dewey was already Professor of Philosophy. Dewey was only four years his senior, and there developed a friendship between the two which lasted until the death of Mead in 1931.

Apart from his occasional contributions to learned journals in the fields of sociology, philosophy, psychology, ethics and education—about seventy articles between 1894 and 1931—Mead left no major work. Even when lecturing Mead used very few notes, and in consequence any reconstruction from his lectures would have been extremely difficult were it not for the fact that a number of his students early realized the vital importance of what Mead was teaching. As a result some of them made very full notes of his lectures, and these have been edited and published by the University of Chicago Press. These works cover the whole field of Mead's particular interests—social psychology, social philosophy, the history of ideas, and systematic pragmatism.

In his Introduction to Mead's *Mind, Self and Society*, Professor Charles W. Morris says that

"Philosophically, Mead was a pragmatist; scientifically, he was a social psychologist. He belonged to an old tradition—the tradition of Aristotle, Descartes, Leibniz; of Russell, Whitehead, Dewey—which fails to see any sharp separation or any antagonism between the activities of science and philosophy, and whose members are themselves both scientists and philosophers"[1].

It is perhaps in the area of social psychology that Mead has made his most distinctive contribution. Mead was very much concerned with the *determinants* of the individual's behaviour, with what it was that made any person act in a particular way. Mead was also concerned with the relations and inter-relations of human behaviour to the more intimate contexts of interaction in which the individual found himself. In other words, he looked for the *normative components* of the determination of social interaction. We are reminded here somewhat of Durkheim's search for, and eliciting of, norms in society.

Mead had studied under Royce, and Royce, like Hegel, stressed the social nature of the self and of morality. Mead, as we shall see presently, regarded the self as a social rather than as a purely psychological phenomenon. The self and the mind were both social emergents, that is, they were generated in a social process without remainder.

But although this self with which he is concerned is a *social product*, it is, nevertheless, an individual identity. Our very sense of difference from other people, whom we internalize in a web of relations, is in the nature of a social product. Mead was also very much concerned with the problems of communication, for language, in the form of vocal gesture, provides the very mechanism for the emergence of mind and the self. It is language that makes the distinctively human society possible. Since, to Mead, the essence of all human experience is social, he attempts to define the various dimensions that help to make up the facts of an individual's actions when he is in the presence of others. This is the very nature of social psychology[2].

B. THE IDEA OF THE SELF

In *Mind, Self and Society* Mead maintains that it is social intercourse which makes us human beings. Aristotle claimed that man was a "social (or political) animal", and this is virtually the burden of Mead's discussion of the development of the self. An infant, for example, has no idea of himself as a separate being; he has been referred to as "a bundle of needs arising out of inner tensions, and capacities to respond to stimulation"[3]. The infant is not yet a self, an Ego, or an "I"; for to become an "I" in the fullest sense there must be social interaction.

Mead's position is behaviouristic; he suggests that the non-human animals interact with one another, and that the behaviour in one animal causes behaviour in another. To put it another way, he suggests that the action of one acts as a cue to the action of another. This is what happens when animals play or fight. Mead further argues that animals act without *intention*, whereas the peculiarity of human interaction is that it is purposeful; and the means of communication from gesture to language are meaningful. In *Mind, Self and Society* he says:

"The dog only stands on its hind legs and walks when we use a particular word, but the dog cannot give to himself that stimulus which somebody else gives to him. He can respond to it but he cannot himself take a hand, so to speak, in conditioning his own reflexes; his reflexes can be conditioned by another but he cannot do it himself. Now, it is characteristic of significant speech that just this process of self-conditioning is going on all the time"[4].

"Intention", "meaningful" and "significant" are, however, rather question-begging words. The researches of August Krogh[5] and Karl von Frisch[6], for example, in the realm of the language of bees, and even the dialects within their language, indicate that whilst such behaviour may be instinctual and without "intention", it certainly cannot be said that it is not meaningful and significant, unless very special definitions are given to those words so as to preclude such behaviour. Moreover, the songs and other calls of birds are not merely joyous outbursts—they make up a complex communications system, with the various sounds suited to various types of message. Dr W. H. Thorpe, however, argues that whilst even complex songs may depend primarily on the inherited make-up of a bird,

"The evidence is far from negligible that the songs of some thrushes, the warblers and the nightingale exhibit elaborate esthetic improvement far beyond what strict biological necessity requires. ... Much of it, of course, may be merely part of the trial-and-error process of learning, but in those cases of vocal imitation where new phrases are produced only after long delay and apparently without specific practice, another influence must be at work"[7].

Without attempting to draw too many conclusions from this esthetic improvement far beyond what strict biological necessity the "process of self-conditioning", and that it is meaningful and significant.

Mead goes on to argue that human beings make gestures which are *calculated* to elicit a response, and that this comes about by the individual taking on the role of the other with whom he is interacting. Gradually the child, for example, acquires the capacity to respond in a kind of *imaginative* way, to his own projected conduct. He rehearses within himself exactly what he is going to do, and inwardly he responds to himself. Should the response that he obtains prove to be unsatisfactory, then he tries again until an act is pictured in his mind which elicits within himself the reflection of the satisfactory response which, in turn, he hopes to draw forth from the real Other outside him. He can then make a sign, a gesture or sound which is meaningful, in the sense that it is calculated to produce the desired effect.

Now, it might be argued that any animal can produce sounds or gestures "calculated" to produce the desired effect, but no doubt Mead would reply that "calculated" in this context does not signify "intentioned", "reasoned" or even "imagined", but simply "adapted to", "suitable for", or "determined to" produce a particular effect. In other words, there is a deterministic cause and effect relationship in animal behaviour, but there is not, as in human behaviour, any cognitive recognition of it, or any intention or mental calculation.

Mead further maintains that among the gestures the human animal makes is Speech, which is audible both to himself and to the person to whom he is speaking. In speech the individual is able to respond to himself with the expected response of the Other more easily than in the case of other bodily gestures. "The vocal gesture, then, has an importance which no other gesture has"[8]. According to Mead the meaning of what we are saying is the tendency to respond to it—

"You are always replying to yourself, just as other people reply. You assume that in some degree there must be identity in the reply. It is action on a common basis"[9].

A person directs behaviour towards himself, converses with himself and passes judgement upon himself. Thus, the self, which does not exist at birth, arises in social experience as a result of taking on the role of others.

The self is not primarily the physiological organism[10]. And although the physiological organism may be essential to it, at least we can think of a self without it. The self is essentially a social structure, and it arises in social experience. Indeed,

"After a self has arisen, it in a certain sense provides for itself its social experiences, and so we can conceive of an absolutely solitary self. But it is impossible to conceive of a self arising outside of social experience"[11].

Mead points out that the conversation of gestures is the beginning of communication, and that the individual begins to carry on a conversation of gestures with himself: he says something which calls out a certain reply in himself, and that in turn makes him change what he was going to say. This is what Mead terms "significant speech". Thinking is thus preparatory to social action. It is interesting to note that Mead considers that Spearman's "X factor" in intelligence is simply this ability of the intelligent individual to take the attitude of the other, or the attitudes of others generally, thus realizing the significance of the gestures and symbols in terms of which thinking proceeds; and so being enabled to carry on with himself the internal conversation with these gestures and symbols.

C. THE DEVELOPMENT OF THE SELF

A child at quite an early age begins to place himself in the position of others, but it is done in a very imitative and uncomprehending manner. For example, he may copy his father by "reading" the newspaper, but as likely as not it will be upside-down. This stage is rather meaningless for him at first, except that he wants to do what others are doing within the family circle, and in this he finds some identity with the Other. At this early stage, however, there is little self-awareness or self-observation.

Around the third year of his life the selfhood of the child develops, as in his daydreams; and in his play with dolls, toys and other children he begins to assume the roles of others. And in his taking on the roles of others he finds himself in the position of being tolerably able to act towards himself as others do. He thus becomes an object to himself. In this form of play he has

"a set of stimuli which calls out in itself the sort of responses they call out in others. He takes this group of responses and organizes them into a certain whole. Such is the simplest form of being another to one's self. It involves a temporal situation. The child says something in one character and responds in another character, and then his responding in another character is a stimulus to himself in the first character, and so the conversation goes on. A certain organized structure arises in him and in his other which replies to it, and these carry on a conversation of gestures between themselves"[12].

He takes the place of his mother, his father, his brother or sister and of the heroes in his life in a whole variety of roles, or series of

selves. His power of integration and generalization are at a minimum, and we find, in consequence, very little consistency in his
behaviour, and no stable self has yet been formed.

Play represents, then, a simple succession of one role after
another—a situation which is quite characteristic of the child's
own personality. The Game, on the other hand, introduces a
definite unity into the organization of other selves; it is, in fact, an
illustration of the situation out of which an organized personality
arises, for in it the child becomes an organic member of society.
"The importance of the game is that it lies entirely inside the
child's own experience . . ."[13]. There follows, therefore, a
development of unity and the building up of the self.

Mead exemplifies this process by a person playing a ball game;
each one of his own acts is determined by his assumption of the
actions of others who are playing the game. What he does is controlled by his being everyone else on that team, at least in so far
as those attitudes affect his own particular response. We get, then,
an "Other" which is an organization of the attitudes of those
involved in the same process. Mead points out that this organization is put in the form of the rules of the game, and this of course
is true. All children like rules, and take such an interest in them
that if they are lacking in any particular game they will invent
them on the spot. But, of course, as the child understands the
nature and the finer points of the game better, so he will take on
the role of others not merely in an understanding of the rules of
the game, important though these may be. If the game is cricket
and he is bowling, he must so understand the functions of each of
his fielders that he will be able to place them precisely where he
knows the batsman will send the ball; he must thus understand
fully the role of the batsman. His wicket-keeper must also be fully
aware of the type of bowling he is going to send down so that
should the batsman miss he will be able to deal with the situation.

"In his game he has to have an organization of these roles; otherwise he cannot play the game. The game represents the passage in
the life of the child from taking the role of others in play to the
organized part that is essential to self-consciousness in the full
sense of the term"[14].

The organized community or social group which gives to the
individual his unity of self is referred to by Mead as the Generalized

Other; and the attitude of the Generalized Other is the attitude of the whole community. In a ball team, the team is the Generalized Other in so far as it enters, as an organized process or social activity, the experience of any one of the individual members of it. As a member of the team the individual anticipates the behaviour of all the other members; he plays a number of roles simultaneously, a generalized role of a number of people. These roles, as we have said, are built around the rules, objects and techniques of the game, and as the individual appropriates these rules and techniques so he generalizes his behaviour—he plays the role of the Generalized Other.

The team with its rules is thus a prototype of the organized community; and eventually the whole community of which he is a member becomes the Generalized Other with which the child becomes identified. As this identification takes place so the values of his society become incorporated into his neural system, or internalized. Thus the self, viewed in this way, consists in an organization of the roles taken over from the community as a Generalized Other.

A prerequisite of the fullest possible development of the individual self is the getting of the broadest activities of any given social whole, or organized society as such, within the experiential field of any of the individuals involved or included in that whole[15]. The separate roles, of which we spoke earlier and which are now organized and internalized, become what we call "social attitudes". These social attitudes imply that the social process, with its various implications, is in fact taken up into the experience of the individual and in consequence that which is going on in society takes place more effectively because the individual has rehearsed it[16]. Not only does the individual fulfil his role better under these conditions, but he is able also to reach back upon the organization of which he is a fundamental part.

D. THE "I", THE "ME", AND THE "OTHER"

Mead never tires of emphasizing that the self-conscious personality that gradually evolves is a *social* product. But, once the self starts to develop, a hard central core comes into being and grows harder as the years go by. Mead makes the claim that each child has its own innate range of potentialities, and that he will receive the impact of society in his own particular way. This means, inevitably, that the Generalized Other will not be exactly the same for everyone, and that the understanding of the roles of others will be conditioned by individual experience.

Mead indicates further that each individual has his own biological needs for food, drink, sexual satisfaction and protection. These may well, from time to time, conflict with the demands of the Generalized Other. If the socialized attitudes which go to make up the Other have been absorbed and internalized, then the individual may well come to terms with his own conflicting needs. If these attitudes have not been absorbed, then the ensuing conflict may resolve into anti-social or deviant behaviour; and some form of reconditioning may have to take place in order that the individual may internalize the accepted norms of social behaviour.

Once the organization of the self is under way it then proceeds under integrative principles of its own. Mead accepts, of course, that in the normal person this process of self-integration has due regard for the needs, the demands, the "rules" of society—but all selves are different, and the "rules" will therefore be interpreted differently even within the same society. There are, however, umpires within the society to ensure that deviation from the accepted interpretation is not too wide. Mead further maintains that when we reflect upon ourselves we become possessed of a cherished object, with merit and prestige; and thus we have the power of reasoning, we acquire standards, and we have the power to reflect upon them.

The self is not so much a substance as a process in which a conversation between the "I" and the "Me" takes place, as it were. The "Me" is the more or less integrated set of attitudes and ideas of other people which we have built together as our conscious experience, and from which we choose roles to represent our own ideas of ourselves. Many of these are roles which we know the community has come to expect us to perform. The "I" is the self as actor or initiator, the agent of change; without the "I" there could not be the notion of novelty or unexpectedness in experience. While differing aspects of "Me" depend upon my social and cultural training and the particular configurations of time and place, the "I" represents the sense of self-identity in the possessor of the experiences[17].

In a stable society the generalized image, which Mead calls the

Generalized Other, and sometimes simply the Other, is relatively settled, and the varieties of interpretation are few because the main roles are appreciated and well understood. But in a heterogeneous society and a changing society we have a whole series of generalized others—such societies are those to be found in large cities like Chicago, London, Liverpool, etc. Mead suggests that only by taking the attitudes of the Generalized Other towards himself can man think at all. The self-conscious individual takes or assumes the organized social attitudes of the given social group or community to which he belongs, and toward the social problems of various kinds which confront that group or community at any given time.

In his valuable book entitled *Human Groups*, Professor W. J. H. Sprott remarks:

"It will be seen that Mead's account is not unlike the tripartite analysis of the self proposed by the psycho-analysts. The 'generalized' other is like the 'super-ego', whilst Mead's spontaneous 'I' is like the psycho-analysts' 'id'. The 'me' is certainly not like the psycho-analysts' 'ego', but that is because the two systems were constructed for different purposes"[18].

It is of some interest here to note that both Freud and Mead were concerned with the effects of social experience upon the self. The Super-Ego represented for Freud the internalization of the external authority of parents, teachers and so on; the Generalized Other was for Mead the internalization by the individual of the attitudes of the whole community, whereby he obtains his unity of the self.

E. THE CONCEPT OF ROLE

We have said that according to Mead the self is constituted in the act of adopting the attitudes of others; to be another is to play his role. For Mead it must follow that there is no human nature outside society. What the personality internalizes is an object system, a role-expectation for the self and for the Other. This role-expectation is the basic unit of the social system; and two or more complementary role-expectations make up a Role System, which is the smallest type of social system studied in sociology. In *The Philosophy of the Act* Mead maintains that it is the capacity of the human individual to assume the organized attitudes of the community towards himself and towards others that distinguishes the duties, rights, customs, laws and the various institutions and role systems in human society from the physiological relationships of an ant nest or a beehive. Mead goes on to add that

"The attainment of this attitude on the part of the individual is responsible for the appearance of a situation in which new values arise, especially within which society deals with the individual as embodying the values in himself. This situation is expressed in the appearance of institutions, e.g., the church, government, art, and education"[19].

Mead thus suggests that social control is internalized, since the essence of all human experience is social; hence perception and communication are social. The internalization of the Other, "the taking of the role of the Other", is an intrinsic aspect of human thinking; and leadership in any form in society becomes the prerogative of the individual most able to internalize the roles of others. The leader is a "multiple participator".

In Section 33 of *Mind, Self and Society*[20], Mead considers some of the social foundations and functions of thought and communication. Communication involves participation in the Other, that is, taking the role of the Other. This requires the appearance of the Other in the self and the identification of the Other with the self. This implies, in turn, the reaching of self-consciousness through the Other. This participation in and identification with the Other is perhaps expressed best by the word "empathy" (cf. German *Einfühlung*), although Mead himself uses the word "sympathy"[21]. "It is through taking this role of the other that he is able to come back on himself and so direct his own process of communication"[22]. As the individual becomes self-conscious so he becomes self-critical; and, through self-criticism, social control over the individual behaviour or conduct operates by virtue of the social origin and basis of such criticism. Self-criticism is essentially social criticism, and behaviour controlled by such self-criticism is essentially behaviour socially controlled.

F. GESTURE, SYMBOL AND LANGUAGE

In his discussion of Mind[23] Mead considers at some length the origin and development of language. He criticizes Wundt's theory of imitation and states that "Imitation as a general instinct is now discredited in human psychology"[24]. Moreover, there is no evidence of any general tendency on the part of forms to imitate each other. He accepts, however, that there is a tendency to imitate among men, and in particular to reproduce vocal gestures. Imitation depends upon the individual influencing himself as others influence him, so that he is under not only the influence of the other but also the influence of himself, in so far as he uses the same vocal gestures. The vocal gesture has an importance that no other gesture has; for whilst we cannot see ourselves when our faces assume certain expressions, if we hear ourselves speak we are more apt to pay attention. A man hears himself when he is irritated, for example, using a tone that is of an irritable quality, and so he catches himself.

When someone significantly says something with his own vocal process he is saying it to himself as well as to everybody else within the reach of his voice. It is only the vocal gesture to which one responds, or tends to respond, as another person tends to respond to it; and it is, therefore, the most fitted type of significant communication.

Language mediates; it is a principle of social organization which makes the distinctively human society possible. Mead links this possibility closely with the facts of the organism, including, in the human case, the dependence of the organism on other organisms and on an environing context in which organisms are sustained. The "I" and the "Me" are perceived as engaged in an inner dialogue to which the "I" contributes an unpredictable and creative element. The "Me" is a somewhat ambiguous concept, compounded of the "I" as object and of the incorporated social attitudes.

The Generalized Other opens up many vistas for the way in which we structure our social world. Mead speaks of the "normalcy of multiple personality"[25] (cf. Durkheim's normalcy of crime); there is a normality about the internalization by the individual of the multiple personalities of his society, particularly through the media of gesture, symbol and language. Social phenomena, says Mead, are facilitated by language which is the instrument of meaning *par excellence*; and symbolization provides the indispensable medium of higher-level communication.

In our thought we are "more or less unconsciously seeing our-

selves as others see us. We are unconsciously addressing ourselves
as others address us; in the same way as the sparrow takes up the
note of the canary we pick up the dialects about us"[26].

To Mead the critical importance of language in the development of human experience lies in the fact that the stimulus is one
that can react upon the speaking individual as it does upon the
other. So that, for example, if one person speaks of a dog to
another person he is arousing in himself the same set of responses
as he is arousing in the other individual[27]. This organized set of
responses, which represents thought or mentation, is something
that an animal (it is assumed) is incapable of arousing. The animal
does not think; he does not put himself in a position for which he
is responsible; he does not put himself in the place of the other[28].

Adjustment between human beings is made through communication, and the central factor in such adjustment is "meaning".
Meaning arises and lies within the field of the relation between
the gesture of a given human organism and the subsequent behaviour of this organism as indicated to another human organism
by that gesture. Meaning is implicit, if not always explicit, in the
relationship among the various phases of the social act to which it
refers, and out of which it develops. And its development takes
place in terms of symbolization at the human evolutionary level.

Symbolization, says Mead, constitutes objects which were not
constituted before; indeed, it constitutes objects which would not
exist except for the context of social relationships wherein such
symbolization occurs.

"Language does not simply symbolize a situation or object which
is already there in advance; it makes possible the existence or the
appearance of that situation or object, for it is a part of the
mechanism whereby that situation or object is created"[29].

The social process is concerned with relating the responses of one
person to the gestures of another, as the "meanings" of the latter,
and it is in consequence responsible for the rise and the existence
of new objects in the social situation. These objects are dependent
upon or constituted by these meanings.

Mead warns against a too subtle attempt at solving the problem
of "the meaning of meaning". Meaning is not to be thought of as
a state of consciousness, or as a set of organized relations existing
mentally outside the field of experience into which they enter.

Meaning must be conceived as having its existence entirely within the field itself. The response which one organism makes to the gesture of another in any given social act is the meaning of that gesture. Mead adds that it is also in a sense responsible for the appearance or coming into being of the new object—or the new content of an old object—to which that gesture refers[30].

G. SOME IMPLICATIONS FOR EDUCATION

Mead's sociological theory of the self does not begin with a philosophic position such as the idealist's. For Mead the self is

"not a metaphysical entity, it is a process of behaviour and response realized in time. It is not innate or given from birth, it is built up from experience and it gains its definition in response to and in opposition to the social process in which it is set"[31].

Karl Mannheim, who was considerably influenced by the social psychology of Mead, goes on to say that Mead does not deny to man a unique psychological endowment—this he undoubtedly has. It is this psychological endowment that enables him to become self-conscious; but only the external, social field in which he dwells can provide the form or context of that self-consciousness or personality. To Mead the mind is a social emergent, and he has gone so far as to add that

"mind is nothing but the importation of this external process into the conduct of the individual so as to meet the problems that arise"[32].

Thus Mead emphasizes the great importance of the social *milieu* in the development of the individual. In the discussion of the aims of education it is frequently, and sometimes rather loosely, claimed that the important goal to achieve is the fullest possible development of the personality, the eliciting of innate qualities, and so forth. But according to Mead the self is not a seed in us, called "personality", which must be carefully and tenderly nurtured, and allowed the maximum freedom for growth. Nothing could be further from reality. The type of environment will determine the type of personality. A social environment which is permissive will shape and evolve one kind of personality; an environment which is authoritarian will elicit another. According to Mead, permission is not the *removal* of social influence so that the innate or "natural" personality may have a chance to develop (cf. Rousseau's "naturalism"); permissiveness merely replaces one kind of social influence for another.

This would seem to imply that we can have ultimately, in our society—indeed, *will* have—the sort of personalities we want to evolve according to the social context or environment that we provide for the growing child. This is a frankly naturalistic interpretation of personality, and not in any way a supernatural one. It is a behaviouristic approach to the nature of the self and the meaning of personality. The self, the child, emerges out of social experience. The conclusion drawn by Karl Mannheim is a very important one:

"Responsibility is not a quality with which we are born but emerges out of the chances we have had to learn, according to our degree of maturity, how to act responsibly, so that as time has passed we have been able to develop a concept of what it means"[33].

It is obvious from the foregoing, on the basis of Mead's analysis, that it is very vital to provide within the educational framework, which is the most important part of the society to which the child belongs, the right sort of chances for the learning of responsibility. This kind of experience can best be achieved in the community life relationships of people.

Thus, a child does not possess a self at birth, and in consequence its early behaviour is diffuse and probably best considered in terms of "cycles of activity". The infant has to learn what it can do, and how to do it, from the responses which others give to him and by the satisfaction which he experiences within himself. At this very early stage he has no self-awareness or self-observation; and his behaviour flows out of him to others in an urgent desire for the immediate satisfaction of his rudimentary needs.

Gradually the infant begins to show signs of becoming aware of others when he includes in his actions some anticipation of their response; and so he directs and controls his actions accordingly. He will use the whole apparatus of his face, his hands and his toes and at times he will show signs of recognition by smiles and gurgles. Slowly he is learning to control and direct his behaviour in terms of what others expect of him, and this is one of the most

K

vital elements in the educational process. The individual must come to recognize and to develop the self-regulating and unifying function of this aspect of his experience.

Mead emphasizes that the sense of identity emerges not out of action by the individual person, but out of *interaction* after one has perceived other people and established some sense of relationship with them and some idea of how actions or behaviour are called out. Only when this sense of being able to *initiate* is present can we really say that there are the beginnings of selfhood. Moreover, the kind of action which is initiated must arise out of a choice of possible actions, or else it would seem to be determined and no question of choice or initiation would arise. Selfhood is possible, therefore, only when an infant has had a sufficiently long experience; and this in turn implies a relatively long independent existence. It is clearly, then, one of the tasks of education to provide the sort of social context and choice of experience that will help the child to initiate activity.

We can no longer treat children as if they were little adults, somewhat deficient in morals and needing to be disciplined in order to get them into the proper attitude. In the words of Mead himself, the infant

"cannot have the whole self-consciousness of the adult; and the adult finds it difficult, to say the least, to put himself into the attitude of the child. This is not, however, an impossible thing, and our development of modern education rests on this possibility of the adult finding a common basis between himself and the child"[34].

The differences among people involve the recognition of varieties of experience. One has to recognize more and more that differing societies vary in their standards, their values and evaluations, from the Hopi Indians, the Samoans and the Papuans to the sophisticated New Yorkers and Londoners. Different types of personality are formed by different types of society: it becomes, therefore, increasingly important to study the multiplicity of "patterns of culture"[35] in order to see what sort of personality, what type of self, each is capable of producing. It is important, too, to see what changing effects culture-contact may have upon a society and upon individuals within that society. The selves that we are, are to a great extent the product of our social contacts; it is from society that we get the indispensable tool of language, our interests and our basic moral standards; selves change with the changes of society. Mead has emphasized the educational importance of culture *milieux* in the following terms:

"The getting of this social response into the individual constitutes the process of education which takes over the cultural media of the community in a more or less abstract way. Education is definitely the process of taking over a certain organized set of responses to one's own stimulation; and until one can respond to himself as the community responds to him, he does not genuinely belong to the community"[36].

Mead has made it quite clear in *The Philosophy of the Act* that "the individual and the society are selectively and causally determinative of the environment, and this determines the individual or the society"[37]. Neither, says Mead, can be explained in the terms of the other except as the other is determined by it. Thus Mead's social philosophy and psychology seek to steer a course between the Scylla of "an impossible solipsism" and the Charybdis of "an equally impossible determinism".

Education must prepare for change; change within the culture-patterns, change within the basic moral standards, change within the core values of society. One of the principles that educationists are becoming increasingly aware of is that the mediation of subject content is not, *per se*, enough—however necessary. We must educate for fluidity, for mobility, for plasticity, for change. One of the essential elements in the education of the future is the inculcation of the ability to absorb new situations, new experiences, new ideas, and the capacity to initiate activity. All cultures have hazards of internal dissension, human misery and mental disease: these social facts are, like all others, capable of being internalized by any single individual member of society. A part of the essence of education is to develop means of building the self in such a way that it cannot only adapt itself to change, but can also *initiate* change, and can present within itself an opposing force to such hazards as those referred to above which challenge its identity.

Mead emphasizes the part which the kindergarten has to play in the social development of the small child[38]. A small child plays at being a mother, a father, a teacher, a milkman, an Indian, a burglar; that is, at taking on a variety of different roles. The roles which children assume in kindergarten are made the basis for training: they are very temporary roles and a child will pass with considerable fluidity from policeman to crook. He will say something in one character and respond in another, and a certain organized structure arises in him, and in his "other" which replies to it. It is perfectly true that role-taking may be purely for amusement, purely for play; but gradually the process of role-taking becomes a process for the better understanding of the "other", or in anticipation of taking up that role later on.

"This outcome is just what the kindergarten works toward. It takes the characters of these various vague beings and gets them into such an organized social relationship to each other that they build up the character of the little child"[39].

The educational importance of role-taking becomes increasingly clear in our ever-growing society. It is vital that we understand other people, that we become members "one of another", that we do not only see ourselves as others see us, but also see others as they see themselves. We must get inside people's skins, feel what they feel, know what they know, so that when they approach us in their role we have the fullest possible understanding of what they seek from us and how best we can come to terms with them. The face-to-face relationships which we every day encounter, the "I-Thou" interaction in which complete identification is found with the "other"[40]—these are the basic data of living together in harmony. Such harmonious living demands a deliberate educational policy: the multitudinous and intricate roles of society must go through a process of simplification so that our pupils may fully understand them. This raises the whole question of initiation for our society; and part of this process of simplification in roles is to be found in tradition, and in the transformation and re-interpretation of approved personality traits and accepted character types.

All this points to a far deeper and wider understanding of our society than is at present the case; it points to courses in civics, social studies and sociology at all levels. The Newsom Report (1963) was fully alive to the necessity of getting the child to understand more thoroughly the social milieu in which he lives, and for realistic role-taking. In its Recommendations[41] it proposed that:

(a) In the final year the school programme ought to be quite deliberately outgoing. It should form an organized initiation into the adult world of work and leisure.

(b) The special functions of films and of television as both sources of information and stimulus, and as social and educational forces, should be carefully exploited at all levels —in University Departments of Education, in Colleges of Education and in all schools.

(c) Experiments should be carefully studied which will enable pupils over the age of fifteen to participate to a limited extent, under the auspices of the school, in the world of work in industry, commerce, or in other fields.

(d) All links with, and knowledge about, the youth employment service, further education, the youth service and adult organizations need strengthening.

(e) Schemes for augmenting the personal advisory and welfare service to young school leavers should be encouraged.

(f) All secondary schools need teachers with special knowledge of, and responsibility for, careers work. Both adequate time and facilities should be available to do this effectively.

(g) Courses, conferences and schemes for enabling teachers to gain some familiarity with industry are a prerequisite.

It should be noted that all these recommendations are, in one way or another, involved in social interaction and role-taking.

We have seen that Mead emphasized the great importance of the organized game in developing a definite unity in the organization of the self. In the game, as distinct from unorganized play, the child has to take in all the roles of the other players. Mead states that

"The game represents the passage in the life of the child from taking the role of others in play to the organized part that is essential to self-consciousness in the full sense of the term"[42].

What goes on in the game goes on in the life of the child all the time; he is continually taking on the attitudes of those about him, especially of those who in some sense control him and on whom he depends. In fact, Mead reminds us[43], the morale of the game takes hold of the child more than the larger morale of the whole community. The child takes part in a game and the game expresses a social situation into which he can completely and wholeheartedly enter; and its morale may exert a far greater hold on him than that of the family of which he is a part, or than that of the community in which he has been brought up and in which he now lives.

This complete identification with the roles of other members of the game is one of the strongest identifications which the child or the developing self makes. The team is the Generalized Other; it provides the rules and the limits of the individual's activity, and he has complete identity with them. This would indicate the educational value of the game as such: it is a means of internalizing the roles of other participants in the game itself, and by transference it is a means of finding identity with other human groups. The process of the Generalized Other is applied by the individual child in the family, the class, the school, the club, the church and so on. Eventually, if this transference is successful, the individual finds identification with the macrosociety—that is, the larger society of which he is a member.

There is a very real sense, if Mead's general theories are valid, in which battles, projects, enterprises, and all organized efforts in which a number of people work together in a variety of roles, are "won on the playing fields". A team game becomes a serious, organized project in which each member must so fully understand the role of the other that he finds complete identity with it. A game, as we all know, frequently goes wrong because one or more members of the team fail fully to appreciate the roles of the others, and therefore their *own* role.

"The importance of the game is that it lies entirely inside the child's own experience, and the importance of our modern type of education is that it is brought as far as possible within this realm"[44].

This is life in miniature, and the organized teams and team games of the school have a function in preparing the pupil for the more serious organized group of the business firm, the factory, the research department and so on. Those who fail to make this internalization of the role of the Generalized Other become ill, maladjusted, deviant, delinquent or positively criminal. Mead claims, however, in his article "The Psychology of Punitive Justice", that the criminal does not seriously endanger the structure of society by his destructive activities. On the other hand,

"he is responsible for a sense of solidarity, aroused among those whose attention would otherwise be centred upon interests quite divergent from those of each other"[45].

This statement approaches very close to Durkheim's discussion of the "normality of crime" in *The Rules of Sociological Method*[46].

Bound up with the question of taking on the roles of others is the great problem in our society of communication—communication, that is, between different groups of people, with differing viewpoints, prejudices, standards and ideals. It is the problem of communication between the scientist and the non-scientist, between the technologist and the layman, between the employer and the employee, between the religious and the non-religious, between the old and the young, and between the "with it" and the "square". This is, once more, the question of role-taking, of getting into the position of the other. Only a really enlightened education, able to range the great variety of social roles and *niveaux*, can help solve the difficulties of class barriers and struggles, colour bars and political doctrinaires. This is an age of formula seeking: we must educate, therefore, for adaptability, understanding, reciprocity, plasticity and empathy.

Mead seems to imply, generally speaking, that education is the development of unity within the self, and the ever-growing building-up of the self through social interaction. The most effective form of teaching can be found in community life, in which the child experiences the complex relationships of people. Neither social attributes nor personal qualities are acquired simply by taking thought or by understanding them intellectually. They are acquired in action, in role-taking or social interaction, and in the internalization of the Generalized Other. It would seem to be the task of the educator to plan learning so that responsibility is being understood through action, and through accepting the role which you know others expect you to play. According to Mead we cannot be ourselves unless we are also members in whom there is a community of attitudes which control the attitudes of all. We cannot have rights unless we have common attitudes, and it is one of the functions of education to establish a sense of community through the internalization of common attitudes. Selves can exist only in definite relationships to other selves.

"No hard-and-fast line can be drawn between our own selves and the selves of others, since our own selves exist and enter as such into our experience only in so far as the selves of others exist and enter as such into our experience also"[47].

For Mead the structure of the individual self reflects the general behaviour-pattern of the social group to which the individual belongs. There is a common structure of selves: we are members of a community: we are members one of another. And this must be the tenor of our philosophy of education, which, in this case, arises out of what Mead regards as an indisputable fact: the self is a sociological phenomenon. "One has to be a member of a community in order to be a self" might be regarded as the text of Mead's philosophy as well as social psychology. As a basis for the theory of education it implies throughout a sociological approach to both learning and living.

REFERENCES

1. Mead, G. H.: *Mind, Self and Society*. The University of Chicago Press, Chicago and London, 1934; 13th Impression 1965, p. ix.
2. *Ibid.* pp. 1–8.
3. Sprott, W. J. H.: *Human Groups*. Penguin Books (Pelican), 1958, p. 23.
4. *Op. cit.*, p. 108.
5. Krogh, A.: "The Language of the Bees". Scientific American Offprint, No. 21, August 1948, published by W. H. Freeman & Coy.
6. von Frisch, K.: "Dialects in the Language of the Bees". Scientific American Offprint, No. 130, August 1962.
7. Thorpe, W. H.: "The Language of Birds". Scientific American Offprint, No. 145, October 1956, p. 6.
8. Mead, G. H.: *Mind, Self and Society*, p. 65.
9. *Ibid.* p. 67.
10. *Ibid.* p. 139.
11. *Ibid.* p. 140.
12. *Ibid.* p. 151.
13. *Ibid.* p. 159.

14. *Ibid.* p. 152.
15. *Ibid.* p. 155.
16. *Ibid.* p. 179.
17. *Ibid.* pp. 192ff.
18. Sprott, W. J. H.: *Op cit.*, p. 26.
19. Mead, G. H.: *The Philosophy of the Act.* The University of Chicago Press, 1938; 5th Impression, 1964, p. 625.
20. *Op. cit.*, pp. 253–60.
21. *Ibid.* pp. 298–303; 366.
22. *Ibid.* p. 254.
23. *Ibid.* pp. 42–134.
24. *Ibid.* p. 52.
25. *Ibid.* p. 142.
26. *Ibid.* p. 68.
27. *Ibid.* p. 71.
28. *Ibid.* p. 73.
29. *Ibid.* p. 78.
30. *Ibid.* p. 78.
31. Mannheim, K. & Stewart, W. A. C.: *An Introduction to the Sociology of Education.* Routledge, 1962, p. 97.
32. *Mind, Self and Society*, p. 188.
33. *Op. cit.*, p. 94.
34. *Mind, Self and Society*, p. 317.
35. *Vide* Benedict, R.: *Patterns of Culture.* Routledge, 1935; Mead, M.: *Growing up in New Guinea.* Penguin Books (Pelican), 1942; Mead, M.: *Coming of Age in Samoa.* Penguin Books (Pelican), 1943.
36. *Mind, Self and Society*, pp. 264–5.
37. *Op. cit.*, p. 153.
38. *Mind, Self and Society*, pp. 152f.
39. *Ibid.* p. 153.
40. Buber, M.: *Between Man & Man.* Fontana Lib., Collins, 1961; *I and Thou.* T. & T. Clark, 1937.
41. Newsom Report: *Half Our Future.* H.M.S.O., 1963, pp. 72–9.
42. *Mind, Self and Society*, p. 152.
43. *Ibid.* p. 160.
44. *Ibid.* p. 159.
45. Mead, G. H.: "The Psychology of Punitive Justice". Article reprinted in *Theories of Society*, ed. Talcott Parsons *et al.*, Free Press, Collier-Macmillan, 1965, p. 882.
46. Durkheim, E.: *The Rules of Sociological Method.* Free Press of Glencoe, Collier-Macmillan, 8th Edition, 1964, pp. 64–75.
47. *Mind, Self and Society*, p. 164.

BIBLIOGRAPHY

A. BOOKS BY GEORGE H. MEAD

The Philosophy of the Present. Chicago: Open Court Pub. Co., 1932. (Edited by A. E. Murphy).
Mind, Self and Society. Univ. of Chicago Press, 1934; 13th Impression, 1965. (Edited by C. W. Morris).
Movements of Thought in the Nineteenth Century. Univ. of Chicago Press, 1936. (Edited by M. H. Moore).
The Philosophy of the Act. Univ. of Chicago Press, 1938; 5th Impression 1964. (Edited by C. W. Morris).
Social Psychology. Univ. of Chicago Press, 1965. (Edited by A. Strauss).
"The Psychology of Punitive Justice". Article published in *The American Journal of Sociology*, No. XXIII, 1917–18, pp. 577–602. Reprinted in *Theories of Society*, ed. by Talcott Parsons *et al.*, Free Press, Collier-Macmillan, 1965, pp. 876–86.

B. OTHER BOOKS OF REFERENCE

Mannheim, K. & Stewart, W. A. C.: *An Introduction to the Sociology of Education.* Routledge, 1962 (especially Chapter IX on "The Social and Cultural Concept of Personality").
Sprott, W. J. H.: *Human Groups.* Penguin Books (Pelican), 1958 (especially Chapter 2).

CHAPTER 13

KARL MANNHEIM (1893–1947)

A. HIS LIFE AND WORK

Until he became a refugee from Nazi totalitarianism Mannheim had been Professor of Sociology at the University of Frankfurt-on-Main, and he had been considerably influenced by Marxist ideology. After his arrival in England he became a lecturer in Sociology at the London School of Economics, and from 1940 onwards he lectured part time at the Institute of London University, where in 1946 he was appointed to the Chair of Education.

Mannheim was a very enthusiastic planner. In the words of S. J. Curtis,

"His opposition to the Nazi totalitarian planning led him to the view that if we were to combat it successfully a free democracy such as ours would have to plan for freedom as thoroughly as the Germans had planned for world domination"[1].

It was the persistent purpose of Mannheim to show, throughout his teaching, that our post-war society must be planned, but that we must at the same time preserve the maximum freedom of the individual possible. This was the dilemma and the task as he saw it. Moreover, the democratic planning of education was, in his view, an essential part of the social and economic planning that he advocated.

Mannheim further considered that planning of this sort would be carried on by a minority—by the cultured élite. He certainly sought the means very earnestly, in conjunction with other sociologists and educationists, for social reconstruction after the Second World War, and Dr W. Boyd has remarked that Mannheim had a "masterly sense of dynamic sociology"[2]. Mannheim attempted to outline some of his ideas for reconstruction in *Man and Society in an Age of Reconstruction*, published in 1940, and in *Diagnosis of Our Time*, published in 1943, in which he made it clear that a planned society depends upon a *transformation of man* and that education is the chief means for bringing this about.

In *Man and Society* he claimed that the planners could recruit themselves only from already existing groups, and that everything could, therefore, depend upon which of these groups with their existing outlooks would produce the energy, the decisiveness, and the capacity to master the vast machinery of modern life. Mannheim felt that it would not be through those human groups in which traces of primitiveness operate without restraint, but through those which have, by gradual education, developed both their moral and rational capacities so far that they can act, not merely for a limited group, but also for the whole of society, and bear the responsibility for it. Thus the planning would be in the hands of a "minority élite". He went on to say that

"Sociologists do not regard education solely as a means of realizing abstract ideas of culture, such as humanism or technical specialization, but as part of the process of influencing men and women. Education can only be understood when we know for which society and for what social position the pupils are being educated. Education does not mould men in the abstract but in and for a given society"[3].

B. THE EDUCATIVE SOCIETY AND SOCIAL CHANGE— SIR FRED CLARKE

Sir Fred Clarke became Director of the London University Institute of Education in 1937. He was a convinced Christian and an Anglican, and he was very conscious of the contribution which sociology might make to the development of educational thought. In particular, he believed that there should be planning in education. In this sphere his guides were not the pragmatists such as John Dewey, but the philosophical idealists such as W. E. Hocking, the sociologist Karl Mannheim, and Christianity.

In his book *Education and Social Change*, which was published in 1940, Clarke stated that

"we propose to accept unreservedly what may be called the sociological standpoint and to exhibit as well as we can its concrete application to the field of English education"[4].

He advocated the unification of the social system as a step in the planning of a much more "collectivist" social order. Moreover, he saw the need for an educative society in which there was no sudden transition from the shelter of the school to the hard and cold reality of the world outside. He urged the reform of secondary education in order to give each child full opportunity for development free from class distinctions and traditional inequalities, and to ensure the abolition of the false antithesis between cultural and vocational education.

In agreement with Mannheim, Clarke envisaged a planned social economic order under effective democratic control; an order in which each person would master some of the techniques needed in an industrial society. He visualized, too, a society in which education was continued and continuous—partly in school, partly in part-time education with the co-operation of industry, and partly in adult education. Clarke wanted the new education to be adventurous and to fight against the increasingly obvious dangers of the mass society and of machine production. He firmly believed that the English institutions, including the Educational System itself, were flexible enough to be adapted to the new conditions. He saw the function of secondary education in society as one of maintaining and enhancing *social unity*, at the same time providing for effective *social differentiation* and continuous re-adaptation.

Clarke regarded culture as the whole life-medium with which education was concerned—the whole social inheritance, beliefs, habits, moral and aesthetic standards, institutions, manners, techniques and vocations. It was one of the main tasks of education to hand on the cultural values and behaviour-patterns of the society to its young and potential members. Unfortunately, there was always a "cultural lag", as Ralph Linton had pointed out— the failure of education to keep up with technological change. Clarke was also fully aware of, and concerned with, the dichotomy of education for work and education for leisure.

In 1948, the year after Mannheim died at the age of fifty-four, Clarke published his *Freedom in the Educative Society*. In this book he developed further the theme of planning for freedom in an English society, which he likened to the Platonic educative society. An "educative society" was one which accepted as its overmastering purpose the production of a given type of citizen.

"The type itself may be defined with varying degrees of precision and detail. But, whatever the type may be, that society may be called educative which consciously directs its activities and organizes every department of its life with a view to the emergence of citizens bearing the characters of the preferred type"[5].

Clarke, however, agreed with Professor W. E. Hocking that, whilst education should be for the type, it should also make possible development "beyond the type"[6]. Clarke maintained that a true culture would emerge from the common life and experience of a healthy society. A common purpose of that society would define itself, and this should be heeded both within the school and outside. The whole content of education should be relevant to it, and the teachers chosen should be its especially sensitive representatives. Clarke seemed to think that education could not create a new society, it could only reflect the one in which it existed. He believed that there should be an increase in the emphasis on *specific functions* rather than upon individuality, as contrasted with the view of Sir Percy Nunn. There should be in education deliberate training for "citizen consciousness", and this fact reinforced the claims of sociology to take a place in the field of studies covered by education.

Clarke deplored the ever-increasing gulf between the two general types of activity—work and leisure. Leisure, he said, was conceived as something completely divorced from work, and he saw the remedy in the "Christian" doctrine of work which takes its ideal from God as a worker who found satisfaction with his work. Clarke held that we should train our pupils to become responsible citizens, whose prime duty it is to produce honest and faithful work. But, it must be said, one has to face the fact today that the work of thousands of our workers is repetitious, mechanical and full of drudgery, and that there can be for most no satisfaction expressed in any single, final product. People are now in the phase, much more so than when Clarke produced this book, of really living *only* in their period of leisure. In the words of S. J. Curtis,

"It is essential that practical ways of humanizing and socializing this kind of work shall be found and one looks to education to assist in making this discovery"[7].

C. MANNHEIM'S *Diagnosis of Our Time*

Mannheim published his *Diagnosis of Our Time* in 1943. It is, from any point of view, a stimulating and thought-provoking book, and it demonstrates how the author and Sir Fred Clarke were working and thinking along similar lines. It is worthwhile looking at the "diagnosis" in some detail since it represents the fruits of discussions which Mannheim conducted during the Second World War with intelligent people of a variety of professions.

In Chapter One of this book Mannheim outlines the significance of new social techniques. Our society is ill, he says, and we are living in an age of transition from laissez-faire to a planned society.

"The planned society that will come may take one of two shapes: it will be ruled either by a minority in terms of a dictatorship or by a new form of government which, in spite of its increased power, will still be democratically controlled"[8].

We are living in a mass society using a large variety of social techniques; and modern techniques tend to foster centralization and therefore minority rule and dictatorship. Mannheim insists that techniques are neither good nor bad in themselves, and that not all planning is evil. There can be planning for conformity and planning for freedom and variety; no great society can hope to survive if it fosters only conformity. But a new social order cannot be brought about simply by a more skilful handling of the new social techniques; it needs guidance by the *spirit*, which is always more than a system of decisions on technical issues. According to Mannheim we need a new militant democracy with the courage to agree on some basic values which are acceptable to everybody who shares the traditions of Western civilization. These agreed basic values must be brought home to the child with all the educational methods at our disposal.

Mannheim further insists that there is a growing disappointment with laissez-faire methods, which are destructive in the economic field where they have always produced the trade cycle and devastating unemployment. He also feels that the efficiency of Fascism and Nazism is devilish; and he has grave doubts about Communism which, although it works and is efficient, and has great achievements to its credit as far as the State and the masses go, never seems able to relinquish its dictatorship or allow the State to "wither away". Between Laissez-Faire and Totalitarianism Mannheim sees the possibility of a Third Way.

In Chapter Two he discusses some of the conflicting philosophies of life. In particular he points out that there is no agreed educational policy for our normal citizens: the further we progress the less we know what we are educating for, whether for some religious ideal, for specialization, or for all-round personalities with a philosophical background. He considers that the system of working primarily for profit and monetary reward is in the process of disintegration; the masses are craving for a stable standard of living; they want to feel that they are useful and important members of the community.

In this chapter Mannheim goes on to investigate the causes of our spiritual crisis, but without rejecting the views of religious and philosophical idealists, or those of the Marxists (that the crisis is simply the "noise" made by the clash of economic systems), he concludes that economic and class factors alone are not responsible for the crisis in our valuations. It is true that no remedy for the chaos in valuations is possible without a sound economic order; but this is not enough, for there are a great many other social conditions which influence the process of value creation and dissemination. Valuations are partly the expression of subjective strivings and partly the fulfilment of objective social functions.

Next he discusses some sociological factors which upset the process of valuation in modern society. In the midst of a rapid and uncontrolled growth of society, Mannheim saw an educational tradition and value system which was still adapted to the needs of a parochial world. In the transition of society from simple conditions to more complex ones, the value of social justice must prevail. The increase in the number of group-contacts and in social mobility was leading to the dropping of values into the melting-pot. And, in consequence, value creation, value dissemination, value acceptance and value assimilation have become more and more the concern of the conscious ego. But, says Mannheim,

"You cannot create a new moral world mainly based upon rational value appreciation, i.e. values whose social and psychological function is intelligible, and at the same time maintain an educational system which in its essential techniques works through the creation of inhibitions and tries to prevent the growth of judgement"[9].

The solution is a *gradualism* in education; but it is no use developing child guidance, psychiatric social work and psychotherapy if the one to guide is left without standards.

Mannheim discusses the meaning of democratic planning in the sphere of valuations, and the need for *consensus* of values. The democracies must give up their complete uninterest in valuations, for democracy can function only if democratic self-discipline is strong enough to make people agree on concrete issues for the sake of common action, even if they differ on details. Consensus is far more than agreement on certain issues—consensus is common life. Mannheim believes that if a society were to invest as much energy, for example, in the mitigation of race and group hatred as the totalitarian societies in fostering it, important achievements in the elimination of conflicts could be accomplished. We need, he suggests, a moral substitute for war: one of the lessons we can learn from the Second World War is how many psychological and institutional forces can become operative in society, if integration is really wanted.

In Chapter Three Mannheim considers the sociological function of youth in society. Static societies rely mainly on the experience of the old; dynamic societies will rely mainly upon the co-operation of youth. As long as there is a will to make a new start, it will have to be done through youth. Youth is a revitalizing agent; youth comes to the conflicts of our modern society from without, and it is this fact which makes youth the predestined pioneer of any change in society. The special function of youth in this situation requires a far greater articulateness in the realm of ideas:

"The whole educational edifice, with its emphasis on examinations, marks, memorizing, or inventories of facts, is busy killing the spirit of experimentation so vital in an epoch of change"[10].

But Mannheim felt that the democratization of culture would benefit mankind only if the *quality* of culture were to be preserved. The problem of preventing the process of levelling down cultural standards was a very serious one, for any expansion of culture which was too rapid might lead to an assimilation of its contents which was totally inadequate, and "to superficiality and a rapid decline of established standards"[11].

Chapter Four deals with the problem of social awareness and the function and role of education and sociology in the development of such awareness. To Mannheim education was becoming *integral* in two repects:

i. by integrating its activities with the activities of other social institutions;
ii. by having regard to the wholeness of the person.

He went on to enumerate some of the reasons for the need of sociological integration in education. There was a lack of contact between thinker, artist and community; there was an urgent need for a fundamental regeneration of our society; in a changing society like ours only an education for change can help. This consists in an undogmatic training of the mind, which enables the person not to be driven by the current of changing events but to rise above them. In this process the teacher is not so much a schoolmaster as a *lifemaster*.

Mannheim then considers the role of sociology in a militant democracy. He finds that there is a lack of awareness in social affairs and a lack of comprehensive sociological orientation. The leaders of the nation, including teachers, should be educated in a way which will enable them to understand the meaning of change. In the present situation no teaching is sound unless it trains man to be aware of the whole situation in which he finds himself, and able after careful deliberation to make his choice and come to a decision, for

"the aim of social progress is not an imaginary society without a governing class, but the improvement of the economic, social, political, and educational opportunities for the people to train themselves for leadership, and an improvement of the method of the selection of the best in the various fields of social life"[12].

Chapter Five deals with mass education and group analysis. In the sociological approach to education Mannheim considers that educational techniques develop as part of the general development of "social techniques". Education is a technique of influencing human behaviour, a means of social control; and democracy must learn to use the forces of group interaction in a positive, cathartic way. In problems of group analysis Mannheim sees room for socio-analysis as distinct from introspection. Socio-analysis refers the individual case to the family constellation and to the whole configuration of social institutions. It also makes more conscious use of group interaction. Mannheim considers that disintegration of personality generally corresponds to disintegration in society; individuals are determined by society, and society is made up of individuals. And the mental climate of a given society as a whole may be the source of unbearable tensions in the individual.

In Chapter Six Mannheim analyses the systematic strategy of the Nazi German society for the production of a "New Order", and the manner in which German Youth Groups were developed in order "to perpetuate the psychological attitude of adolescence"[13]. Mannheim suggests that we have something to learn from such group organization.

It is in Chapter Seven that Mannheim produces an attempt to show the implications of his social philosophy. The chapter is divided into two parts: Part One is concerned with Christianity in the Age of Planning, and Part Two with Christian Values and the Changing Environment. In the first part Mannheim asserts that Christianity is at the cross-roads, and asks the question, "Will it associate with the masses or side with the ruling minorities?" He personally sees in a planned democratic society the need for spiritual integration, and claims that

"Only a generation which has been educated through religion, or at least on the religious level, to discriminate between immediate advantage and the lasting issues of life will be capable of accepting the sacrifice which a properly planned democratic order must continually demand from every single group and individual in the interests of the whole"[14].

Mannheim thinks that it is better for the Christian Faith itself if it is not identified with one particular party but rather carries its spirit into all.

Generally accepted values must be based upon tacit or explicit *consensus*. In the past, custom represented such a tacit consensus, and where this is vanishing and can no longer be maintained, it becomes necessary for new methods to be developed, in which persuasion, imitation, free discussion, and consciously accepted example will play a role. Mannheim speaks of the concepts of Christian Archetypes; he says that fundamental Christian attitudes have not been laid down in terms of rigid rules, but have rather been given in concrete *paradigmata*, that is, patterns, examples or models, which only point in the direction where Right is to be sought. As a result, there is scope left for creative contribution in every new epoch.

In the second part of this chapter Mannheim discusses the necessity of planning for religious experience and for spontaneity of life. He considers that there are four essentials in the sphere of religious experience:

i. Personal communion with God.
ii. Personal relationships.
iii. A pattern of social life.
iv. The persistence of conventions.

Mannheim considers whether one of the remedies for the dehumanizing effects of "a civilization of busybodies" may not be some form of complete or temporary withdrawal from the affairs of the world; there must, he insists, be guardians of the spirit, to whom the purity of the deeper experience is more important than its contemporaneity; there must be suitable secular orders into which active participants in political and business life may withdraw for periods of contemplation[15]. In our personal relationships we must be fully alive to the need for mutual help, personal inspiration, and the restoration of neighbourhood, fellowship and community. And the pattern of social life, which is always more than the "sum of atomized units", must be permeated with the spirit of a continuous give-and-take between the individuals and the pattern. And whilst there is a place for certain conventions in "ritualistic orthodoxy", Mannheim sees the pluralistic approach to planning alone as satisfactory. To plan for freedom is to provide an "elastic mould" for the growth of society, and to utilize a rich variety of approaches.

He then goes on to consider the question of valuation and paradigmatic experience. A man may be impeccable from the point of view of morality, and yet not be religious; whilst an immoral man can sometimes have deep religious experiences. The religious focus is not an ethical or moral experience, nor yet a way of regulating behaviour or conduct, but a way of interpreting life from the centre of some paradigmatic experience (e.g. sin, redemption, suffering, love of the Cross and so on). In the despiritualization of modern life Mannheim sees the evaporation of primordial images or Archetypes which have directed the life-experience of mankind through the ages[16]. It is the disintegration and disappearance of these Archetypes without anything else to take their place which leads to the break-up of modern life-experience and human conduct.

"Without paradigmatic experiences no consistent conduct, no character formation and no real human co-existence and co-operation are possible. Without them our universe of discourse loses its articulation, conduct falls to pieces . . ."[17].

And if in our mass society neither the school nor the church and religion provide codes, patterns of behaviour and paradigmatic experiences and ideas, it is the cinema, the television and other commercialized institutions which take over the role of teaching people what to aim for, whom to obey, whom to copy, how to be free and how to love.

Finally, Mannheim analyses some of the concrete issues which are subject to revaluation—the problem of survival values, of asceticism, of the split consciousness of self-assertion and self-denial, of privacy in the modern world with its growing influence of mass existence, and of shared experience and mass ecstasy. And he concludes with the observation by Ruskin that "there is no wealth but life". Fundamental democratization claims for everyone a share in real education, which Mannheim conceives as one that no longer seeks primarily to satisfy the craving for social distinction, but enables us adequately to understand the pattern of life in which we are called upon to live and act.

D. GENERAL FEATURES OF MANNHEIM'S THOUGHT AND EDUCATIONAL THEORY

Truth and Social Determinism: Mannheim clearly agreed with the pragmatists in denying the possibility of arriving at Absolute Truth, and he extended this view to religion and mystical experience. To him all truths were dependent upon specific social factors, and since these themselves were perpetually changing so, of necessity, was truth. In general, he was in accord with the Logical Positivists and philosophical analysts who argue that no statement can have meaning unless it can be verified in sense experience, and that any discussion about the reality of the sense world or of mind is largely meaningless, a waste of time, and in the technical connotation of the word "nonsense"[18].

To Mannheim all thought was socially determined, and he considered that the personal contribution of the individual was of little importance in comparison with the patterns of thought (paradigmata) predominant in the group to which he belonged. All thought which is of real importance is "situationally based". What impressed Mannheim were not our personal ideas so much as the enormous pressure exerted upon the individual by social patterns of thought and behaviour. Professor M. V. C. Jeffreys has said that

"the sociological method tends to eliminate from the picture the distinctive human quality of behaviour. The approach is one that highlights the irrational elements in behaviour; the more irrational the behaviour, the more easily can it be accounted for in terms of social pressure. Little light is shed on the problem of how man can become more rational and responsible"[19].

But this statement ignores the fact that the irrational elements in human behaviour are as distinctive as the rational and equally as important and instructive. Moreover, it is patently incorrect to suggest that the sociological approach has little light to shed on how man can become more rational and responsible: indeed, this is one of the main aims of the whole exercise, although the sociologist *qua* sociologist may leave the solution of the problem to the social philosopher and the educational philosopher. If, as Mannheim maintains, thought is socially determined, then society must clearly seek to determine thought in the right way, and on the basis of Logical Positivism this will mean a careful analysis of every new situation as it arises.

Planning and Social Integration: Whilst opposing the Fascist and Communist regimes, Mannheim was equally opposed to laissez-faire. There was, he said, a Third Way. This was a way of consciously directed planning in order to preserve freedom and the democratic way of life. But planning means planners, and this at once lays emphasis upon an élite and the possibility of making the centralization of power and minority rule much easier. Planning was not to be regarded as utopian; rather, it accepted the present determined state of society as its datum. But though it was not "totalitarian", the planning that Mannheim conceived would be *total*. Mannheim was, in fact, advocating the planned guidance of the lives of the people on a sociological basis with the assistance of psychology, both individual and social.

He pleaded for sociological integration in education and contrasted his views with those, like Nunn's, whose emphasis was upon the self-realization of the individual as the supreme aim of education[20]. He felt that the old liberal concept of education, with its "fostering of the free development of personality through the unhampered unfolding of innate qualities"[21], was too aloof from history to be of any real value in the concrete situations of life.

"Whoever tries to state such eternal values very soon realizes that they are bound to be too abstract to lend concrete shape to education at a given moment"[22].

In his *Education and Society* A. K. C. Ottaway remarks, *à propos* the question of social planning in education, that planning does not necessarily imply complete conformity or regimentation; one can plan for variety and harmony[23]. Democracy must be militant in its exclusion of those "who wish to abuse the methods of freedom for abolishing freedom"[24]. The real problem is not ultimately that of planning or no planning, but of how to plan without destroying the freedom and initiative of the individual[25].

Basic and Core Values: Mannheim saw no need to dictate everything that people should think; he felt, rightly or wrongly, that there was enough agreement over basic values, inherited both from classical antiquity and from Christianity, which should be widely propagated. He considered that the more complicated values could be left open to discussion, personal choices or experiment. But one wonders whether there is really such wide agreement as Mannheim suggested in regard to these core, or basic, values. When one considers the somewhat fluid state at the present time in relation to such problems as sexual morality and behaviour, and the changing standards of social conduct generally one becomes a little suspicious of any facile conclusion about "generally accepted" core values. And yet, in a sense, Mannheim was right. We all know, for example, that war is wasteful as well as soul-destroying; we are all agreed that hatred can lead only to further hate and enmity; we accept, in principle if not in fact, that the maxim "Do unto others as you would that they should do to you" is not merely a piece of pious pleasantry but, in reality, the most utilitarian criterion for achieving the greatest happiness of the greatest number; whilst the value of truth quickly becomes evident when we try consistently to tell lies for any length of time. On the basis of his philosophy Mannheim would probably claim little more for his "core" values than the fact that they represent the most civil and pragmatic way to live. And that is something.

The Function of Youth: Mannheim felt that we were too attached to tradition and that, in consequence, we tended to neglect the dynamic energies of youth. More and more youth had to be integrated into the social life of the larger society, and this would involve much stronger links between the school and that society in order that there might be a more gradual social initiation. This would mean, too, the discovery of social roles appropriate to the status of the adolescent. There can be no doubt that this question is still one of the most urgent and difficult in our present society—the problem of the initiation of youth. The full implementation of the 1944 Education Act in respect of County Colleges would do much to help solve this particular problem. In the words of the Crowther Report, *15 to 18*, published in 1959:

"There are four strands that should be woven into the curriculum of county colleges: an appreciation of the adult world in which young workers suddenly find themselves; guidance for them in working out their problems of human relations and moral standards; development of their physical and aesthetic skills; and a continuance of their basic education, with vocational bias where appropriate"[26].

But, sound as this suggestion obviously is, the social awareness implied in this and in other parts of the Crowther Report is something that should begin on the day that a child enters the Infants

School and should continue throughout his school career. Social attitudes are not imbibed suddenly on a course, nor yet naturally during the years of adolescence; they have to be inculcated in actual social and community living. It is not merely in the last year at school that the programme has to be outgoing, although the Newsom Report may be right in suggesting that some special attempts in this direction should be made during the final year[27]. This is a process that should be going on all the time. Civics, current affairs, modern and local history and social studies should, in some form or another, feature in the school programme from earliest days. Only in this way can youth begin to visualize its own role and function in our society.

The Growth of Personality and its Roles: Mannheim follows very closely the thought of G. H. Mead in regard to the self. The self is not given at birth or at any other time, but it emerges out of our social experience. Man has a unique psychological endowment to enable him to become self-conscious, but only the external field in which he lives can provide the form which that self-consciousness will take. The stages of individual development outlined by Mead—those of more or less automatic imitation, of play, and of organized game—are closely connected with the concept of role-taking.

Mannheim also follows the social psychologist, J. L. Moreno, who suggests that it is more desirable to think of the role as a point of reference than the personality or the ego, because these are less concrete and, as he says, wrapped up in "metapsychological mysteriousness"[28]. Moreno, however, asserts that man is a *creator* and he claims that education must take its stand on this belief, and just shape what it does according to this principle. In this connexion Mannheim emphasizes the importance of thinking of the curriculum as an instrument by means of which we can help children to spontaneous achievement (as in art, music, dancing, etc.), rather than to the avoidance of failure, or even more seriously to the confirmation that poor standards are inevitable.

In a world in which the hours of work are gradually becoming fewer, in which work itself is for the masses at least becoming less and less creative, and in which the hours of leisure threaten to become as monotonous as those of work itself, the only viable solution is one in which a premium is placed upon individual skills, latent, trained and acquired, and upon sheer creativity.

The Value of Groups: In his writings Mannheim emphasized repeatedly the vital and basic importance of groups for normal social activity as well as for psychotherapeutic purposes. It is in the group that the sense of unique oddity and failure are reduced; and in this connexion Mannheim saw the value of psychodrama and sociodrama for diagnostic as well as therapeutic purposes. But, in general, it is within the primary groups that the individual gradually develops his self-awareness and his sense of role-relationships. It is through the group that we acquire status for ourselves; gradually also we associate a sense of guilt or disapproval with one role and approval with another. As time passes we internalize this set of preferences and begin to work out consciously and unconsciously a scale of aspiration. In the post-War society we have seen the development of groups of all types—from beatnik groups and "pop" groups to groups concerned with personal therapy and social reintegration. Within the schools the value of the small group for all types of work has been fully exploited as over against the old "class audience" concept.

The Bipolarity of Education: Mannheim speaks of the bipolarity of education, by which he means that we must educate for both conformity and originality. By conformity he means the willingness to submerge one's aggressiveness and individuality in the interests of the group and social "belongingness". Conformity means adjustment of the self for common effort, and a desire to be obedient and subservient to the common will. But, at the same time, we must educate equally for originality, for creativeness, for responsibility and for spontaneity. But Mannheim warns that

"Education for spontaneity must lead us on to realize more and more that we are members one of another. If it does not it leads to neurosis and psychosis"[29].

With all this in mind he suggests that we must seek in education to provide curricula which have sound cultural justifications; that is, they must be firmly based on the social situation of the learner, which involves the pattern of inherited culture, the unique content of contemporary culture, and the culture of the foreseeable future. The whole web of social relationships is a part of this intricate cultural pattern, and only a full awareness of what this implies will ensure a society and a world in which individuals accept their responsibility for others[30].

Education as an Inter-Disciplinary Study: In his prefatory remarks to *An Introduction to the Sociology of Education* Professor W. A. C. Stewart says:

"At the risk of being cloven by a sociological spade or a psychological pick, I would say that if ever any study was inter-disciplinary it is education"[31].

He goes on to point out that Mannheim saw man as a biological, psychological and sociological organism, influenced by and conditioned to the stimuli about him. In consequence, if man were to have a total comprehension of his own impulses, and a mastery of the social format, he must study life whole. Such a *Weltanschauung* would involve the use of disciplines such as philosophy, psychology and sociology. Education is mainly a social business; it is a dynamic process concerned with social and personal experiences. These experiences require analysis, selection, reflection and evaluation. Thus it is that philosophic reflection, psychology and sociology become the fundamental studies which collectively provide a corpus of knowledge for a deeper understanding of education as a whole.

In his *Education and Contemporary Society* H. L. Elvin considers, in an interesting and most suggestive way, the academic disciplines that are relevant to the study of education and society. He maintains that these are especially sociology, psychology, social philosophy, and comparative education—all to be studied in the light of history[32]. It was precisely this synoptic and integrative view that Mannheim had in mind. And without the overall information and knowledge that these disciplines enabled one to achieve, he considered that it was impossible to make a sound and balanced judgement on educational problems and policies.

Education for Society: Education has gone through the various phases of being teacher-centred, subject-centred and child-centred. We are now entering a phase wherein education is becoming more and more society-centred. In Mannheim's own words:

"Education can only arise out of a social situation. . . . If the need for education arises out of people living together, one of its aims has to be to enable them to live together more successfully in the widest sense of these terms. . . . Education, then, is dynamic on both sides in that it deals with adaptable development of individuals and equally with a changing and developing society[33].

But he makes it clear that in a democratic state we must guard against the notion that education should be substantially the same for everyone; indeed, equality of opportunity coupled with education according to age, ability and aptitude must lead to a "differentiated educational system rather than greater conformity"[34].

Mannheim stresses the importance of obtaining a sense of common purpose between the home, the school and the society. We must seek to eradicate the concept of "compulsory" education for a particular period of our lives, and accept much more freely the "compulsive" quality of education during the whole of life. In this sense of common purpose, and in underlining the educative fabric of the whole society, Mannheim suggested that educators must seek to harmonize the *apparently* antagonistic elements in that society—school and life, work and leisure, action and reflection, self-control and self-expression, individuality and co-operation, change and tradition.

Morality and Religion: Mannheim pleaded for a new morality in the planned society. This would be achieved only if the deepest sources of human regeneration assist in the rebirth of society. Mannheim felt that the existing institutional forms of religion were unable to bring about the reconstruction of man and of society: there must be a return to the genuine sources of religious experience, for

"Only if the rebirth of religion, both in terms of popular movement and a regenerated leadership, coincides with the forthcoming social transformation can it happen that the new democratic order of this country will be Christian"[35].

It is in this connexion that Mannheim speaks of the paradigmatic experiences, those decisive and basic experiences which are felt to reveal the meaning of life as a whole. He feels that the erstwhile paradigmata of the Hero, the Saint, the Sage, the Virgin and so on, have lost their inspirational force in modern times, and that we need to plan and recreate patterns that will be the source of vitality and life.

The Butler Education Act of 1944 accepted, in principle, that there was a need to promote religious and moral life within society through the framework of the school, and so it made compulsory each day in all State schools an assembly for the purposes of collective worship, and also certain curriculum time for Religious Instruction. Agreed Syllabuses were subsequently framed by Local Education Authorities to meet the need for general guidance in terms of subject-matter as well as method. Whether Religious Education in schools since World War Two has done anything to recreate the paradigmata of which Mannheim spoke, and whether such patterns have become the new spiritual source of vitality and life one may certainly beg to doubt. Two things, however, in this connexion seem fairly clear: one is that both content and method of Religious Education seem to be at fault[36]; and the other is that there is a growing opposition to the compulsory element in Religious Education, even with the saving "contracting-out" clauses in the Act. This opposition does not come merely from atheists, agnostics or humanists, but also from people with firm religious convictions, who feel, nevertheless, that the entire process of Religious Education as practised at the moment is misconceived[37].

To use the Religious Education period as one in which moral instruction is given within a religious framework is, as H. L. Elvin has pointed out,

"logically precarious, for although religions have their closely associated moral codes and outlooks, religion and morals are not identical any more than theology and ethics are. And the attempt to keep the religious framework but to do something different leads to a forcing that is sometimes rather absurd. ('What can Amos tell us about Rachmanism?' as I saw on one draft syllabus)"[38].

If it can really be said that Religious Education has been *planned* in Mannheim's sense of the word, he would certainly be very disappointed with the results of that planning to date. But it may well be that there are some dimensions and incommensurables in life that cannot be planned in normal curriculum terms—and we certainly cannot legislate for them.

The Value of Sociology: Mannheim advocated that there should be a planned guidance of the lives of people and that this should be on a sociological basis with the aid of psychology. Social education was the planned use of a wide range of social forces and institutions to create the democratic personality type necessary to guarantee social integration in a reconstructed society. Sociology taught us how to find out; it taught us not to take social influences for granted, but to regard the social environment as a set of patterns to be explored for their educational significance. We might then exploit them for our educational purposes. Since the prime need of our contemporary society is for *consensus*, the first task of social education is to achieve this. The conflict and confusion of values which Mannheim observed in society stemmed, he held, from the social disorganization brought about by industrialism; at the same time it represented the widespread disorganization and disorientation of individuals.

Mannheim's solution to the problems he diagnosed has been referred to, by Mrs Jean Floud, as the "gospel of salvation through sociology"[39]. But the fact is that Mannheim saw education as a part of the totality of conscious processes which were rapidly replacing the unconscious techniques; with the fading of tradition in the most important spheres of life, he maintained that

"The principal contribution of the sociological approach to the history and the theory of education is to draw attention to the fact that neither educational aims nor educational techniques can be conceived without a context, but rather, that they are to a very large extent socially directed"[40].

The Training of Teachers: If Mannheim's thought was not totalitarian, at least it was total. He saw society whole and integrated, and education was something that permeated all its groups and institutions. He considered, therefore, that the training of teachers should no longer be concerned *primarily* with the "tricks of the trade" and with method[41], but rather with the fullest possible education of the educator, with his social education and with his education for living. Mannheim would have approved wholeheartedly of the change of title, in 1965, from "Training College for Teachers" to "College of Education"—recommended originally by the Robbins Report[42]—which at least implied a change of viewpoint.

Mannheim considered that a knowledge of sociology and social psychology was essential to all teachers or educators. A true educator must understand the way in which human nature can be moulded by society; the concepts of conditioning, deconditioning and reconditioning; the essentially *moral* problems arising from human relationships; primary and secondary groups; the forces which make for control in a society; the relationships between freedom, authority, discipline and control; and the differing systems in the various sub-cultures of society in the realm of values.

"With the greater participation of the student in the learning process, it also follows that the incentives upon which learning is built will tend to move from constraints, external rewards like marks, prizes, ranking, towards mobilizing interest. If these things are true, then the way in which teachers are prepared has also to change. The methods of training can no longer be based upon the imparting of tricks of the trade but have to be transformed into a social education which primarily calls for the development of an all-round approach to the pupil whereby a widened horizon and human understanding of the person become more important than the simpler assessment of intellectual progress. The emphasis is now no longer on instruction and learning but rather on development of living. The educational institutions themselves have to become true societies and the course for the preparation of teachers has to be modified to take into account those changes"[43].

It is perhaps not without significance that in many of our Colleges of Education a minor revolution is going on in the realm of curricula and syllabuses, and that the trend is more and more towards a fuller understanding of life, of society, of its institutions, its *mores*, and its problems.

E. SOME CRITICISMS OF MANNHEIM'S VIEWS

Mannheim has been attacked and criticized, quite naturally, at varying levels. The proliferation of his Germanic mind led him into many fields—philosophy, psychology, social psychology, sociology, economics and education. It is not easy, even for the finest minds, to sustain accuracy or acceptance in such a large area of knowledge.

In a very close piece of analysis G. H. Bantock[44] has examined Mannheim's assertion that norms change with the changing order and are not themselves "absolute". We shall not here examine further the terms employed and their precise connotation; it is, however, important for the reader to consider their meaning. What is here emphasized by Bantock is the fact that social movements, like economic laws, are *tendencies*. Norms *tend* to change; but not invariably, and not for everyone. Moreover, this is a factual-judgement and not a value-judgement. We still have to ask the very pertinent question, "Ought norms to change?" And if not, what should be done about it?

Reality is, for Mannheim, Becoming. In social action it is efficiency which appears to be his criterion. And in the realm of moral judgements it is consensus which seems to be the ultimate guide. But as Bantock points out:

"The view that group consensus provides the best source of ethical truth, then, seems to rest on the assumption that group opinion transcends individual view-point, affording that comprehensiveness which permits a more objective synthesis; and this manifests itself, according to historicist moral theory, in action which accords with the evolving social situation"[45].

But, again, history has frequently demonstrated that the views of the majority are in no way *necessarily* superior to the views of the minority; and even if K. R. Popper has not given the final *coup de grâce* to historicism at least he has ably demonstrated its poverty[46].

Mannheim's contention that all truths are dependent upon specific social factors, and his conclusion that the personal contribution of the individual is of little importance in comparison with the patterns of thought predominant in the group to which he belongs is a classic example of *reductio ad absurdum*. It proves too much. It means, in the last analysis, that his own views were quite insignificant compared with the ideological standpoint of the Nazi society from which he was forced to flee; and that his own attempt to provide a Third Way as over against the society of laissez-faire, in which he took refuge, was doomed to failure.

There is always a danger in pushing any particular theory too far. There is obviously a great deal of "truth" in Mannheim's point of view; the more complex a society becomes, the more its institutions require planning. All planning requires planners, and there is never any guarantee that once the planners begin to limit freedom, as they must inevitably do, they will know where to draw the line. Again, it is true that social and group factors are of considerable importance in the shaping of people's ideas and development. And yet history is replete with the ways in which individuals, at many very different levels, have changed the course of events, have acted upon groups and even upon the whole patterns of society. One must, perforce, agree that education for "self-realization" can be a pretty meaningless affair; for the very concept of "self" is problematic. But education for social integration does not, *ipso facto*, eliminate "self-realization". Both terms obviously require further and closer definition, although it has always, perhaps, been evident that there is, and can be, no self-realization *in vacuo*. Man is a social animal, and he must ultimately realize himself in and through other people. The philosopher John Macmurray thinks that an isolated self is an unreal abstraction, and that there are only "persons in relation"[47]. If we wish to consider the self we must do so directly as a person, for the distinctive characteristic of selfhood is to be personal. This "personality" has significance only through and in a context of face-to-face relationships. This seems to accord fairly closely with G. H. Mead's social psychology, and with Mannheim's "Social and Cultural Concept of Personality"[48].

Finally, the whole question of the training of teachers is very much under review at the present time. It is unfortunate that we are going through a period when the priority is quantity rather than quality, but there are many signs that Mannheim's view of "teacher education" is gaining ground—the increased length of the course to three years for all but mature students; a fourth year for students selected to do a B.Ed. Course; a greater emphasis on the study of society generally, and on some of its institutions and problems in particular; the study of one subject in depth as well as a number of basic subjects in a very general way. In the

L

words of M. L. Jacks, who complained that the trained teacher was too often the untrained human being:

"The era of the training of teachers is past: our business today is with the education of the educator"[49].

REFERENCES

1. Curtis, S. J.: *An Introduction to the Philosophy of Education.* U.T.P., 1958, p. 201.
2. Boyd, W.: *The History of Western Education.* A. & C. Black, 7th Edition, 1964, p. 453.
3. Mannheim, K.: *Man and Society in an Age of Reconstruction.* Routledge, 1940. Quoted by Bantock, G. H. in *Freedom and Authority in Education.* Faber, 1952, p. 37.
4. Clarke, F.: *Education and Social Change.* Sheldon Press, 1940, p. 1.
5. Clarke, F.: *Freedom in the Educative Society.* U.L.P., 1948, p. 13.
6. *Vide* Hocking, W. E.: *Man and State.* New Haven, Yale University Press, 1926.
7. Curtis, S. J.: *A Short History of Educational Ideas.* U.T.P., 4th Edition, 1965, p. 535.
8. Mannheim, K.: *Diagnosis of Our Time.* Kegan Paul, 1943, p. 1.
9. *Ibid.* p. 24.
10. *Ibid.* p. 42.
11. *Ibid.* p. 45.
12. *Ibid.* p. 72.
13. *Ibid.* p. 98.
14. *Ibid.* p. 102.
15. *Ibid.* p. 126.
16. Cf. Jung, C. G.: *Archetypes and the Collective Unconscious.* Routledge, 1959, *passim.*
17. *Diagnosis of Our Time,* p. 136.
18. *Vide* Ayer, A. J.: *Language, Truth and Logic.* V. Gollancz, 1946; Joad, C. E. M.: *A Critique of Logical Positivism.* V. Gollancz, 1950; Curtis, S. J. & Boultwood, M. E. A.: *A Short History of Educational Ideas.* U.T.P., 4th Edition, 1965, pp. 620–622; Curtis, S. J.: *An Introduction to the Philosophy of Education.* U.T.P., 1958, p. 29.
19. Jeffreys, M. V. C.: *Mystery of Man.* Pitman, 1957, pp. 19–20.

20. Mannheim, K. & Stewart, W. A. C.: *An Introduction to the Sociology of Education*. Routledge, 1962, pp. 47–50.
21. *Diagnosis of Our Time*. pp. 56–7.
22. *Ibid.* p. 56.
23. Ottaway, A. K. C.: *Education and Society*. Routledge, 1962, pp. 86–7.
24. *Ibid.* pp. 86–7.
25. Cf. Curtis, S. J.: *An Introduction to the Philosophy of Education*, p. 210.
26. Crowther Report: *15 to 18*, (Volume I). H.M.S.O., 1959, p. 195.
27. Newsom Report: *Half Our Future*. H.M.S.O., 1963, p. 72, para. 210.
28. *Vide An Introduction to the Sociology of Education*, pp. 93ff.
29. *Ibid.* p. 113.
30. *Ibid.* pp. 107–13.
31. *Ibid.* p. ix.
32. Elvin, H. L.: *Education and Contemporary Society*. C. A. Watts, 1965.
33. *An Introduction to the Sociology of Education*, pp. 17–18.
34. *Ibid.* p. 25.
35. *Diagnosis of Our Time*, p. 106.
36. *Vide* Loukes, H.: *Teenage Religion*. S.C.M. Press, 1961; Goldman, R.: *Religious Thinking from Childhood to Adolescence*. Routledge, 1964; Goldman, R.: *Readiness for Religion*. Routledge, 1965; Acland, R.: *We Teach them Wrong*. V. Gollancz, 1963.
37. *Vide Religious and Moral Education*. Printed by Blackfriars Press Ltd., Leicester, October 1965. A pamphlet produced by a Group of Christians and Humanists, putting forward some proposals for County Schools.
38. Elvin, H. L.: *Op. cit.*, p. 196.
39. *Vide* Judges, A. V. (editor): *The Function of Teaching*. Faber, 1959, pp. 40–6. An essay by Mrs Jean Floud on "Karl Mannheim".
40. *An Introduction to the Sociology of Education*, p. 159.
41. *Ibid.* pp. 12–13.
42. *Vide* Robbins Report: *Higher Education*. H.M.S.O., 1963, p. 119, para. 351.
43. *An Introduction to the Sociology of Education*, p. 32.
44. Bantock, G. H.: *Education and Values*. Faber, 1965, p. 121.
45. *Ibid.* p. 129.
46. Popper, K. R.: *The Poverty of Historicism*. Routledge, 1961.
47. Macmurray, J.: *Persons in Relation*. Faber, 1957.

48. *An Introduction to the Sociology of Education*, pp. 87–9.
49. Jacks, M. L.: *Total Education*. Kegan Paul, 1946, p. 146.

BIBLIOGRAPHY

A. BOOKS BY KARL MANNHEIM

Ideology and Utopia. (In German 1921). Routledge, 1954.
Man in an Age of Reconstruction. (In German 1935). Routledge, 1940.
Diagnosis of Our Time. Routledge, 1943.
Freedom, Power and Democratic Planning. Routledge, 1951.
Essays on the Sociology of Knowledge. Routledge, 1952.
Essays on Sociology and Social Psychology. Routledge, 1953.
Essays on the Sociology of Culture. Routledge, 1956.
Systematic Sociology: An Introduction to the Study of Society. Routledge, 1957.
Mannheim, K. & Stewart, W. A. C.: *An Introduction to the Sociology of Education*. Routledge, 1962.

B. OTHER BOOKS OF REFERENCE

Bantock, G. H.: *Freedom and Authority in Education*. Faber, 1952 (especially pp. 38–53).
—: *Education and Values*. Faber, 1965 (especially pp. 118–52).
Clarke, F.: *Education and Social Change*. Sheldon Press, 1940.
—: *Freedom in the Educative Society*. U.L.P., 1948.
Judges, A. V. (editor): *The Function of Teaching*. Faber, 1959. (Chapter 2 on "Karl Mannheim" by Mrs Jean Floud.)

CONCLUSION

We have surveyed, in brief, some of the outstanding thinkers from the age of Socrates and Plato down to modern times. Our study has been in the fields of philosophy, psychology and sociology, and each discipline has in turn been applied to education. Nothing more than an introduction has been attempted, and it has been left to the student to pursue the study of both disciplines and thinkers through a variety of books, both original and critical. Some of the bibliographies have been fairly detailed in order to assist those students who may be pursuing a line of research into the work of one of the thinkers, or into some branch of study here touched upon. More and more the student in training requires guidance in reading over a wide area, rather than exhaustive text-books on any particular aspect of education. He needs the discipline of both wide reference and reading in depth; he needs to study the disciplines in themselves, and for themselves, as well as for their application to educational theory. Perhaps most of all the student in training, and the teacher who is practising, must realize that it is very rarely that our educational problems are solved in isolation. By this we mean that there is no purely philosophical answer, or a completely psychological solution, or a sheer sociological one. As we face educational issues we need to bring all our disciplines and resources to bear upon them. Doctrinaire solutions based upon nothing but political postures, economic emergencies, or upon psychological theories or metaphysical and religious prejudice, are inevitably partial, if not specifically harmful.

If our society is to survive with anything like an integrated culture, amidst the ever-evolving sub-cultures and mass cultures of our time, then educators themselves are primarily responsible for understanding these movements in their society, and for seeking to absorb and to modify them in some way. If we are honest with ourselves we shall admit that there are elements in our society which we not only do not like, but which we also know to be harmful to the health and ultimate happiness of our community. Nor do we have to be seers, prophets or evangelists to delineate these elements; some of the most forthright, as well as constructive, in the field of human values are people who call themselves "humanists", and who base their value-judgements upon a scientific investigation and critical analysis of things as they are, and as they could be; yes, and even as they *ought* to be. But the teacher, whether humanist, Christian, agnostic, existentialist, Zen Buddhist or whatever, must make judgements of value, and he will inevitably have some effect upon his pupils through his own attitudes, character, personality and values. If, in Pilate-fashion, we seek to wash our hands of all moral and value-judgements in our teaching, and remain simply in the realms of logic, scientific method, statistical social analysis and an amoral psychological behaviourism, we must not be surprised if the less intelligent members of our society (who cannot understand logic and statistical analysis, but who are quite prepared to accept amoral behaviourism) become depraved, deviant or delinquent; nor must we be too amazed if some of the more intelligent, who can wield logic and use statistics only too well, defend their anti-social behaviour with current pseudo-scientific theory.

A disciplined teacher, with some breadth of culture and experience, and with a sense of values arrived at through a free-ranging of truth wherever it may be found, is likely to produce disciplined and educated pupils, as well as good citizens.

NAME INDEX

SUBJECT INDEX

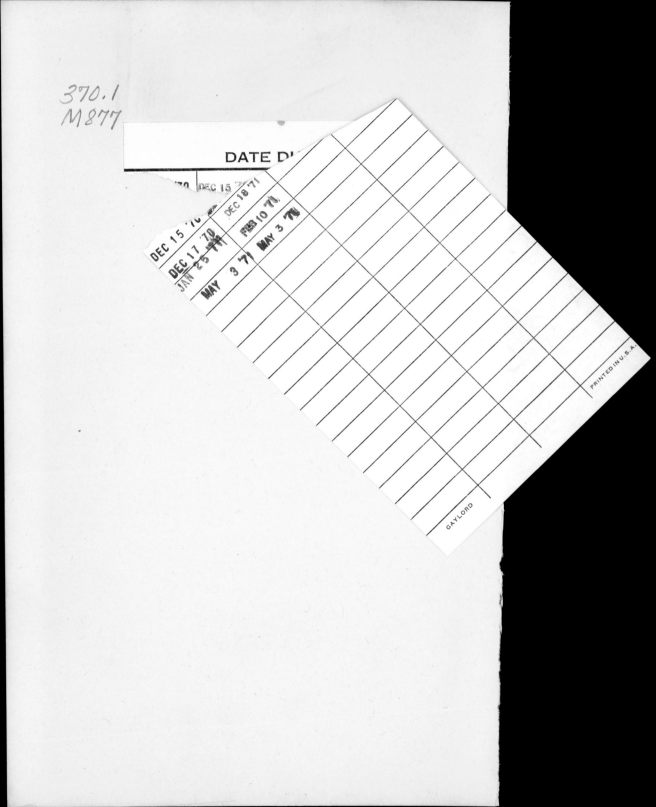